EASTERN INFERNO

EASTERN INFERNO

The Journals of a German
Panzerjäger on the Eastern Front,
1941–43

Edited by
CHRISTINE ALEXANDER
and
MASON KUNZE

CASEMATE
Philadelphia & Oxford

First published in 2010.
This edition published in the United States of America in 2022 by
CASEMATE PUBLISHERS
1950 Lawrence Road, Havertown, PA 19083, US
and
The Old Music Hall, 106–108 Cowley Road, Oxford OX4 1JE, UK

Paperback Edition: ISBN 978-1-63624-220-0
Digital Edition: ISBN 978-1-61200-024-4

A CIP record for this book is available from the British Library

Printed and bound in the United States of America by Integrated Books International
Typeset by DiTech Publishing Services

For a complete list of Casemate titles, please contact:

CASEMATE PUBLISHERS (US)
Telephone (610) 853-9131
Fax (610) 853-9146
Email: casemate@casematepublishers.com
www.casematepublishers.com

CASEMATE PUBLISHERS (UK)
Telephone (01865) 241249
Email: casemate-uk@casematepublishers.co.uk
www.casematepublishers.co.uk

Contents

Dedication		vii
Preface		ix
Foreword		xi

Journal I	Operation Barbarossa and the Battle for Kiev	1
Journal II	March to the East and the Winter of 1941–42	69
Journal III	Frontline Warfare and the Retreat After Stalingrad	129

Final Documents	183
Suggested Reading	187

Dedication

This book is dedicated to my grandfather, Hans Roth—a man who, in the midst of a horrendous war, thought it important to leave a legacy behind for all those who would never have a chance to meet him. Because of his diaries his child, grandchildren and generations to come will have a tiny glimpse into the life of this man. For this, I am truly grateful.

May these diaries prompt the reader to think about how they too can leave a legacy for those who come after them.

Mom ... to you, may you one day read the words of your father in this book, and may it bring a deep peace that makes your heart complete. From your children Marc, Mason and me, you have been the best mother one could ever have. We love you more than words can express.

Avana Fullerton and Matthew Fullerton—may the words in this book give you a connection to your great grandfather. I love you both so very deeply and am so proud of you both. May you carry on an incredible legacy of your own and pass this book to all who come after you. Taylor Alexander, Jordan Alexander and Whitney Alexander—words cannot express the joy of sharing my life with you. I love you all. May God continue to bless our lives together.

Frank Alexander, my husband and the man of my dreams—you have captivated my heart completely. I love you! Thank you for putting all the pieces of the diary in order.

Special thanks to:
Jeff Rogers for digging into the diaries and giving us the valuable in formation needed to put this book together. Jeff, I am so thankful for all your time and passion you put into reading the diaries and helping us get this book in order.

Jan and Ada Goerike, thank you for your hard work in translating the diaries from German to English.

We also owe special appreciation to Håkan Henriksson in Sweden, and to John Calvin of wwiiphotos-maps.com for their expertise and generous assistance with additional photographs to illuminate the path and experiences of Hans Roth during the war.

And last but not least—I want to thank our special friends at WW2 Forums (www.ww2f.com) Carl Evans, Eric Brown, Christopher Jensen, Slava Gurdzhi and David Mitchell who so willingly shared with us their knowledge of the Second World War which helped us decipher some of the meanings and information needed to bring a perspective on the events in which my grandfather was a part.

CHRISTINE ALEXANDER
Granddaughter of Hans Roth

Preface

War stories have always fascinated me. As a young boy, I would sit in front of the television for hours, completely mesmerized by old black and white footage of World War I and World War II. I must have seen "Tora! Tora! Tora!" and "The Guns of Navarone" a hundred times—I could never get enough.

But never could I have imagined that a firsthand account of World War II, which no movie or footage could match, was collecting dust in my very own home. It wasn't until I helped my mother move, 30 years later, that I discovered this hidden treasure.

My mother grew up during the 1930s and 40s and has always been reluctant to tell me, my brother, and my sister anything about her childhood in wartime Germany.

It was with the same apprehension that she handed me the set of three diaries, in perfect condition. She told me they were my German grandfather's personal journals. They were written in German, which I could not read, so I had the first five pages translated as soon as possible. I could hardly wait to see what the diaries contained—and the results were nothing short of amazing.

Even the translator, a native German speaker, was shocked after translating only a few pages.

I was holding a firsthand account of brutality, carnage and death, combined with the hope that, one day, life would return to the way it was before the war.

They weren't just the words of a German soldier on the frontlines of the Eastern Front; they were also the words of my grandfather, Hans Roth. A grandfather I would never have the privilege to know, except through the contents of his diaries.

Hans Roth was in his early thirties when he was drafted into the German Army. His life had previously consisted of all a young man could dream of. He was the owner of a successful graphic design office in downtown Frankfurt, husband to a lovely wife, and father of a beautiful, five-year-old daughter named Erika.

His wife, my grandmother, was forced to work in an ammunition factory, as were many other German women during the war. They were sometimes left there for days at a time, so children were left alone at home to fend for themselves.

The Red Cross took my mother to a large farm, along with other children, where a family watched over them.

It has taken over five years, and multiple translators, to decode the contents of the three diaries.

One of the translators could only bear to complete a small bit of her translation before retiring from the project. She told me the diaries were too vivid and emotional for her to continue translating them.

I soon discovered that my mother hadn't read most of the diaries. They were the words of her dad, a dad she really never had the opportunity to get to know.

Her only memory of her father was of a figure bending down to kiss her while she slept and whispering, "Auf wiedersehen, liebling Erika," as he left for war.

For my mother, reading these diaries meant meeting the father she never had met and reviving all the grief and pain of his absence.

Still, to this day, she has chosen not to read them.

MASON KUNZE
Grandson of Hans Roth

Foreword

The German Army's invasion of the Soviet Union during World War II that began in June 1941, became the largest and bloodiest land conflict in history. Its huge numbers of men—at least seven million involved in the initial onset—and thousands of tanks and aircraft stretched across endless expanses of steppe. Just as a television picture is composed of millions of dots, the campaign's vast savagery was the product of countless acts of brutality by millions of individual men. Yet, lengthy first-hand recollections of this conflict are rare as few lived long enough to share them.

Hans Roth took the time to keep a journal of his service in the Wehrmacht, while fighting in some of the fiercest battles that characterized the war on the Eastern Front. His insights provide a stirring glimpse into the daily life of Germans soldiers as they fought a desperate war.

Hans Roth loved his wife and his daughter, the latter whom he had seen very little of since he was called up for duty in the Wehrmacht to serve in the *Panzerjäger* (anti-tank) battalion of the 299th Infantry Division. His love for family was expressed often in the journals he kept, and he longed to see them, mentioning them regularly as he wrote. While Hans did write home as often as he could (he mentions these letters throughout his diaries), I must suspect he withheld in these letters most of the horrors he experienced, saving them instead for the detailed journals he privately maintained.

Hans's story begins in the late spring days of 1941, as the 299th Infantry Division, assigned to the German Sixth Army, prepares to invade the Soviet Union. As Operation Barbarossa unfolds, the 299th finds itself entangled in the desperate fighting south of the Pripyat Marshes. Roth sees firsthand the waste of human lives, by both the German and Soviet armies. Later that summer, he is involved in the reduction of the Kiev Pocket, becoming one of the first German troops to enter the Ukrainian capital. After a dire winter of bitter cold, he and the men of his division support the northern shoulder of Sixth Army, as it makes its drive to Stalingrad and gets locked into that desperate struggle. When the Red Army launches a massive counteroffensive, trapping Sixth Army against the Volga, the 299th Division and Hans Roth are outside the pincers of the Soviet envelopment. As Soviet hammerblows continue, Roth witnesses the collapse of the Italian Eighth, Hungarian Second, and Romanian Third Armies on the northern flank, as the men of these formations melt into the countryside. His unit is ultimately transferred to Second Army, then Second Panzer Army, in their attempts to hold the southern flank of Army Group Center after the destruction of Sixth Army at Stalingrad. He then participates in the fierce battles for Kharkov, Voronezh, and the Orel salient while detailing the horrendous fighting that characterized combat on the Eastern Front.

Throughout his narratives of the German campaigns, *Gefreiter* (private), later *Feldwebel* (corporal), Roth takes great effort to describe his surroundings, writing much about the Ukrainian and Russian people, including their hardships, and the contrasts between their lives and the one he knew before the war. At first their lifestyle seemed foreign to him, but after living among them for nearly two years, he grew accustomed to their pastoral ways. He was witness to the summary execution of captured partisans, expressing some remorse at their deaths, but fully understanding that the nature of the war meant that these same people could have been the cause of his death.

While lacking the polish of later published personal accounts, Roth's monograph has the advantage of being written as the events happened and not after the war, when memories can be muddled and remembrances altered by later experience. This is the strength of Roth's work, as his thoughts are unaltered; the stark events recorded don't undergo a metamorphosis to fit later sensibilities.

Hans Roth eventually disappeared into the cauldron that became known as the Destruction of Army Group Center. He undoubtedly was working on his fourth journal when he lost contact with his family in summer 1944. His three completed ones had been placed in safekeeping back home, with the last one ending in July 1943. Little is known of his service after that date, except what was included in letters home, but these did not cover the horrors of the war as his journals did. The location of Hans Roth's grave is unknown.

However, the journals he kept provide a memorial for him and the millions of soldiers whose lives came to a horrific end in a war far from home.

JEFFERY W. ROGERS

The Iron Cross, Second Class, awarded to Hans Roth on November 3, 1941, along with its accompanying certificate. *(Photos courtesy of Christine Alexander and Mason Kunze)*

Im Namen des Führers und Obersten Befehlshabers der Wehrmacht

verleihe ich

dem

Gefreiten
Hans R o t h ,
Stab Pz.Jg.Abt.299

das

Eiserne Kreuz 2.Klasse

Div.St.Qu.........,den 3.November 1941.

(Dienstsiegel)

Generalleutnant und Div.Kdr.

(Dienstgrad und Dienststellung)

The War Merit Cross, 2nd Class, with Swords, awarded to then-Corporal (Feldwebel) Hans Roth on November 15, 1943, with certificate. *(Photos courtesy of Christine Alexander and Mason Kunze)*

IM NAMEN DES FÜHRERS

VERLEIHE ICH

DEM

Feldwebel
Hans R o t h,
Stab/Pz.Jg.Abt.299,

DAS

KRIEGSVERDIENSTKREUZ
2. KLASSE
MIT SCHWERTERN

Div.Gef.St. , DEN 15.11.1943

(DIENSTSIEGEL)

Generalleutnant und Div.-Kdr.

(DIENSTGRAD UND DIENSTSTELLUNG)

Operation Barbarossa
and the Battle for Kiev

Editors' Note:

In Hans Roth's first journal, the 299th Infantry Division, in which he served under General Willi Mosel, is poised at the Bug River in Poland, waiting for the launch of Operation Barbarossa, Germany's massive surprise attack on the Soviet Union. The division is part of Walter von Reichenau's Sixth Army, which will comprise the left flank of Field Marshal Gerd von Rundstedt's Army Group South.

The Germans had arrayed three army groups: North, with Leningrad as its ultimate objective; Center, aimed straight at Moscow; and South, with its first objective Kiev, and then the industrial regions beyond. Army Group North had one panzer group, which was assisted by the proximity of the Baltic Sea in cutting off Soviet forces. Army Group Center had two panzer groups deployed on each wing, which performed an impressive series of encirclement battles at Brest-Litovsk, Minsk, and Smolensk, propelling the Army Group halfway to Moscow within weeks.

The German high command underestimated the challenge for Army Group South, however, as it only had one panzer group, with a huge expanse of territory to cover and no natural obstacles against which to pin enemy concentrations. Further, the Soviet forces in the south, under Marshal Semen Budenny, were the largest of any sector, consisting of over a million men, not counting reserves. All across the front, the Germans were shocked by the numbers of artillery pieces, tanks, and planes the Soviets developed, which far exceeded pre-war estimates, as well as by the ferocity of Soviet resistance. This was especially true in the south.

The result was that while spectacular gains were quickly made by Army Groups North and Center, Army Group South found itself in a difficult, confrontational slog against Budenny's forces. The First Panzer Group, under von Kleist, could not effect encirclements by itself, even as the vast expanse of the steppe diluted its fighting strength. The initial stage of Operation Barbarossa in the south relied primarily on infantry divisions, which forged gradually across the territory, snowballing numerically superior Soviet forces before them until finally arriving before Kiev, where scenes reminiscent of the trenches of World War I were reprised.

Reichenau's Sixth Army was the primary instrument of the advance, until in July the high command decided to employ the panzers, along with Seventeenth Army, in a subsidiary encirclement battle against a Soviet salient at Uman. Successfully completed on August 8, with the capture of over 100,000 prisoners, this truncation of Budenny's forces opened the door to further advances near the lower Dniepr and the Black Sea, including the entranceway to the Crimea.

Meantime, Sixth Army had fought its way through Korosten, Zhitomir and other towns to the outskirts of Kiev, where it found itself in a veritable death-grip with the Soviets' Southwest Front, which was considerably larger in both men and firepower. While most accounts of the onset of Barbarossa describe spectacular advances by the German panzer divisions, Roth describes the pure hell undergone by the infantry divisions of Sixth Army, as they waited for their high command to devise a solution to their original miscalculation.

* * *

In the journals that follow, which were translated from the handwritten versions, occasional punctuation and paragraph breaks have been added for clarity. For certain idioms or technical references, explanations have been added [in brackets] where possible. The titles assigned to the journals themselves are the editors' and were not part of the originals.

Gefreiter (Private) Hans Roth. *(Photo courtesy of Christine Alexander and Mason Kunze)*

[ON THE JOURNAL'S FIRST PAGE]

Once again we are close to being deployed on another difficult assignment. I am hoping that what follows will become my diary. In it, I will recount the daily events just as they occur, without any embellishment. I am still not permitted to write such things to my wife, but will tell her later.

12 June 1941, Łasków, Poland

12 June, 1941: After an extremely exhausting journey that lasted several days, we arrived in Łasków [Poland], about 8 kilometers from the Russian border. Our march went from Kiacz-Wielki via OpatówLublin-Krasnistaw-Zamosc-Hrubiczo, to our current location. The dust and heat are terrible.

Łasków, which is nothing more than a small hick-town with an unmistakable Ukrainian feel to it, is populated by friendly and clean people. The houses [*blockhüssen*] are small, single-story constructions with thatched roofs. As wood and straw are the most common construction materials, both the barns and the houses are made from woven willow. The rooms, small but cozy, are always whitewashed or painted light blue with woven straw mats and beautiful local flowers decorating the ovens, walls, and ceilings. Vibrant embroidered pillows and curtains in their blaze of color create a warm but simple atmosphere in the tiny rooms. We pitch our tents in the barn and enjoy some well-deserved peace and quiet.

13 June: Drive to Zamosc in order to take position. The beauty of the town's market is remarkable. The rich baroque façades of the town hall and center, though unfamiliar to me, are delightful. Truly a wonderful style! Russian churches with their onion domes are found everywhere along the way. The street signs and store fronts are mostly bi-lingual—German and Ukrainian.

14 June: Received orders to drive to the Bug River. With the main intelligence unit [*Offz.-Erkundungstrupp*] already on location there, I am ordered to map out our observations of the enemy's positions. On my way there, the construction and support units [*bau-und-pionieren trupps*] were feverishly working on the roads in disrepair, rushing to build a corduroy road across the swamps and mud.

I arrive in Piaseczno around noon. The forest there has already been taken by the Russians. The Russian flag, with its hammer and sickle, waves within a stone's throw. It is unimaginable what would happen to our cohorts if the Russians were to get the idea to send out a reconnaissance unit to explore the area. We know all too well that this is possible.

How should we handle this? The Russian bunkers and machine gun positions are just 100 meters away, facing ten soldiers and a few *pionieren* [engineers]. The river is the border—past it, the abyss. If the Russians do come, we will be unable to retreat, as we are without vehicles. Are we the scapegoats who are supposed to be slaughtered by the Russians [as an excuse] for the German attack? Similar situations took place in Poland. A truly honorable death sentence! Nevertheless, we sleep peacefully. We do not even bother to set out guards. Why should we, only to anticipate the inevitable?

My dear Rosel, if I wrote to you about such events, you surely would not find any peace of mind. How good it is that you do not know about this.

15 June: The situation is becoming more and more serious. Russian scouts were on our side of the river last night, close to our encampment. Gauging from the footprints in the sand, it must have been a group of at least twenty men. What a fine mess we have gotten ourselves into! Should we fire at them?

We are now no longer able to make a move without being noticed. They track our every movement with their *scherenfernrohr* [scissor telescopes] all day long. We have to sneak like Indians to the riverbank in order to accomplish our task. This is how I will have to map out the enemy's positions and establish the artillery sectors tomorrow, which should allow us to complete our assignment. I hope that will be the result!

16 June: What luck we have! I was able to finish my task without any disruption from the Reds [*die Roten*]. I now also know the location of where we, along with our *pionieren*, are going to traverse the river. Once again we will be part of the first wave! Since the mission is intended to surprise the Russians, the attack will probably commence in a few days. The forest to our rear is filled with intense activity. Heavy artillery has been placed in position. Our panzers have also arrived. Flak cannons were set in place last night.

There is a great deal of activity on the enemy side as well. The Reds have strengthened their positions, and given the noise from the opposing forest, they appear to have rolled their tanks into position. I am extremely tired tonight and it is still unbearably hot.

Hans Roth on leave with his wife Rosel. *(Photo courtesy Christine Alexander and Mason Kunze)*

17 June: It is raining, which is a blessing for the local farmers, but bad news for us. Where there were paths yesterday there are muddy creeks today, which reach up to the top of my jackboots.

Our commander [General Willi Moser] arrives at noon. He brings bad news, declaring that we have to stay put for a few more days. The weather clears up in the evening, and a stroll down to the bridgehead on the Bug wonderfully relaxes my nerves, which have suffered greatly under the tension of the past few days.

I now know the day of the attack. It will unfold on June 21, and stretch across an expansive front. What will the following weeks bring? I think of my dear family with longing. As I have asked myself so often in the past, I wonder if my longing actually comes from simply missing the comforts of civilian life. I thought about this on my way down to the fortifications on the Bug: such an idea is not possible. Time and time again I envision Rosel and Butziben [daughter Erika]. How else could the true love that speaks from each line of her letters touch me so deeply? These two people are the most precious things that life could have taken away from me.

My thoughts are with Father and Mother, these two kind beings; the love between is us great. With gratitude I think of all the good things they have done for Rosel and me. God willing, I will get through the coming weeks—for their sake.

18 June: It is now becoming serious. Under the cover of night, the entire division will move into attack formation. Reinforcement troops from the 528th Infantry Regiment arrived today around noon—young guys with fresh faces. For some of them, the sun will shine for only a few more days. Such is the soldier's fate! I expect the attack to occur across the front on Sunday.

This new day has already brought great joy to me—two lovely letters from my dear Rosel and one sweet letter from Hanau.

19 June: My most recent observations lead me to assume that our section [of the front] should expect great resistance. Will our surprise maneuver really succeed?

Further to the rear, farmers are forced to leave their fields and property. Our troops might also have to advance tomorrow. It is atrocious. The farmers' wives hurl themselves on the ground, pulling their hair. All this damn crying! There is no way we can help them!

Hurray! The greatest battle of all times will start the day after tomorrow!

20 June: Our cabin is being abandoned. The division has arrived; final preparations for the strike on the Bug fortifications.

21 June: The attack starts tonight at 0300 hours. We are attached to the von Kleist group [*1st Panzergruppe* commanded by Field Marshal Paul Ludwig Ewald von Kleist]. Our assignment: a rapid putsch in wedge formation, regardless of casualties...

For the moment there is a quiet, wonderful, twilight peacefulness over the countryside. The huts in the village will be on fire in a few hours; the air will be filled with the howling and screeching of shells. The impact of the shelling will tear apart the fields and roads.

How amazing it is that we are once again part of this offensive—fighting under Kleist. Farewell my wife and sweet Erika. Farewell my beloved parents. You will be in my thoughts tomorrow. Do not worry; a soldier's luck will be with me.

22 June: All of a sudden, at exactly 0315 hours, and apparently out of the blue, an opening salvo emerges from the barrels of hundreds of guns of all calibers. The howling and staccato of Stalin's arsenal fills the air as if Armageddon had begun. It is impossible to comprehend one's world in such an inferno.

Our homeland is still innocently asleep while here death is already collecting a rich harvest. We crouch in our holes with pallid but resolved faces while counting the minutes until we storm the Bug fortifications ... a reassuring touch of our ID tags, the arming of hand grenades, the securing of our MPi [*machinenpistole*: submachine gun].

It is now 0330 hours. A whistle sounds; we quickly jump out from undercover and at an insane speed cross the 20 meters to the inflatable boats. In a snatch we are on the other side of the river where rattling machine gun fire awaits us. We have our first casualties.

With the help of a few *sturmpionieren* we slowly—much too slowly—eat through the barbed wire barriers. Meanwhile, shells fire into the bunkers at Molnikow [Ukraine].

We finally get out of this mess. In a few short steps we are able to advance to the first bunker, arriving in its blind spot. The Reds fire like mad but are unable to reach us. The decisive moment is near. An explosive specialist approaches the bunker from behind and shoves in a short-fused bomb into the bunker's fire hole. The bunker shook, and black smoke emerged from its openings, signaling its final doom. We move on.

Molnikow is completely in our hands by 1000 hours. The Reds, hunted by our infantry, disperse quickly to Bisknjiczo-Ruski. Because the crossing of the river by our panzers is progressing slowly, we are ordered to cleanse the village of any remaining enemy combatants. The area is combed house by house. Our shelling has caused terrible damage. The Reds, however, have also done their fair share.

Slowly, our nerves grow accustomed to the all too familiar gruesome images. Close to the Reds' customs house lies a large mound of fallen Russians, most of them torn to shreds from the shelling. Slaughtered civilians lie in the neighboring house. The horridly disfigured bodies of a young woman and her two small children lie among their shattered personal belongings in another small, cleansed house.

I am compelled to think of you Rosel and Erika, when I witness such horrible images. How wonderful it is that we are able to exterminate these murderous beasts. How good it is that we have pre-empted them; for in the coming weeks these bloodhounds might have been standing on German soil. It is inconceivable what would have happened then!

We have taken our first prisoners—snipers and deserters receive their deserved reward.

After our panzers arrive, we proceed with our attack under nothing more than light fire and make our advance via Motkowicz-Myskzów, approximately 40 kilometers from the front. We meet serious resistance near Biscupicze.

Helmulth Pfaff and his 14th are pressed hard by enemy tanks. With many casualties, he has had to retreat to Biscupicze. According to his observations, we should expect an attack from 50—some heavy—tanks. We move into hedgehog formation at sunset. Although everyone is extremely exhausted after the first day of fighting, no one thinks about sleeping. It is an uneasy, restless night.

23 June: The morning starts with light artillery fire. The Red tanks still have not left their deployment area. We can apparently expect panzer and Stuka [*Sturzkampfbomber*] support at around 0800 hours. This good news has noticeably raised our morale.

In the interim, our Luftwaffe comrades deliver a bit of entertainment. Dogfight after dogfight is fought over our heads. One after another, nine Russian bombers are shot down and crash to the ground in flames. This is the precision work of which [fighter pilot Werner] Moelders and [Adolf] Galland are true masters.

The Russian tank attack commences at noon, with the German counterattack starting thirty minutes later. Never have we experienced anything like this: 100 Russian tanks are fighting against us. The most important thing is to keep the blood cool and the nerves calm. We eliminated four tanks within a short amount of time. Approximately 20 Stukas dive bomb, howling from the skies, to attack the Russian tank line. By the afternoon, the battle is decided to our advantage. More than 60 enemy tanks stand burned out or crushed all over the battlefield. Most of the enemy units retreat back to Babicze. We follow close behind them during the night so that we will be able to encircle them.

24 June: Encirclement of the enemy has been achieved by dawn and continues to close in, despite the desperate attempts by the Reds to break through. The battle culminates around 0900 hours. The tremendous pressure on the enclosed division worries us. The Russians run like maniacs against our lines. The situation becomes extremely critical around 1000 hours, with the enemy encirclement being breached to the southern end of the valley basin.

Artillery fire has been ordered, and just minutes later, scores of heavy shells hiss and howl over our heads. A wall of black smoke stands before us. The smoke is at times white, and occasionally holes are torn into it from the shrapnel. The entire valley swills from the impact of the shelling. We are able to reach the first buildings in Babicze under the cover of the well positioned fire. The damn spiral mines [*spiralminen*] explode one after another in angry thunder right before us and over our heads. That sound—that nasty and poisonous sound from the swarms of artillery shelling. With our faces contorted by anger, we jump into the Reds' shrapnel trenches. Anti-tank grenades hammer into their fortifications. All goes crazy now and chaos erupts. The shelling from the Reds spews forth clouds of shrapnel which blow over us…. And from these swirls of fire rain down showers of metal into the small pond right in front of us.

Ratas [Soviet fighter planes] appear and attack us. Thank God, no casualties. We reach the middle of the village around noon. Resistance from the Reds has been broken—an entire Red division has been destroyed. Clusters of dead and wounded soldiers are blocking the street. The number of our own casualties is also high. We are so exhausted we could pass out. Despite this, we reassemble and continue to advance without any noteworthy resistance, to the village of Lokacze. The welcome there is not very pleasant, as wild gunfire was awaiting us. Damn snipers! House after house must be cleansed with hand grenades. Fanatics fire at us until the roofs collapse over their heads and they are buried under the rubble. Others escape their houses at the last minute as human torches. They either collapse dead on the street or are beaten to death. Within the hour the entire village has transformed into an ocean of flames.

A thought comes to mind about our infantry during the slaughtering: how many innocent men have been sent to kingdom come? It is a bizarre thought. Our lancers go out and get drunk.

As soon as the first house goes up in flames, dead bodies can be found lying on the street. Soldiers destroy and shoot about mercilessly until plumes of smoke cover the horizon. I believe that this raiding by the infantry brings balance to the extreme exertion of marching and fighting. At the single shot of a sniper the exhausted men return to life. With their nerves pulverized, they have forgotten the barbarian heat, forgotten all that damn traipsing about. An infantry soldier recently said to me, "You see, I was terribly tired, now I am fresh again. It went back to being a good party!" Yes, yes, this "party" makes me sick to my stomach.

25 June: What I would give to be able to sleep in! After only two hours of sleep we are back at it. We have received orders to rush and break through enemy lines to the south of Lutsk. Will we be successful at crossing the River Styr?

Our rapid advance in narrow wedge formation has created a terrible situation for us: only the banks along the road are able to be cleansed of enemy troops. There is no time to comb the neighboring forests, which is precisely, however, where the enemy combatants are reassembling. Time and time again there are small battles to the rear of the front line.

Supply convoys are being attacked and obliterated by the enemy far behind our own line. Red aircraft are hanging over us today like flies. It is a miracle that their relentless attacks have caused only a few casualties.

We reach the Styr around noon. The Reds have broken the river. The flooded territory is kilometers wide, rendering a crossing of the river for our panzers impossible. Attempts to use floating bridges are futile. The enemy fires unremittingly at our bridgehead.

A sad day for me! Four dear comrades have fallen: Walter Wolff, Horas, Muegge the always good humored, and Schielke. Many have been badly wounded. I myself am spiritually and physically totally exhausted! If my dear Rosel could see me like this—dirty, jaded, thirsty... I think she would cry out of pity for me. Our beloved homeland [*Heimat*] will never fully comprehend what we have accomplished during this campaign. They do not have the slightest idea of the difficult terrain we have experienced, nor the types of battles.

We have just had another attack from a Red *Tiefflieger* [low-flying bomber]. Gruber was killed. He had just married his bride eight days ago by proxy. The night is restless. Hell must be loose to the rear of the line. The sky is blood red; relentless rumbling and thunder are indicative of the heavy battle occurring all around us.

Our panzers roll in to provide reinforcement. At present, we receive news that the battle for Lutsk has commenced. At dawn, we notice dark, smoky clouds hanging over the riverbanks close to the village.

26 June: Latest observations in the morning bring no changes to the situation. It is still impossible to get the vehicles across the river. We receive orders from division HQ and are commanded to cross the Styr near Lutsk, despite the chance of meeting strong Russian tank forces there. Very well; we take off toward our destination—all by ourselves, without the support of heavy artillery and infantry, which will cross the river by way of the floating bridges.

The constant attacks from the enemy are sickening. Enemy aircraft, mostly bombers, suddenly attack, as if they were coming from right behind the hedges. All of the drama is over within seconds: first, the incredible thunder of detonations; next, the hammering of on-board cannons from the bombers; and finally, the smell of dark and foul smoke along with the hissing and singing of shrapnel over our heads. In the end, the wounded are shrieking, and the show is over. That is how it went five times until we arrived in Lutsk.

The number of casualties is considerable. Slowly, we enter the village, all while keeping our left and right flanks secure. We are able to take a short break in the town center. The time is used to collect the injured and take a swig from our canteen.

The beating that the town has taken from the Stukas and heavy artillery is extensive. The local prison is a gruesome sight. Prior to their retreat, the Bolshevik mob staged a terrible bloodbath. More than a hundred men, women, and children were slaughtered like cattle. Never will I forget such appalling images. These are the dead of our enemies, for those bloodhounds and murderers would prey on English priests!

Meanwhile, a few comrades have pulled the remaining *Rotarmisten* [Red Army soldiers] and Jews from their hiding places. A solo gun performance echoed across the square and with that, the mob ascended to the heavens of "the English High Church."

We move on. Together with our panzers, we advance slowly to the east side of the village, where Russian tanks suddenly appear. PaKs [anti-tank cannons] have never before been brought into position so quickly. Our panzers are deployed; we lie atop them, packed with hand grenades in order to eliminate the approaching infantry. After an hour of battle, the attacking behemoths and their accompanying fighters are either destroyed or have fled. Unfortunately, we too have suffered the loss of some of our panzers. I was on top of one of them, but was incredibly lucky that it did not catch fire. Such an episode is typical for the entire damn Eastern campaign. The panzers that have been able to make a quick advance are already in Lutsk, approximately 40 kilometers from here.

Lutsk was captured by our troops this morning, and the area around the town has been cleansed of enemy troops. So where did the enemy tanks and infantry suddenly come from? This Asian mob is sly and cunning; every hour brings an evil surprise—a large pile of *scheisse* [shit]. We are no longer safe anywhere. There is not a single hour of peace and quiet. It is true that I am not a coward. Fear is a term unknown to me. It is rather eerie, however, to ride alone on a messenger motorcycle through large stretches of forest that have yet to be cleansed.

Over the past few days the Reds have shot many messengers on their motorcycles, dragging them off their bikes in order to torture them terribly and then to kill them. The rashness of the Russian strategy can be seen in the following example:

> This afternoon, when Russian tanks appeared, the crew of one of our panzers climbed out to position its cannon. When we returned, we found it all in flames. A civilian who was in hiding had set it on fire. He was captured and also set on fire.

There is strong ground and aircraft activity from the Russians during the evening. We hear rumors that we have been encircled by enemy tanks. *Scheisse, scheisse!* Stay calm and wait and see!

27 June: Russian anti-tank guns (7.5–22 cm) hammered our positions the entire night. Once again, a night without any peace and sleep. By dawn, the Ratas are present in large numbers; however, none of their firing succeeds at making it into our holes. Like drunken men, they move in, veering to the right, then sharply to the left. We fire like crazy. We know very well what these maneuvers mean—they're sniffing about our positions. Soon they will either take us under well targeted fire, or the heavy flounders [*flundern*] will dive down and dribble a dozen or so bombs into our holes. We are therefore ordered to immediately change positions, which is not that easy, since we are under machine gun fire.

As expected, a jolly group of heavy bombers appear a few minutes later. Again, everything happens in a matter of seconds. Chunks of earth are propelled into the air just 40 to 50 meters from us. Dirt, mud, roots, and entire sections of ground swirl about in the air. Glowing hot pieces of shrapnel land right at our feet. Jagged bolts of lightning slam into the ground with a loud roar. Though as quickly as it started, it was over. The ghostly silence that follows eats on our nerves. Wounded soldiers are moaning.

What will come next? A third and fourth wave, which uncover our exact positions and blow the living lights out of us? Minutes of anxious waiting follow, but nothing happens. Enemy fire has even started to subside. A single SMG [*schweres maschingewehr*—heavy machine gun] chugs on for a while, and then there is silence. What is going on? Why don't the Reds attack this ridiculous bunch of ours? Shortly after, we are given an answer: Our infantry had hobbled in a forced march to our aid. (Hobbled, because it is impossible to talk about walking when mentioning these poor fellows, who have no shoes to cover their blistered feet.) As courteous as the Russians are, they left the area to our soldiers. Now though, the leaf is about to turn!

28 June: The rest of our motorized groups and most importantly our artillery arrive in the morning. Even more important, though, is the food. The *B-Wagen* have also arrived. We would have suffered terribly had the Russians attacked us with only a few drops of gas left in our tanks.

No enemy contact as we advance. Red fighter planes try to disrupt our convoy every now and then, but these brothers do not dare a true attack today, for we have our comrades from the MGK with us today. It is glorious how they pierce the blue skies with their twin-barrel machine guns. Our *Heeres-Fla* [anti-aircraft forces] stutter as if they are possessed. The gentlemen of the Ratas soon tuck in their tails and disappear while growling ferociously. The farewell they bid with their onboard cannons unfortunately costs us two wounded soldiers.

29 June: The morning delivers an explanation as to why the Russians disappeared so quickly. We have taken a few Ukrainian POWs who had been hiding out in the bushes. They had lost the will to continue fighting, and are better informed

Town center of Dubno, present day Rivne Oblast, Ukraine, summer 1941. *(Photograph courtesy of Håkan Henriksson)*

Summer 1941. Ruins from the relentless bombing in Dubno, present day Rivne Oblast, Ukraine. *(Photo courtesy of Håkan Henriksson)*

about the situation than we are, and what they have to say, as their meaningful grins demonstrate, makes us happy. The Russians are encircled, and since the encirclement is weak around Dubno, they have begun to concentrate their forces there in order to try and break through.

We reach Dubno in the evening following a rapid march. The town is free of enemy troops. Earlier in the afternoon, the Russians were forced to surrender the town after putting up a desperate fight. They didn't leave before vandalizing the town like a bunch of *schweine* [pigs]. Everything has been crushed to pieces. We find a large pile of mutilated dead bodies in the town prison.

A so-called "check of the road" on our sidecar motorcycle almost costs us by a hair's breadth our lives. The Reds need to schedule some extra shooting lessons for their recruits. One should be able to hit a motorcycle with three people from a distance of 150 meters—Yes, yes, when one has joyfully survived, one can make fun of the situation! I think that if our helmets had not been on top of our heads, our hair would have stood straight up—the odds were 100 to 3!

Our artillery has let out some hell-fire in the area where the Russians were retreating at dusk. Along with our 9th Panzer Division, we advance in pursuit of the Russians. Our panzers continue to scope out the area under the cover of night. We stay behind to protect the flanks. Anyone who knows what it means to protect the flanks in a war with the Bolsheviks understands that we will have yet again another sleepless night.

30 June: Against the odds, the night is quiet—quiet according to our standards, as we have grown accustomed over the past few days to quite a bit of noise. Shells fly here and there into the fields behind us. Smaller caliber shots are buzzing right before our feet.

A hellish spectacle takes place near the runway around 0300 hours. Our panzers must have encountered enemy forces, yet the Reds are nowhere to be seen around here.

The sun burns mercilessly onto our heads, our limbs are heavy like lead. How nice it would be to take a nap over there in the shade! The *Alte* [Sergeant] must be capable of reading our minds: "Anyone who is not in charge of the cannons can lie down and sleep." People forget where they are. They just fall down on the spot. Others are able to make it into the barn, simply to collapse onto the floor and fall sound asleep.

It is evening when we wake up, our stomachs growling. Here are my words of praise to our cook—the *Rudolph* [playful reference to the most dominant stag]. He is always with us on the front lines, and he is just as tired as we are, yet he is the one who has prepared a nice meal of pork while we were sleeping. Cries of joy arise from our troops, which is followed by a scolding from our superior officer. The cook is nonetheless touched by our delight. The meal that followed allowed us to almost forget the dead, which were lying a hundredfold everywhere.

German soldiers atop a wrecked Soviet T-34 tank in the vicinity of Dubno. *(Photograph courtesy of Håkan Henriksson)*

Shortly after dinner, something terrible happens. One of those damn 122-caliber cannons, which has been plowing around quite regularly, crashed into Group Franke. As the foul smoke retreats, the horrible sight is revealed. There amongst the chaos, between the tree trunks, shards of metal, and pools of blood, lie eight dead comrades. Franke himself lies half buried in the ground in a trench, staring obtusely at the chaos. He lashes about at us as we try to dig him out, yelling: "What do you want from me? I'm staying with my men." The poor guy is close to insanity. After a short time he passes out. He has lost a lot of blood—almost too much blood. A piece of shrapnel has smashed his arm. Life is funny, it was the last Russian shell that struck our camp and caused all of that damage—not a single shot was fired that night!

1 July: It is quiet again this morning. I am lying in the grass looking into the beautiful, blue summer sky above me. Tiny white clouds are sailing west, toward the homeland. The grass has a strong scent. Bumblebees and honeybees are flying from flower to flower. It is similar to peacetime in the Weil Valley. Do you remember, dear Rosel, how we used to lie next to each other under the sun on the slopes of the valley? You would talk so eloquently and passionately about the life of the ants. I wonder what you are doing right now. I long for you so much.

A reconnaissance group returns, and has brought prisoners with them. Most of the prisoners are wounded. The unit discovered a few enemy positions. Most of the prisoners were taken from local pig farms, where they had been attempting to hide.

The Russian soldier is a very strange creature. We Germans will never understand them. On the one hand, they are an immeasurably good natured, helpful, and hospitable people. On the other, they are sadistically gruesome. A German-speaking Ukrainian once told me regarding this: "A week ago, Russian heavy artillery was being put into position in Dubno, when a small child ran

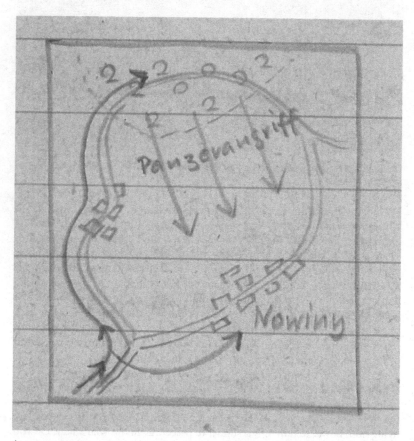

As a reconnaissance cartographer, Hans Roth took great care to depict the 299th Infantry Division's various plans of attack. Here in his first journal was an illustration of the encirclement of the town of Nowiny with its coinciding panzer attack.

in front of one of the caterpillars [*raupen*] and fell. The Russian operating the vehicle saved the child from being rolled over at the last minute. Tears of joy ran down the soldier's checks for the successful rescue. He picked the little girl up into his arms, gave her some candy and took her home to her mother. When he arrived at the house, the soldier destroyed everything, raped the mother, knocked her unconscious, and cut off her breasts. As he left, he gave the little girl some more candy and a small picture of a saint as a farewell."

That's Russia! Who can understand what is going on here? The Russian soldier is a tough opponent who stands his ground until the last bullet. He cannot compare to the bravery of the German soldier who gladly fights for the big goat [*der groß Ziege*].

"Comrade General put me here to shoot. This is why I stand here and shoot." Dispassionate and in no way convinced by [Karl] Marx's philosophy, they stand unexcited in their trenches and shoot. The political commissars in the cities and villages, however, are totally different. Like snipers, they ambush our troops marching through the cities. Good luck to the German soldier who falls into their hands. With sadistic joy they will torture him to death and then mutilate his body beyond recognition. We have already witnessed such atrocious scenes. I pray to God that I will not be taken prisoner.

2 July: It is quiet again today. No shots have been fired. What is going on? I do not like this silence, it eats at my nerves. The Reds have run away and are surely somewhere plotting an evil plan. We hear no news from reconnaissance.

The heat is making us anxious and aggressive. One even sits in the shade like a pig roasting over a spit. The wind blows the sweaty scent of decay into our noses. Damn the smell of dead bodies!

Today everything is making me crazy! It is noon, and we are sitting around in a daze. We are sweaty and thirsty, yet we have nothing left to drink. The wells are surely poisoned, and the water that we had brought with us was drunk ages ago. Digging new wells during the day is too dangerous.

The evening brings cool air and a better mood. We are looking forward to a good night's sleep in the comfortable barn.

I continue to be suspicious because of the silence. The thunder of cannons is approaching us from the west. West—that is the direction we came from. Something is going on! This comes as no surprise. A motorcycle messenger from the division races up to us. "Alert! Get ready and climb in your vehicles!" We leave camp five minutes later. It is 2100 hours. We depart on the road that we arrived on from Dubno. Meanwhile though, it has become pitch dark. The awful road, ripped open by shellfire, is the biggest challenge for Sepp's driving skills and my good eyes! All of a sudden a sharp jerk and we're stuck in a crater left by a shell. Damn darkness! I hit my shinbones so hard that I am seeing stars. By the time we have pulled the motorcycle out of the hole, our entire convoy has passed and is far ahead. There is no one to be seen around; black loneliness is all that surrounds us. We hear the staccato of a machine gun somewhere in the distance. We pass intersections and forks in the road—nothing, we just keep moving. Thank goodness I know our destination, Nowiny. There are officers sitting in a ditch off to the right side of the road.

"How do we get to Nowiny?"

"You have to turn left!"

And so we drive and drive; it has now been hours. At 0130 hours, we reach a small village. An officer is standing at the last house and stops us. He is terribly anxious and asks us if we are crazy. I take this as a matter of fact, and calmly ask why he is so agitated. The news that he shares does not bring me any comfort: the village and the surrounding area has been cleared by our infantry because an attack of about 200 Russian tanks is expected in an hour. *Scheisse!* Our guardian angel advises us to turn back, as it would be suicide to drive any further.

"We are *Panzerschützen* [anti-tank reconnaissance] and not infantrymen, Herr Lieutenant," and we continue on our way. We drive and drive, no creatures are anywhere to be found. Daylight is starting to appear in the east.

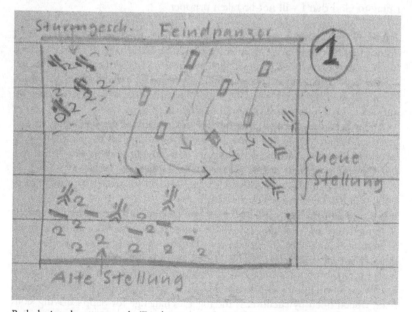

Roth depicts the enemy tank *(Feindpanzer)* attack on July 3, with the infantry's old and new positions, as well as the counterattack by German *Sturmgeschütz* assault guns.

I have a weird feeling in my ass. We should have arrived in Nowiny a long time ago! Before us stands a large forest and I order the engine to be turned off. Intently, we listen into the night. Not very far from us, Russian commands are clearly audible through the humming and banging. A chill runs down my back; the shock almost overwhelms me.

We are in the sector where the Russians are positioning their tanks for the attack! In an instant, we jump on our motorcycle, start the engine, and race off. After an hour we arrive at that infamous intersection. The officers are gone and the *Sturmpionieren* are digging in anti-tank mines. When we arrive, they stare at us as if we are ghosts. We had to turn to the right—not to the left! Five minutes later we rejoin our division in Nowiny.

3 July: It is 0300 hours and the PaKs are being brought into attack formation. We lie in our trenches and await the first wave, which should roll toward us within the next few minutes. Our hearts are hammering in our chests; our foreheads are cold and white. With fire in our eyes, we stare toward the gentle waves in the field from where we expect the attack. Soon masses of Russian tanks will approach. We know all too well that it will be life or death for each and every one of us today.

To surprise our leaders, the Russians have organized an entire tank division and infantry in the adjacent forests. They are going to attempt to break through in this area, since the front line here is extremely narrow. On the double we gathered together an infantry battalion and our tank buster unit, along with ten anti-tank cannons in order to oppose the Russians.

It is now 0330 hours. There, on the hill directly in front of us, the Russians suddenly appear. Slowly, in a zigzag maneuver, the first wave approaches. They have all the time in the world to floor us.

"Aim 70!" Damn it, just keep cool! Patience. Let these *schweine* come closer. 100 meters… 90 meters, 80, now 70 meters. Almost simultaneously, ten shells from our ten anti-tank cannons strike the approaching steel monsters. Is it possible, flames and black smoke are rising from four tanks? Five other tanks are standing motionless. The halt has been lifted; now our task starts. Leave the trenches!

Under the cover of our cannons, we draw closer to the tanks that are still standing, and which are still firing like crazy. The second wave approaches, and there on top of the hill one can already see the third wave. We must retreat, as we are under heavy fire. One after the other, we work our way back from one trench to the next. My comrade on the left throws his arms in the air—he's been hit. The cannon that was protecting us suddenly breaks apart—a direct hit. A comrade lies motionless on the ground right in front of me—dead; and to my right a soldier is also shouting for the medic.

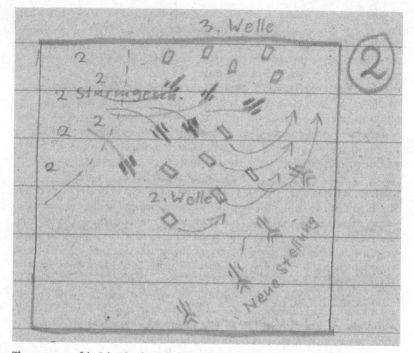

The next stage of the July 3 battle, with the Soviets' third wave (*Welle*) of tanks and the German assault guns advancing.

Just twenty meters to the trench! Please God, help! Will this be the end? They are now shooting shells right in front of our feet. I throw myself down on the ground and hold on to the earth. The ground is being ripped up right before me. I jump up once again, almost stumbling over two comrades who have been torn apart from the shelling. Damn tank cannons! Another impact right in front of me! The shrapnel is howling around my ears. A fist-size chunk shreds my gas mask; more shrapnel severs the hand piece from my machine gun.

And then, I finally make it! I am now in the trench. I suddenly do not care anymore. I throw myself on the ground, face to the sky, and wait for the tanks to arrive and crush me.

Poor Rosel, sweet Erika! ... Your husband fell on the field of honor on 3 July... etc., etc.... Don't think, do not think!

Meanwhile, the following happened in our section: the accurate fire of our cannons fought off the first attack, and our anti-tank cannons took advantage

Photograph taken by an unknown German soldier on 14 September, 1942 in the village of Onufriyvka close to Kremenchuk in present day Kirovohrad Oblast. A group of German soldiers are being awarded the "*Eiserne Kreuz*"—the Iron Cross. *(Photograph courtesy of Håkan Henriksson)*

of the chaos that followed to change their positions. The second wave pushes wild firing toward our previous positions in an attempt to crush us. Suddenly, they receive fire into their flanks from the east. A few heavy tanks are eliminated. They turn immediately to the east and take our current position under fire.

[Side note:] This saves my life. Apart from myself, there was no one else at our former position. Two men succeeded in making it into the woods to the west. The remaining men were lying in the field either dead or wounded.

Moments later, the third wave approaches from the hill, and at the same time, our assault guns advance, firing in turn at the second and third waves.

This situation may be unique to the entire Eastern campaign. The leaders know that only this move alone will be able to save us from destruction. Remaining cool-blooded is the key to success in such circumstances. One imprecise shot can hit our own assault guns and vice-versa; inaccurate fire from our anti-tank cannons can destroy our own assault guns.

Being fired at from two sides, the second wave veers to the north, creating havoc for the third wave. Sixteen more Red tanks are destroyed and the rest attempt to take cover on the side of the hill.

Photograph depicting German soldiers returning from a reconnaissance mission. As Roth describes, the men have camouflaged their helmets with reed and covered their bodies in mud. Taken in June 1943, close to Nikopol, present day Dnipropetrovsk Oblast, Ukraine. *(Photograph courtesy of Håkan Henriksson)*

And then a miracle happens: German SS troops in camouflage jackets appear to our rear. It is the *Leibstandarte* [*Adolf Hitler*]—finally arriving after hours of waiting. They were halted somewhere around Dubno and ordered on a forced march to come to our aid. They had only been in their positions for about ten minutes before alternating rows of Russian tanks and soldiers appeared. The battle lasted three hours. It was a terrible butchery—a man-against-man fight that could not have been any worse.

A bayonet wounds my upper arm. Get the first-aid kit and move on! The sun is burning down on our helmets. I am no longer wearing my jacket. To their surprise, we attack enemy tanks and soldiers, who are dressed in just their shirts and pants. Aircraft arrive and join in on the ground attack with great effect. The entire valley is stirring like a cauldron.

Victory comes that afternoon. The Reds attack for the last time around 1500 hours. The masses charge with a loud "hurrah!" There are no longer any tanks;

with our concentrated fire we mowed them down row after row. The attack is gloriously crushed. The Russians make a final retreat to the north.

As sweet as victory may be, our casualties are numerous. Of the 12 ordnances in the 3rd, seven have been destroyed by direct hits. My knees are soft like rubber. Don't collapse! Although our strength is fading, there is no time to rest. That same night we march on to Rowne.

4 July: Around midnight we stop at a village lying peacefully blanketed in the moonlight. We have not had any enemy contact until here. The plan is to stay here the rest of the night and sleep in the houses. However, we receive warning to move on, as the village may or may not be held by the Russians. Once again, we "rest" in the ditch next to the road. After making several detours, we arrive at our destination at around 0700 hours. We are refreshed after a few hours sleep.

The Russians have retreated a great distance. The division's order of the day is read that afternoon. It is full of praise for our troops' courage during yesterday's tank battle. However, we also receive bad news: 36 comrades fell and many were wounded. The announcement ends on a staggering note: Red motorized units ambushed a supply convoy and annihilated it—53 comrades were butchered. Unfortunately, three of our own panzers arrived on scene too late. Michen, Hufmann, Brosig, Sudback, and Schmidt from our unit died yesterday.

5 July: We continue our march in the morning. Our panzers took Rowne last night and we push forward in a forced march to cleanse the area like any infantry would. The heat is terrible! Our infantry marches in this heat 150km in two days. All the units are working tremendously hard.

6 July: We continue on after midnight. Our pace is extreme; we barely have time to eat and we don't dare think of sleeping. We break through the lines of a few weak enemy forces that are attempting to stand in our way. We leave their destruction to the troops that follow to our rear.

"Push forward! It's all or nothing!" Damn it, what is "all" anyway! What is going on?

During the sparse breaks, we shuffle about on our legs of rubber. The sun is burning mercilessly on our skulls. The engines are humming quietly and radiate the stench of diesel. The dust is so thick that I am unable to see the person in front of me. My eyes tear up and burn. My mug [*fresse*, or face] is crusted with dirt. The damn limestone gets in everywhere.

We reach Korcecz at night. We pass through the town after a short battle. We roll on at a maddening speed. Orders to halt are finally issued after an hour. I feel like I was just put through a meat grinder. I let myself collapse a few steps from my motorcycle. Even the enticing smell coming from the mobile field kitchen is unable to motivate me to get up. Sleep, I just want to sleep!

7 July: Our artillery fires all throughout the night. I think there is danger brewing out on the front lines. The air is thick and I can smell trouble. Rumors are circulating that we are in proximity to the dreaded Stalin Line.

In the early hours of the morning, strings of Russian fighters appear at low altitude. Their on-board machine guns scour our positions, and bomb after bomb is dropped across our lines. Thank goodness there are no casualties.

It calms down around noon—and how about that—we receive mail! After 14 days, a letter from Rosel. I am so happy to have that woman as my wife! Her bravery can be felt in each line. Her good heart gives me much courage and comfort for the difficult hours to come!

I have only one wish: to get home in good health and to thank her.

8 July: *Scheisse.* No sleep again last night. At around 2300 hours, our old reconnaissance group crept forward through the swamps around the Slucz River. We must have looked ridiculous with our painted war faces. On top of our heads we had our *hurratute* [slang for steel helmet] camouflaged with dirt and garnished with reed. We carried a bag with hand grenades around our chest and our machine gun over our shoulders. Our only clothing was a bathing suit. Our bodies were covered in clay from head to toe. That was how we left camp.

We made it to the first line of enemy bunkers without seeing any infantry or trenches. We returned around 0200 hours without ever being noticed by the Russians. I tried to sleep, though with no luck, due to the thousands of disgusting mosquitoes from the swamps that torture us down to the blood. It can drive one crazy! All of that on top of the heat and constant thirst!

Unexpectedly, at 1100 hours a swift attack from the Stalin Line. At the same time, Russian bombers attack at low altitude. We are suddenly awoken from our slumber. The first salvo was alarmingly precise. Wounded soldiers are crying and moaning. Foul-smelling smoke hangs below the trees. Ten minutes later, and the ground near us bursts into the air; fragments of splinters fly into our foxholes. The firewall moves slowly toward the so-called "Tarn Position." Here, shells and bombs create a dreadful bloodbath; 41 dead and 82 wounded lie where our *Kradschützen* [motorcycle infantry] had been positioned. We have to work until late in the evening in order to recover the dead and secure our wounded comrades. My heart aches when I think of their loved ones—their mothers, wives, and children.

We regroup and reposition on the same night due to the large number of casualties. The grand attack against the front lines and the fortifications to the west of Zwiahel [Novohrad-Volynskyi] will commence tomorrow morning. The situation is as follows:

> Our scouts discovered days ago that 5th Army is moving in a forced march toward Zwiahel so as to secure an important crossing over the Slucz River. The crossings are being protected by strong enemy units. However,

thanks to our forced march, we have arrived here first. I now understand the reason why we were marching at such an insane speed during these past few days. The primary Red Army formations are still a day's march to the east of Zwiahel. We must use all our strength to break through the strongholds so as to take the city and river crossings tomorrow. Each and every one of us knows what is at stake. We are ready.

9 July: The big coup was a success. Today, around noon, the town of Zwiahel, and the crossings over the Slucz fell into our hands after fierce resistance—just in time. The initial units of the Russian 5th Army arrived at just about the same time. We could not have asked for anything better than to have the band of fortifications now destroyed. The effect of our 30.5 caliber mortars and Stukas was devastating. Together with the *Sturmpioneren*, we contributed well to the collapse of the bunkers.

The Reds make a retreat to their fortified positions by the woods where the masses of enemy soldiers are regrouping for a counterattack. We, however, are rewarded by having our heads bloodied for our attempt to follow and destroy the Russians; we are outnumbered. With our one and only division we're supposed to hold the city and bridgehead until noon tomorrow. We can only expect the adjoining divisions to arrive tomorrow at the earliest.

The faces of the officers and soldiers are very serious. How far along are the preparations on the other side for an attack? Will the flank reinforcements arrive in time? Nothing but questions for which there are no answers. The situation is grave or even desperate. If the Russians attack now, or during the night, their sheer masses will trample us into the ground. Stories from the Great War about the Russian steamroller [*dampfwalze*] suddenly come to mind. Yes, they will definitely smash us to a pulp of blood and dirt. Again, the orders are made clear: "The town and bridgehead will be held to the last man!"

It is evening. Hour after hour, we expect the attack; however, nothing happens. With the exception of the flashes from cannon fire, nothing out of the ordinary is occurring on the other side.

What is happening? Are the Russians going to miss their big chance once again? Don't they know that their opponents are nothing more than small combat forces? Again, we start to ponder our thoughts, which are beginning to eat on our nerves. At midnight, the order to send out reconnaissance troops comes as a blessing. Soon after, the old caste leaves our lines. The Russians have also sent out patrol units. We encounter one of them during our investigation. We take one prisoner after a brief exchange of fire.

The night is pitch black. Occasionally we hear the whistling of a shell or of tracers flying through the sky. Otherwise it is quiet. It is only between the lines that scouts from both sides are crawling around, trying to sniff their way around the enemy's position and gather information. Upon their discovery, a short burst of a machine gun follows, and then it is quiet again. The damn silence is making me suspicious.

10 July: We returned to our lines at dawn. Interrogation of our prisoner confirmed our suspicions: an entire army lies on the other side. However, they appear not to be firmly entrenched yet.

Someone delivered the mail during the night. A letter received by one of our comrades is passed from trench to trench. In it, someone is complaining about working overtime, the shortage of beer and cigarettes, and other similar matters. How little does that idiot understand about the things that go on out here? Is that the voice of the homeland? They will hear our stories of success at home and Mr. "Indispensible" will say in triumph: "Well, we've done a great job, haven't we?" Let it be said: you local natives, if anyone has accomplished anything it was us! Well, we are indebted to you for our great weapons and ammunition without duds, but the Russians too have good weapons—sometimes even better than ours! The key factor is the spirit and bravery of the person carrying those weapons. None of you guys have any idea of these two things. Shame on you if you think that you have fought these battles and have accomplished such great victories with your overtime! Think about our overtime out here. The reward for some of us was a burning piece of metal in our spine.

The idiot continues to write in his letter to the front that we had it better out here; here, not because he has remembered his manhood, but "because there is an abundance of cigarettes, beer, and schnapps at the front, and the shootings aren't that bad at all!" Such impertinence leaves one speechless! Dear Sir, you are more than welcome to join us! You will shit in your pants because of all these cigarettes and cigars in the air. But enough of that—we have other issues and problems than talking about the whining of a "home-fighter." My anger is blown away when I think of the pure idealism of my parents.

IR 530 [530th Infantry Regiment] receives orders at 1000 hours to push forward from Rzadkowka toward Czykowka. After battling for four hours over every yard, and suffering an enormous amount of casualties, they have to retreat to their original positions. If we hadn't had the heavy artillery, which protected the flanks with an iron curtain, the Russians would have rolled over our entire front line from the flanks.

Unfortunately the Russians have encircled part of the retreating regiment. It is impossible to utilize our artillery; the danger of hitting your own guys is too large. Therefore, "Volunteers are needed!" There is not much discussion among us—comrades are in danger, which is all we need to know.

In company formation we attempt to attack the Russians simultaneously from both sides. We each throw our two smoke grenades at the right moment. The Russians seem to be sensitive to the white smoke. They assume a large-scale counterattack from the west and retreat to their fortified positions. We lose a few comrades who approach too close to the iron curtain that the Russian heavy artillery has erected around our position. We make our way back to our lines with just a small number of casualties.

Arriving at our positions we receive good news: reinforcement divisions have arrived on our flanks. Thank goodness! A huge weight has been lifted from our chests. The attack will commence tomorrow. Wonderful!

11 July: The hellish spectacle starts all over at night. The ground shakes for an hour from the exploding shells. Shrapnel is whistling over our heads. Flares rise into the skies and light up the smoke. They then direct the fire into our vicinity in heavy batteries. What is going on? Do these *schweine* want to attack us as well? Flare after flare rises into the sky. Our faces are white and petrified. No shots are being fired from our side. However, B-officers [*B offizier*] and light and sound measuring troops [*licht und schall messungtrupps*] are working feverishly. The fire then becomes weaker. It must be time for their attack. Our eyes try to penetrate the darkness. Where are the Red flares? Nothing? Everything is as it was before; the fire slowly dies out. It is now quiet, much too quiet for our nerves.

0330 hours: initial fire from 36 batteries suddenly begins. 150 cannons of all size calibers spit their shells across enemy lines. Like the sound of a sawmill, they howl, hiss, and streak through the air. Light flashes along the edge of the forest; these are the impacts of our shelling.

We advance along the train tracks under the cover of our firewall. From there we take over and cover our advancing infantry regiments. The Russians, understanding the importance of such a position, attempt to storm the train tracks. Our shelling has brought them enormous casualties; however, more and more enemy fighters are flocking to the scene. My machine gun barks and spits out its deadly rounds against the attackers. It is magnificent! The railroad embankment provides excellent cover.

Not a single shell sprays its splinters near our heads. *Prima, prima!* [Awesome, awesome!] It is like a shooting range out here, and it goes on like this for a long time. Our mood is excellent. Some are even making cruel jokes. Oh how these young men have become so cold-hearted. Yet one should never forget the gravity of the moment during battle—it might just take its bitter revenge, which is what happened in our situation.

During target practice we completely forgot about the right end of the railroad embankment. Despite all our wild fire, the Russians somehow managed to position a heavy machine gun there—and shortly after, a second machine gun. It cost a lot of our sweat and blood to get them off the embankment. We are unable to bring our PaK into position atop the embankment. All that is available to us are our machine guns and a bunch of hand grenades—a lot of hand grenades. We were able to get them off of the embankment within two hours. We had one dead and one wounded comrade lying over there behind the bushes. And the day had started so well!

It's two in the afternoon, the sky is deep blue. It is so hot that one can see the air coming over the embankment in waves. The train tracks are steaming they're so hot. The ties are slippery and stink from the hot tar. The vapors from the tar are good for the lungs, they say! *Scheisse*! There is a dead body on the ground over there—shot through the chest. Because of the stupid scene at the other end of the tracks, the Russians have had enough time to entrench themselves just 300 meters from us. If we had enough, we could hammer them with grenades. If we had enough...

We've already thrown too many grenades. Two men went back to retrieve more ammunition, but they don't seem to be coming back. Thank goodness—the Russians have lost their drive to keep attacking us. They are occupied with digging themselves in. They're masters at that. I look carefully to the left. What a splendid view. For as far as I can see, there are plumes of smoke above the impact craters from our shells. The artillery from both sides is doing its job at creating a protective firewall. The position of the Russian fire unfortunately tells me that we have only advanced about one kilometer.

Reinforcements arrive at night, as we expect a major offensive from the Russians around sunset. If we are unable to receive protection from our artillery, we will hold the embankment with iron will. We wait and wait, and not a single shot is fired. It is getting dark. I am lying between the tracks in a lookout position. What was that? There is a clang and crashing of pieces of metal. Almost immediately one of us fires a flare. Shots are fired, and shortly after bullets from a heavy machine gun whistle over our heads.

The Russians used the cover of darkness to approach our position to within one hundred meters and commence a hellish concert. The bursts of their machine gun fire are situated only a couple hands wide above the top of the embankment. Series of rounds strike the train tracks. A few projectiles ricochet off the train tracks in sloping trajectories. The singing of infantry carbines can be easily distinguished from the buzzing and hammering of the heavy machine guns.

The damn Russian water-cooled machine guns crackle like a thousand alarm clocks. We carefully bring a PaK into position onto one of the canals below the embankment to our right. A large group of soldiers is also deployed to protect the cannon. (Only five comrades return the next morning after this suicide mission.) We are unable to shoot due to our lack of visibility and our need to save the flares for a later moment. We just lie there and wait. We keep our carbines or machine guns positioned in our arms, our legs bent, prepared to jump up and fire. Our hands grip reassuringly our grenades and ammo clips. The light machine gun crews are sitting alert, ready to tilt the barrel and start firing. As the fire pauses, I realize that it is my neighbor, the "greenhorn," who received the letter earlier today that made me so angry. He rolled down the embankment—dead from a shot to the head. Poor guy! He had just shown me pictures of his young wife this morning.

The shooting, however, has picked up again. New showers of shrapnel are raining down; the air is filled with singing and whining. Ricocheting bullets howl. It sounds like the crackling of a fire or the blazing of spruce trees. The mad fire suddenly subsides. A final few hungry carbines are still spitting their last bullets from their clips—then, absolute silence. We leap up onto the railroad embankment, staring and listening into the night. We cup our hands behind our ears as funnels in order to improve our hearing. Then flares soar up into the sky, burst, and sail slowly to the ground. More flares rise up, and we continue to stare and listen. The stillness is disturbing. We can feel our hearts beating in our chests and temples. Our hands search reassuringly for hand grenades. More flares take off like fireworks.

Now we can see them coming, those Red bastards, that Asian mob. Night attacks are a particular specialty of this gang. Flare after flare shoots into the sky. We open fire from a distance of 150 meters. Our shells slam into the attacker's lines and tear open large holes. However, it is night and the terrain is full of natural obstacles. Wave after wave approaches. A bitter battle of man against man is being waged along the canal to the right of the embankment. The cannon over there is out of ammunition and the Russians finish off its crew. Our machine guns are still able to keep the bastards away from us, but for how much longer? Messengers return to HQ. *Verflucht noch mal!* [Damn it!] Artillery fire is the only thing that can help us here. We shoot signal flares into the sky again and again—in between, enemy flares illuminate the scene. Red tracers also soar into the air in the neighboring sector. What wonderful fireworks, what a grandiose illumination of fear and horror!

We receive orders to retreat to our baseline positions. The entire front line must be pulled back to its original position. Damn it, it is unbelievable that we must retreat—we, the 299th Infantry Division, have to run; German soldiers have to abandon the field to those Russian *schweine!*

Now the drama of the retreat is beginning, which costs us many dead and wounded. We reach our original positions around 0200 hours. Our artillery provides us cover.

12 July: A *Sturmgeschütz* [assault gun] group takes over our section of the front. We are pulled back about 3km. A mass dropping of Russian paratroopers is expected in this area to the rear of our artillery positions, and we are the ones who will have to deal with them.

Shrapnel trenches are dug in great haste. They must be dug deeper since there are no tree trunks in the area to use for cover. This is a dismal landscape. Apparently the Reds cut down all the trees years ago and kept the water, rendering large areas into swamps. Man-high bushes cover the areas of open marshes, but not us attackers.

The Russians, masters of camouflage and the construction of tactical barriers, have erected their HQ alongside a large forest at the northern entrance to this cauldron of a landscape. The perimeter of the forest was left to grow wild and is therefore covered with hedges and swamp bogs. Beneath the hedges, they have dug escape tunnels about two meters deep, which can be flooded in case of emergency. The bunkers for the positioning of their machine guns are grown over with vegetation. Even with the best optical instruments, it is impossible to make them out. A deserter has told us that hundreds of rangers and soldiers worked for years to transform this area into its present condition. Villages that are still indicated on our maps have disappeared.

Trails and roads were mined a month ago. Grass was then seeded above the mines, trails, and roads. Hand grenades that were suspended on wires in the bushes have also ripped apart two comrades this morning.

The shrapnel trenches are complete, the vehicles have been camouflaged, and cannons dug into the ground in semi-circle formation. We await anything that might come. The artillery puts on a great show. The second attack started at 0500 this morning. Howitzers, right before us, incessantly spray their shrapnel into the air. Our very heavy equipment buzzes and rumbles further behind us. Their heavy shells fly close above our heads, targeting bridges, important roads, and mobile ammunition depots, which are 20 to 25km behind Russian lines.

Meanwhile, it is now noon. Brutal heat is bearing down on the trenches and swamps all around us. The blaze of the sun is driving me insane; my eyes burn from all that staring up into the sun. My head hurts as if being pricked by a thousand needles. Damn it! Do not pass out! Hannes!

It is disgusting—our clothes are sticking to our bodies. A stinking broth, a mixture of sweat and eight days of dirt are underneath my helmet and runs down my cheeks only to disappear into my collar. Damn this trench warfare, damn this stupid swamp without any shade or water to drink.

Russian reconnaissance aircraft appear in the afternoon at low altitude. The obligatory attack starts shortly after; however, it does not cause any damage. From time to time they shoot at our position, attempting to locate our ordnance, yet they have no luck.

The enemy fire slowly dies down by sunset. Messengers relay the latest news: the front line has advanced by a thousand meters. We are very excited about the news, even if it is only a kilometer. We have been humbled during these dreadful days.

13 July: Except for having to take turns on watch, we all got a few hours sleep last night. Wow, we got some real sleep! Yes, it really does exist! This of course doesn't mean that these few hours of sleep have really refreshed us. The opposite is true—I feel groggy. All my bones ache from sleeping crouched in a hole. So, get out of the trench and shake those bones. Though most of us don't have the chance to do so, since the Russians plant a round of good morning fire at our position. All of the bushes in front of us have been trimmed—the best gardeners could hardly have done a better job.

Unbelievable, comrade, it could have all gone wrong! Someone tells us that he has seen phantom troops; another reports that they have gone into position behind our lines. Someone else is talking about new weapons and a mysterious DO device that has been brought into position in order to be used for the very first time to break through the tough Russian resistance.

An enormous detonation from cannon fire disrupts our guesswork. A single pounding impact and a yellowish white wall of smoke rises up about 500 meters, blocking out the sun for a short time. Hundreds of missiles—they must be missiles gauging from the smoke tail—howl through the air toward the enemy. A second, third, and fourth round follow soon after. This is a rare spectacle! We have left our trenches and are standing on top of the cover to admire the show. It has beaten the wind out of the Russians, who have not fired a single shot from the other side.

I get more information about the spectacle at noon: the DO device is able to fire multiple rocket-propelled shells simultaneously. The shells are filled with flame-oil. Once the projectile hits the ground the flame-oil splatters everywhere, setting everything ablaze. The effect must be devastating. Despite this, the Russians continue to hold their positions.

Our heads are bloodied when we attempt to break through enemy positions on part of the border. The Reds are beginning their counterattack. We manage to bring it to a halt, though with a number of casualties larger than theirs. We have almost reached the end of our fighting strength. The unbearable heat and the brutality of combat have battered us. We will only be able to take the waves of Russian attacks for a little while longer! We need fresh troops! In the past two days Infantry Regiments 529 and 528 have lost 380 and 304 men, respectively. The replacements are coming too slowly. Enormous projectiles are crashing into our positions. They rip large chunks out of the ground. What an honor it is that these gentlemen are wasting their large calibers on a bunch of poor ants like us.

It is getting serious now. The Reds have brought railroad cannons onto the track in the direction of Zhitomir [Ukraine], where they are out of reach of our ordnance. In the evening, the Russian *schweine* attack us under the cover of heavy fire. They manage to push us back a few kilometers to the outskirts of the town.

I could cry out of anger and frustration. Nothing works anymore. My body does not want to cooperate any longer. My nerves are singing like the wires of a telegraph. Will I ever see my home again?

Today's toll: 20 dead, 11 missing, and 163 wounded. Dear Rosel! My Butziben, keep your dad in dear memory!

14 July: We are ordered to attack this morning at 0800 hours. However, yesterday's thunderstorm has flooded the roads and rendered them impassable. What now? The following radio message arrives around 0900: "Attack postponed. Reorganize into defensive formation!" So, the Russians are going to attack again. Yes. And how badly they attack! The large calibers buzz over into our positions. Whole series of shells are accompanied by smaller calibers and rounds with tremendous shrapnel capacity.

In sequence, bombers drop their eggs at low altitude. Fighters spew forth rounds of machine gun fire into our trenches. It is a hellish spectacle capable of robbing a man of his sanity. Half crazy, we crouch down in our trenches. All around us the ground is being thrown into the air—right before our very eyes. To our left and right, to our rear … flames dart everywhere. My hair is charred. A large chunk of soil flies against my helmet and knocks me out for a brief moment. And then they come, the *roten teufel* [Red devils]. "Hurrah! Hurrah!"

The first ones close in on us to within 50 meters. We clamber out of our trenches. The machine gun crews stay behind to give us cover. Are these the same people? Their faces are distorted beyond recognition. The hate and endless anger against these bloodhounds switches off any sort of thinking. We end the attack half an hour later. I do not remember the details of the butchery. It is unbelievable, but true. We ran forward like homicidal maniacs. We shot, slashed, and beat. We fell down, got up, and stormed forward again. I am just not able to remember all of the details. And look at us! My shirt is torn, my hands and knees are bleeding, and there are traces of blood all over my uniform. On the collar of my left boot hangs a piece of pulverized brain. I have to vomit. Enough! Now comes the reaction. I feel dizzy and have cold chills—nerve fever.

15 July: I slept 20 hours straight and am feeling much better now. Large caliber shells and bombs have changed a great deal the appearance of our position.

I can only wonder about this: I did not notice any of the fire spectacles while I was lying well protected in the medic's tent. I must have been sleeping like the dead.

A shimmering heat lingers over our position. Water sits in large puddles in our muddy trenches and gives off an odor of decay. The air and the ground are alive with insects. Black masses of flies gather on anything edible. Apart from some light artillery fire, it has been a relatively quiet today. The rest has done me well. We are further encouraged by the words of [Sixth Army's Field Marshal Walter von] Reichenau; he sends us his greatest respect for our courage and bravery.

16 July: The front line has not moved. There has been no combat worth mentioning. Every now and then, there are single rifle shots, the chugging of a machine gun, or even a few rounds of artillery. Bombers attack our position around noon. A stockpile of ammunition was hit; the explosion tears eight comrades apart, and many more are wounded. The loud blare of battle is coming from both the left and right flanks. Divisions of fresh troops are apparently attacking there and are making good progress. Will the Russians finally have to run?

17 July: We are blessed with enemy fire this morning. Their shelling hammers into our positions for an hour, and Ratas appear as a surprise. They are flying about twenty meters over our heads and fire into our columns. The spectacle is then suddenly over. Shots are no longer being fired by them; then we get the message that the Russians are retreating. We can't believe it. We've gotten excited over one too many false messages during these past few days. And yet, it is all true. Our artillery fires into units of fleeing Russians.

Orders for an attack arrive in the afternoon. By dusk we conquer a stretch of about 4 kilometers of the Forest of the Dead northeast of Zwiahel. The terrible ten days of trench warfare, with all of its horrors, hours of artillery fire, and bloody man-to-man combat is finally over.

Our eyes are filled with tears of joy.

18 July: The Reds must have had tremendous casualties, since our artillery fire was correctly targeted. Shreds of tree trunks are all over the ground. Our shelling has ripped apart the forest floor. Among the destruction lie hundreds of bodies, demolished gear, vehicles, and every type of gun. Bodies of the hated enemy lie in massive piles in front of their positions. The bodies are blackened and swollen by the heat. The terrible, pungent smell of decay looms over the entire forest. Many, many of our comrades can finally be buried.

Much of the details of the battles during these last days remind me of the grim forest battles in La Besace [France] a year ago, but the Russian is a different opponent than the Belgians and French. At that time, we fought against men who, as soldiers, applied intelligence, endurance, and experience; the enemy here resembles a dull, indifferent, soulless machine of destruction and death. At our leisure, we took the Russians in our vice grip. The French would have learned from experience and attempted to avoid unnecessary casualties. These guys here fight like mad until nothing moves. They never surrender!

This evening we suddenly receive artillery fire out of the blue. I go on watch during the night, those eerie hours. We know that there are still many Russian *schweine* hidden in the forest. The night is pitch black. Every creak in the woods could be a Russian lurking around. I'm at my wits end. Morning finally arrives and brings with it the obligatory artillery fire.

19 July: I'm hungry. Food has been sparse and bad for days now. Cigarettes, the *Kola Dallmann* [a popular cola based candy] of the German soldier, are also no longer available.

It is raining. The damn stench of the dead bodies is worse than ever. We have the worst case of malaria. Reading Rosel's letters is my only joy. I pray to God that I return safe and sound.

20 July: The Reds have moved into a new defensive position which they try to hold onto with all of their might. This is the third line of the Nowograd-Wolynok [Zwiahel] bunkers—part of the Stalin Line. We've gotten a few bloody heads trying to storm those damn concrete bunkers. Because we are so exhausted, they don't expect us to venture into a second round of attacks.

Thank God! We are being replaced by fresh troops. We remain on alert in the forest. We dig our trenches close to a group of artillery cannons which had been moved in as reinforcements.

Since we have always been the first line of defense, we have never had the opportunity to see the firing of the 21cm long barrel cannons at close range. Our eyes and mouths are wide open in awe of these guns—first in awe, then to protect our eardrums. Such a monster requires a crew of forty. It fires up to a distance of 40km. The projectile weighs three centners [approximately 150kg or 330 lbs]. The effect of its shrapnel covers an area of approximately 1,000 meters—enough to yank the molars out of many Russians at no extra charge. A single shot costs about 2,000 Reichsmark. "People, come to the donation box! Who has not donated yet, who still wants to buy a WHW [lottery ticket]?" Two thousand Marks a pop! That is the combined income of the Praunheim and Romerstadt donation boxes. Prepare yourselves collectors, as many more shots are being fired today. And by the way, the cannons here are booty from Czechoslovakia and were manufactured by Skoda. They were built for the Turkish Army but ended up in the German Army. Yes indeed, the Sudetenland Campaign has indeed brought something good.

Our commander gives a speech in the afternoon that fills us with pride.

The 299th Infantry Division has been able to withstand the pressure from the Russian 5th Army for days now. The Russians deployed into battle their elite troops from the Moscow defense force. Their one last task is to push a wedge between us and Group von Kleist. They will fail.

Crucial operations in the south are in jeopardy. We are all now well aware of the situation and will fight, fight until the last man is left standing. We face several difficult hours ahead. Enormous casualties have weakened our fighting power. The Moscow radio station broadcast yesterday that the 298th and 299th Infantry Divisions were destroyed near Zwiahel—nothing more than wishful thinking! It's not over yet! Did we not just beat you by five hours in reaching the Slucz River? Is that your reason for barking into the microphone! You guys could barely run fast enough! We'll teach you how to run, but in the opposite direction.

Soviet soldiers captured by the Germans close to Uman in present day Ukraine, summer 1941. *(Photograph courtesy of Håkan Henriksson)*

Ukrainian women enlisted to help German soldiers at a stone quarry in Postepnoye, Ukraine. *(Photograph courtesy of Håkan Henriksson)*

Unbelievable! Our tired bunch is ordered to rest for a few days in a neighboring village! This good news has caught us by surprise! It's about time! The casualties would otherwise be great.

22 July: We move into the village in separate groups this morning. It has been severely destroyed from our artillery fire. All that remain of its original inhabitants can be found on four or five farms at most. They stand in front of their cottages with curiosity rather than anger in their faces. Perhaps they just have good self-control. They must be curious about what will happen next.

Our first mission is to split up and search for food. "Min Bohn" was very lucky. He found a pack of "Mahorka" [Soviet brand of tobacco]. The good soul is standing out on the side of the road handing it out to us. Everybody gets a small portion.

We sit down and start to split some old newspapers. Some pull the *schweisslappen* [strips of newspaper used inside boots] out of their boots. Soon the entire first platoon is steaming like a train station. This "Mahorka" is really bad stuff, though since all we've been smoking these past few days is grass, leaves, and all kinds of herbs, it tastes like the best Italian tobacco.

We set up camp on a meadow on the outskirts of the village. We pitch our tents and dig foxholes for cover. The "wandering plumber store," guys who are responsible for all of the pots, pans, and cooking equipment, are relieved of their precious load; frying and cooking takes place soon thereafter. After eating, we just sit around, staring into the evening sky not worrying about the front line at all.

No one will ever know how it all started: out of the blue, someone starts singing a song in a clear tenor voice; all of a sudden it gets so quiet that "Min Bohn's" cigarette slips out of his mouth (now that I think about it, his mouth was actually quite wide open). Others start singing along and soon the whole bunch is singing. Some just sit with their arms around their knees; others lie on their backs using their arms under their heads as pillows. The singing becomes louder and louder: "Brave little soldier's wife, we will come home soon!"

The song "My home stands in the most beautiful meadow…" starts up after a short pause, and everyone is singing. Workers, farmers, teachers, and businessmen are all singing together. They have all become comrades in their gray uniforms. With their steel helmets, and in the face of death, they sing this melancholy song line by line, and with devotion. They fill each line with their longing for peace, tranquility, their wives and kids.

They do not have their own words for the emotions that dominate their spirits. It is awkward for them to express their emotions, which is why they sing a song about the house or valley where they were born. There is a gorgeous sky full of stars above me. Those same stars are also right now above my house in Westhausen. Are you thinking of me, my dear Rosel!?

The town of Zhitomyr under German occupation. Panje wagons can be seen passing through in the background. *(Photograph courtesy of Håkan Henriksson.)*

After about ten hours of quality sleep, I get up to take a close look around the village. Groups of refugees, mostly women and children, arrive from all directions; they had been hiding out in the surrounding woods. The men of the village were forced to fight for the Reds and have fallen dead in their houses and on the streets. There are shocking scenes everywhere we turn. Women are looking for their dead husbands and brothers. Children are finding the torn apart bodies of their fathers. Horrible images. A woman with an infant in her arms tries to pull the dead body of her husband into an old foxhole in order to bury him.

An elderly couple is seated at the corner of a house. The old man is hunched over—dead. The *babuschka* [Russian for grandmother] leans against her husband, her eyes fixated on the horror surrounding them. Their sons and grandsons lie inside the house in large, black pools of blood. She has lost her voice, and her soul is forever dead.

A little further away, a group of about twenty comrades lie mowed down from machine gun fire. Two dead fighters gripped in a deadly man-against-man fight lie dead in the neighboring garden. The Red is still grasping onto his bayonet in his rigid hand. Gauging from the wound, he had stabbed the German in the neck. The Red's head is swollen; the German's hands are still clinched around the neck of the Russian like iron clamps. I know all too well the horror of man fighting against man. We are unable to separate all the bodies, so both friend and foe are buried together. In hole after hole we bury twenty-one of our best comrades. Fifty-eight Russians are buried in a mass grave.

The heat is unbearable. The stench of decay is disgusting. We hold handkerchiefs in front of our faces to protect ourselves from it. We have to use force to pull the women and children away from their dead relatives. The risk of infection is also very high.

My knees are weak on our way back home. Is it because of the brutal heat, or the horrific images?

24 July: Alternating periods of sun and rain showers. It is like a greenhouse in the swamps, and we must take quinine tablets to prevent the spread of malaria. After weeks of continuous exhaustion, many symptoms start to take effect during this time of rest. One comrade has nerve fever [febris nervosa]. During the attacks, he jumps up, shoots about, and tries to attack the Reds; but there aren't any. The poor devil is going to be transported further to the rear this afternoon. Most, however, are suffering from serious intestinal diseases (also known as shitting uncontrollably). I am one of them. But this is nothing in comparison to the bloody battles fought during this past week. We are so deeply thankful for having this chance to rest!

25 July: One could wallow in self-glorification after all the laudatory speeches we've heard: "Your admirable accomplishments will find their place in history. Your bravery is unprecedented!" and so on.... It goes like this the entire day. The commander of the division, the commander of the corps, and Field Marshal Reichenau—all of them have suddenly taken us into their hearts. We have been promised French wine, champagne, chocolate, cigarettes, and sardines. Poor old stomach, how will you cope with all of these delicacies? Well, at least we are happy; however, we have done nothing more than our duty.

26 July: We receive good news from the front: the Russians are retreating to Korosten [Ukraine], all while desperately trying to fight.

27 July: Our days of rest are over. We are advancing to Kiev.

28 July: Zhitomir fell after severe street battles. Occasionally Russian tanks advance in order to give cover to the retreating Bolsheviks. Russian fighters and bombers are making our lives miserable. Our convoys are repeatedly rewarding their targets. The Red masses pull back to Kiev, which is apparently heavily fortified.

Once again, there's going to be difficult urban combat.

29–30 July: We advance kilometer after kilometer under light artillery fire and minor infantry fights.

31 July: We take a short break 40 kilometers past Zhitomir. The same subject dominates our conversations: when will this campaign be over? Someone spread a rumor that we will be dismissed after this mess. What an immature religious belief! First, I think that the Russian campaign will last much longer. (I even voice this opinion in contrast to those officers who believe that it will be over within two months). Second, does anyone believe that glorious, veteran fighters like us will be sent home to search for fishing worms in their gardens? We shall see if I am not right on at least one of these points.

1 August: We stop in a small pine forest with a tiny lake. As we will be here for a few hours, we peal our sweaty uniforms from our bodies and jump into the pee-warm, dirty water. But this joy is short-lived—Ratas suddenly appear and hammer quite a few rounds over our heads. Right at the beginning of the attack a hand grenade kills one of our own. What a damn mess! Wet as dogs, we quickly put our clothes back on and take cover under the trees. Just in time—ten Martin bombers appear soon after. All of a sudden there are smoke trails soon followed by detonations. Goddamn it!

We are very lucky. When the yellow smoke clears we can see that exactly where our camp would have been is now covered with craters from the shelling.

The Russian fighters are unpleasantly active these days. We had a bad surprise yesterday afternoon. Three heavy aircraft flew over us at an extremely low altitude. Since they did not fire, we didn't pay much attention. Shortly after, we hear wild machine gun fire to our rear. A team of scouts, including myself, is assembled to go back and see what is going on. As we reach the edge of the forest, we see a group of about fifteen civilians running like mad onto a bridge. Suddenly, something whistles above our heads; we throw ourselves to the ground and simultaneously five or six hand grenades explode with a deafening bang just a few meters away from us. In short bursts we sprint from cover to cover in order to approach the group. With great effort we manage to cut off access to the bridge for this ferocious firing group.

We find the big surprise in the meadow—parachutes. Russian soldiers in civilian clothes had jumped from the aircraft with order to destroy this important bridge. What a lucky coincidence that we caught them and prevented the bridge assault at the last minute. Their boxes full of dynamite would have been enough to destroy an entire city neighborhood. One of the paratroopers has unfortunately managed to escape; a burst from his machine gun killed one of our comrades and seriously wounded another.

2 August: It is not much further to Kiev. We see it on the map and are able to feel it from the desperate resistance we encounter. We are only able to make slow progress. The first line of bunkers lies in front of us. Apparently, there are a dozen or more lines of various fortifications past that. Bunkers, minefields, swamps, automatic flamethrower traps, and who knows what else.

Difficult hours and days are ahead of us, but we have become so stubborn that nothing is able to shock us anymore. We no longer care about the crashing blows, the low hum of bombs dropping from aircraft, and the chirping of machine gun bursts.

Life on the front has made me a fatalist. Now, everything is up to fate; how else could we carry on! Shells have plowed our lines. The ground was propelled into the air just a few meters in front of me. A shower of glowing hot shrapnel rains down on us. Comrades to the left and right have been torn apart; my uniform is splattered with their blood. The blow throws me on my back, yet I am not hurt. Fate! If I've made it alright through the hell of Zwiahel with its 1,000 dead, then things will go well in the future.

3 August: It is our wedding anniversary, dear Rosel! Do you still remember this: One evening, we were sitting outside in the garden at Hausen. It was also August 3, and your stupid husband had completely forgotten that it was our anniversary. I could really tell how upset you were about my mistake.

Here it is again, August 3; a day of non-stop fighting and casualties. Yet, I remember our wedding anniversary. I thank fate for allowing our paths to cross and making you, my darling, my wife and the mother of our beloved Erika.

Please God, let me return home safely, so that I can make up for my mistake and still have time to catch up on everything!

Despite fierce resistance, we manage to break through enemy lines in the evening. We are making good progress.

4 August: We are now about 15 kilometers from Kiev. The Weta Line is before us, and is fortified with all the bells and whistles. Three well-performed attacks are knocked off by the Russians. Indeed, that is not the way to do it!

It appears that there are problems at HQ, as things are not going as planned. There are changes in the command structure, and a few generals are exchanged. The number of casualties is just not in balance with our success. I really do not like this shit.

5 August: We are digging in. There is heavy artillery fire all day long. Under the cover of night we are able to get closer to the line of bunkers. Thank goodness everything goes well and without much notice by the enemy.

We take position without much fighting in the Glewacha Forest at about midnight. Everything must be dug into the ground by morning. The bunker cannons and the Caucasian snipers snub out anyone who can be seen in the daylight.

6 August: Heavy fire starts as expected around 0500 hours. I am sitting in B-position [*beobachter*, or observer] and am able to see our impending doom as no one else can. The sap [short trench dug from the front-trench] is right at the edge of the forest. From here, the terrain slopes gently down to the Weta River. That damn river looks like it will drink a lot of blood (perhaps mine too). Behind the river is an enormous anti-tank trench filled with barbed wire.

Well camouflaged bunkers line the trench. The firing is coming from them. Death is rolling toward us. A crushing wall of fire crawls slowly, very slowly, up the hill. These *schweine* shoot with a precision that could have only been learned through intensive training. Halfway up the hill, the firewall now reaches a tree-covered farmhouse. Cracking and splintering is heard when tree branches, wooden beams, and bricks go swirling through the air. The stinking firewall moves on.

Do not lose your nerves now, Hannes! I estimate that death will be arriving any minute now. Everybody has been warned. We claw our fingers into the dirt. We have sweat on our forehead out of fear. God, if we were at least able to defend ourselves! And then all hell breaks loose. There is a howling, an enormous roar, thundering, cracking, and the humming of thousands of splinters.

Foul-smelling smoke floods into our trenches. Did this last seconds or minutes? I cannot say. I pull my nose carefully out of the dirt to see that the firewall has moved on. I remain deaf for minutes. There is something wet on my face—blood! Thank goodness it is just a scratch. Our position is in chaos. The tree trunks we used for cover have been torn to shreds. Portions of the trenches have been filled back up with dirt. One position received a direct hit. Two comrades were killed and three were wounded. Overall, we are lucky; it could have gone worse.

This afternoon, artillery is brought into position in the forest to our rear. There are many cannons in addition to some mammoth calibers, which are probably mortars that will be used here for the very first time. The new cannons are hidden from view of us soldiers. Night falls and single shells are fired toward the enemy positions. One could call it a trial run. It is nice that our barbarians are letting us hear something from them.

We receive orders to attack tomorrow at around 2300 hours. My God, that is going to be tough. And to be honest, I am sick of it.

7 August: Officers are standing next to the long-barrel cannons, howitzers, mortars, and grenade launchers. They pressure the crews by staring at their wristwatches. The short hand is going in circles... The final minute has just started; it seems to have no end! Hundreds of barrels spit their deadly loads into the sky. Howitzers, mortars, and large caliber long-barrel cannons begin their work. There is thundering and howling as death races toward the saps, bunkers, cannon positions, machine gun nests, and trenches. Our artillery hammers down on the Weta fortifications for thirty minutes.

We switch to the attack at exactly 0510 hours. Like many times before, we work hand-in-hand with the *Sturmpioneren* and the *Flammenwerfer* [flamethrowers]. Against our expectations, everything went excellently. The entire attack unfolded as if it were on the training field in Ohrdruf. Within an hour we are under the cover of the anti-tank trench on the banks of the Weta down from the wildly flaming bunkers. Our grenades fly through the bunker openings. Loads of explosives and flamethrowers polish them off.

Surprise! Three bunkers have been cleaned out and a nice breach has been opened after just two hours. Now how does that sound? My dear gentlemen, we shit a great deal in our pants during this nice scene from *Wochenschau* [German weekly newsreel]. Quite a few have thrown their arms into the air, did an about-face—such an awkward movement—and fallen down stiff on the banks of the Weta River. And by the way—we attacked the bunkers dressed as Adam [i.e. naked]. I wonder if these Red officer whores were decent enough to cover their eyes with their hands! Either way, it was necessary because of the mud in the river. What did the sergeant used to say: "I can determine a soldier's character from the state of his uniform." Yes, dear Fips, come to us and tell us about your "states." Maybe you could fetch the clothes of the brave soldiers from the other side of the river. You see, we honored your wishes and spared our clothes. We miss your groveling speeches.

We roll up Russian positions one after another. The hill across the Weta is firmly in our hands by the afternoon. Only the village of Potschtowaja and the bridge are still occupied by the enemy. It has been planned to take the bridge in a swift action, since it is crucial for our motorized units. This time it is someone else's job to attempt this risky undertaking. We'll provide the fire protection. These guys go in forcefully. By nightfall the bridge and village are cleansed of enemies. We are in charge of guarding the bridge after midnight. This is not without danger, since the Russians are placing well targeted fire onto the bridge and village. Finally, after a few hours we are relieved and take positions to guard the northern exit.

Potschtowaja is in flames. We hear the crackling of the fires. Cows are bellowing somewhere out in the distance. They must be trapped in their barn and are burning alive. The wind drives thick clouds of smoke toward us. A trail of smoke is over the entire village. The fire glows red; the heat takes our breath away. Every other house is on fire. The cracking of rounds left behind by the Russians can be heard among the sizzling and crackling. We climb over hot debris. The wall of a house collapses nearby. Wounded soldiers are being carried past us. The fires light up a Red Cross flag. The singing of an airplane is above our heads.

8 August: It is raining. The trenches that were dug so quickly are full of water. One lies in his dirt hole like a sack. Our uniforms are saturated with dirty

Rosel and Hans in the Black Forest.

Hans and Rosel with other German soldiers in the Black Forest. *(Photo courtesy Christine Alexander and Mason Kunze)*

yellow water. We lie trembling from the cold and fear in our "bathtubs" or "water caskets." Volley after volley is fired to the other side. There are explosions all around us. They look like the arborvitae found around the Frankfurt central train station—"trees of life"!

That is ironic … death is walking through our lines here! We have twelve dead within half an hour. Goddamn it! If only at least the rain would stop. I cannot stand much longer looking at the red soup in the holes of our fallen soldiers. I don't like tomatoes, but I do love tomato soup.

Disgusting. One could puke his guts out! The same comrades who attacked the bunkers on the Weta yesterday, full of bravery, are now lying ripped apart in their holes. When a comrade receives that final blow ripping his guts out, one should no longer look at him. Whatever follows, does that not belong to him and his heroic efforts? It is ugly, plain awful. I am tired, tired of all that is around me.

The regiment led an attack north of the cobblestone road this morning. These brave guys have made good progress, although under great casualties. They took Gatnoje and are near Schuljany at the gates of Kiev. It is too bad that they have left us here. The Russians have adjusted their fire excellently, aiming at both our positions and the road.

It is noon and relatively quiet at the moment. They have stopped bothering us with the damn small calibers. They are probably out of ammunition. However, three huge ones arrive regularly every five minutes. Judging from the size of the craters, they must be coming from railroad cannon, which have demolished this fine road.

Our mood is much better. The rain has stopped and even the sun has come out, which makes everything much better. At least we can leave our holes. Someone makes a joke and we laugh. Life does go on!

Russian tanks have been announced. I take B-position under a burned-out roof, crouched there with a scissor telescope. For five minutes everything is forgotten, the artillery fire and the danger. What a few minutes!

The battle of Kiev has reached its climax. A plain stretches all the way to the outskirts of the city. There are only a few outcroppings of trees and small rolling hills in the landscape. The radio towers are clearly visible behind the forest. To the left there are the suburbs of Schuljany and Mikoiska, and the big city with its 850,000 inhabitants, its beautiful churches, and the citadel behind a few trails of smoke along the horizon.

Down there is the battle. I see Russian artillery fire around every small forest on the plain. A cloud of shrapnel hangs over a crack in the ground like a ball of cotton. *Waffentruppen* are attacking a bunker over there. The drama comes to an end when the fire from a flamethrower appear. It is strange to sit up here so far away from the man-to-man battle—so far away and yet so close through this telescope. It is odd to see the death struggle of comrades without my own life being threatened.

A scissor telescope is a great device! A little twist of the knob and another individual scene of the brewing battle comes into focus. The Red dogs attack a howitzer position. Friend and foe are butchering each other. I can see the infantry lines near Gatnoje. They are installing a machine gun position on the road out of the village. The firewall then rolls alongside the cobblestone road. Gray clouds hover over the Terempki Forest. The humming of fighter planes is in the air.

The sum of all the individually observed scenes, with their stirring images, truly deserves the name "battle" ... tramping horses, rattling engines, mud-covered motorcycle messengers, the burning torches that were once houses, the angry barking of machine guns, the wounded who turn their eyes up to the heavens, the recoiling of the cannons' hot muzzles, dark fountains of soil and smoke, the hissing of shrapnel, the humming of shells.... Bawling, roaring, crackling, moaning, whistling, heaving—it's the 8th of August—day two of the battle of Kiev!

9 August: The morning begins with a mass attack from Russian bombers. I haven't seen anything like this before. At times, there are 40 to 50 planes in the sky at once. I am automatically driven to think about the futuristic drawings in War of the Future [*der Krieg der Zukunft*], a magazine that I read years ago. "Dominik in the battle of Kiev"—one could laugh if the situation wasn't so serious. [Soviet Field Marshal] Budenny has released his swallows for the Kiev air show. There is a droning and buzzing so loud that one cannot hear oneself think. The Ratas, those agile bi-planes, and the Martin bombers, attack German positions with bombs and their on-board cannons. For the first time, they are also releasing shells and catapult bombs, which hit the ground before the plane is even over head. *Scheisse*, comrades! We must rethink our entire cover strategy. We must learn.

We receive orders to attack at around 1000 hours. It smells like trouble! The division apparently got stuck after making good progress yesterday. The roaring of artillery is deafening; three groups receive orders to wind their way through the minefield in order to make contact with our over-extended front line. My group's task is to reach the Terempki estate by 1130 hours. The commander and his adjutant, who arrived from Gatnoje, have already taken position at the estate early this morning. We do not have to hear a speech to know that the passage through the minefield will not be easy. Three curtains of artillery fire are released over the field through which we have to pass—not to mention the shrapnel, mines, and bombers. There is no time for discussion; we pick up our equipment and weapons without saying a word.

A moment later we begin our mission, walking in single file. Without the cover of clouds the sun burns hot. The mugginess is driving us mad. We bring two TO [communications] units along as per our orders, which will be part of an observation post near the front line. These poor guys are carrying such heavy boxes on their backs. Little Arthur collapses after a few hundred meters. Dear God—how will we accomplish this mission? We reached the first artillery curtain, but have not yet crossed it. Don't give up now! One of our comrades places the heavy box on his back and we continue, passing by the carcasses of stinking horses and dead soldiers. Many mangled corpses are lying in our path. They have black and swollen faces.

We now move off the cobblestone road. Everything was going well up to this point. Four enemy aircraft then suddenly appear, flying so close to the ground that we can feel the slipstream from their propellers. These *schweine* stalk us for about five minutes. Why are we throwing ourselves into the mud? They're flying so low just to have a headcount.

Their sporadic fire does not cause any harm. Our group appears to be too small to be worth a real attack. They turn away and drop their bombs further down the cobblestone road.

At the barn (ask any Kiev fighter for the barn at Gatnoje and he will walk away in silence with his memories of the wretched brick walls covered with mangled and bloody bodies)—this awful place—we take a break since it is the only source of shade on the entire field. A cigarette is hastily smoked. It is said to calm one's nerves; however, it has no such effect on us. We have a clear view of our path through the mine-infested field, past the shredded forest, all the way to our destination, the ruins of Terempki. The three murderous curtains of enemy artillery fire are most intimidating. I suddenly do not like the taste of my cigarette anymore. *Scheisse*. It is all a bunch of *scheisse*. Little Arthur is so excited: the tension inside him is so intense that he starts telling jokes. It is well known that quiet and shy guys turn into jokesters full of quick repartee under such circumstances. He has come up with lines that he could not have created otherwise, even with half an hour of thinking. But what does it matter, we have to move on. Orders are orders; they are performed as they are received.

My group reaches the Terempki estate at 1120 hours. There is not much talk about how we got there! It is a miracle! With luck on our side, we walked past hundreds of mines and crossed an artillery curtain which offered us only small amounts of shrapnel. We have arrived and are in one piece, except for a few scratches. My poor *ToFu* [*Funker*: radio operator] men took much longer. Their backs are bloody from the heavy boxes. How many times during these few kilometers did we have to throw ourselves down on the ground for cover? One is mistaken if he thinks that we could quickly recuperate from the horrors of our march.

When it rains it pours—shell after shell howls toward us and smashes the pathetic ruins of the Terempki estate. Debris is swirling through the air.

Our comrades have organized dugouts in checkerboard style. Our sap position is close to the last house, in the middle of a vegetable garden with half a dozen shredded trees. We have to crawl in order to reach our cover holes. We barely made it into them by the time the sky was suddenly filled with those damn bi-planes. They approach in squadron formation from the right of the forest. They fly lower and lower. The machine guns rattle to the tune of the planes' engines. They are good at this, these *schweine*! I can see the pilots stretching out of their seats and over the fuselage in order to scan the ground and throw their dreadful hand grenades. My stomach starts to churn. The coffee I drank this morning isn't sitting well with me. They come down even lower, fly over our position, and turn toward the forest. Their red stars on the bottom of the wings sparkle in the sun [...] just lay still, very still! My steel helmet is feeling increasingly heavy. How long has it been since I slept? I cross my arms behind my head and lie on the ground with my eyes closed. The soil is pleasantly cool....

Damn it. I actually fell asleep in all of this commotion. Yes, I even dreamt. We were on a walk, you and I, Rosel. We were standing on top of a rock similar to our favorite place in Falkenstein. We were overlooking a plain that was filled with smoke and fire. You were leaning against me and started to cry silently. Well, dreams are sometimes weird. Nonsense! My brave Rosel does not cry because of smoke and fire.

The enemy ordnances have been plowing into our position for hours now. The wind drives suffocating clouds of smoke over us. The Reds are shooting with all that they have—large chunks, small chunks, shells.... Their fire is landing very well. So well in fact, that one can see our dreadful tarpaulins scattered all over. At times a hand with stiff and cramped fingers or a boot sticks out from underneath them. Ladies, these are your husbands and sons who are lying stiff and torn apart. You are perhaps enjoying the sunny day at this moment, the babble of your children or their sparkling eyes. You have no idea that soon you will receive a letter that renders your life unbearable. Do not think about this! God help me! Do not think about this! We know that the suffering of our wives and mothers is greater than ours here in this downpour of shrapnel.

The artillery fire suddenly stops in the afternoon. This is understandable; even the toughest butcher must have a break for breakfast. I can imagine how they are sitting over there, with grins on their devilish faces black from the soot; I can imagine their smacking while they eat. "Let's get back to business," says comrade commissar as their dirty and greasy paws reach for the shells and stroke the cool steel which tears apart the damn fascists.

Just wait you damn bloodhounds. Soon it will be our turn!

We use the break from the firing to our advantage. Doors, fences, boards, and beams are hauled in from the surrounding area in order to build covers for our holes. Earthen walls are reinforced. Anything capable of catching splinters is arranged around the holes—buckets, barrels, chairs, benches...

As we put the final touches on our fortification, the air is all of a sudden filled with the roaring of approaching shells and their impacts. Terempki is nothing but a sea of surging black smoke. The last remaining bricks are being tossed into the air. Heavy Russian shells slam again and again into its ruins. I have counted 243 blows within half an hour. 243 times 500 shards—that makes 121,500 red-hot glowing pieces of metal which are flying over the ground, and which can rip apart everything in their way. Maybe one of you can tell me if there remains a hand's-width portion of space within a 1,000 meter radius that has not been penetrated by the death carrying iron shards.

It is impossible to describe the horror throughout the hours until the evening. I press myself to the bottom of my hole, half mad from fear and horror. Doesn't anyone have a bit of compassion for us miserable bundles of humans who are almost insane and who are holding on with their teeth in the dirt?

For God's sake, if it has to be, at least let me die instantaneously! The moaning and the shouting of the wounded are faintly audible through the howling and crashing. You poor guys! Who do you think will be able to help you? The one who leaves his cover will be rattled with splinters like that old bucket up there.

It is finally getting dark and quiet after long and horrific hours. Life is coming back to our position. Spades clatter, flares rise into the sky, and moaning and shouting rise from the trenches and holes closest to the front line. Paramedics run out with their stretchers. Groups are sitting together in holes and carve crosses. Fires die down and every now and then there is a crackling from the burned out houses and barns. Again and again a whimpering or a cry cuts through like a razor.

10 August: The barrage starts up again suddenly in the morning. From one moment to the next, the air is filled with whistling and howling. A fist presses my head into the ground. A hammer slams into the soil with a roar. The earth trembles and the muddy ground buckles until it finally bursts…. Six large calibers came to within 30 meters of us. It smells like mud and gunpowder. If there is still a God in Heaven, I am begging him to finish us off. Bring this to an end. Just end it… I cannot take this any longer! Someone amongst us must have gone crazy. He jumps out of the trench, throws his arms wildly into the air, and laughs. He finally jumps into the barbed wire and breaks down after being hit by repeated shrapnel as the next rounds of shells arrive. Poor devil! What got into you? I know so much about you: you are married with four children; you have not had a vacation in over a year; you had it … it is all in the past now!

Damn—I cannot go on like this much longer! And then I go and do something completely crazy. I take a bottle that still has a bit of schnapps in it, sit up on the edge of the trench, and take a big sip. I take my time in closing the flask and throw it into the trench of the neighboring group. I also attached a short note stating: "Are there any bastards [*scheissekerle*] there? Please pass this on." The bottle with its little note works wonders. After about ten minutes it lands back in my hole. Someone added to the note: "There aren't any *scheissekerle* here."

Suddenly, a large group of aircraft appears, followed by a wonderful surprise. Three Messerschmitts are quickly approaching. I don't care about the shrapnel and raise my head to watch. Dogfights [*luftkampf*]—open-air theater! What's this? The three veer off! Are the German fighters wimping out [*deutsche Jäge kneifen*]?! The *Roten hunde* [Red dogs] triumph. They come down low, machine guns rattle, and the wounded cry out. This drama is repeated a dozen times this morning. It isn't surprising that a few of the desperate guys who have lost all their nerve take up their weapons and shoot at the cowards in the retreating Messerschmitts.

The artillery fire dies down a little around noon, though the Reds continue to fire aimlessly at our position. A delivery of food makes its way toward us. The second one didn't make it—direct hit. The guy paints a colorful picture of blood, pea soup, and brain. Enjoy your meal! Just take the food with you, comrade. My appetite has disappeared.

What assholes these guys are! They still exist. They come and make our lives on the front miserable with their bloodthirsty stories. We are busy enough with our own stories up here. We have left plenty of blood yesterday and today and do not care what is happening in the rear at the moment.

The terrible artillery fire starts up again in the afternoon. And then the most horrible thing happens; there is a sulfurous flame, a deafening explosion, and the beams of our cover are torn to bits. The force of the air presses us against the trench walls; clumps of dirt cover us. I am still half numb when I push through the shredded beams and climb out. Only then can I see the full picture. The neighboring bunker, approximately three meters from us, has taken a direct hit. I see a large crater, which extends all the way up to our dugout. Stinky, yellow smoke boils over the area.

God damn it. Are they all dead? Most importantly, is he dead—our dear lieutenant? Half mad, I leap into the crater. Pieces of uniform and limbs are sticking out of the dirt. I start digging hurriedly in the dirt using my bare hands. I grab a hold of Huebner's head, which has been severed from the rest of his body. Finally, I find our "Little one" buried up to his neck. In a mad rush, Rueffer jumps into the hole; within seconds we are able to free him from underneath the mass of earth. If only he would stop his terrible screaming, our dear little lieutenant! We have never heard him shout so loud before. He only has a few minutes left to live. His lower body and legs are crushed to a pulp. While we try to lift him out of the hole, a shell slams into the ground right next to us in a loud roar. A shower of shards rains down over us. Rueffer collapses and the lieutenant's body slides on top of me. He is no longer screaming. A fist-sized piece of shrapnel has smashed into his face. Even in death he has protected me—his best comrade—with his own body.

Everything inside of me is numb. A film covers my eyes. I do not care anymore. Even if they demolish the rest of our small group, at least it will be over. Peace, eternal peace. The memories of these hours of horror will no longer torture me.

Orders to retreat come in the evening. "The division will retreat to the Weta Line in the night and regroup in defensive formation." One order, one cold sentence, which hits us like the strike of a whip. Soldiers on the front understand what it means to take back a piece of land that has been soaked with the blood of comrades: this was hard-earned, meter by meter, under enormous casualties.

Under the cover of night, my group—I have five men left in my group—feels their way back through the crater field. This is how it must have appeared at Verdun in 1918. The Reds continue their wild firing into our position; however, we are able to reach the cobblestone road by midnight. Nobody is talking, nobody is smoking. As per division orders, smoking is prohibited when aircraft are present. Talking! Everyone has enough to do with his own thoughts and with carrying his equipment.

We finally reach Potschtowaja. This place was also badly hit. Some in the group are wounded. I was just about to lie down in a hole to sleep when a comrade approached me. "You are ordered to go to the commandant." Two other group leaders are also there. The old guy salutes us and asks us, "Who will volunteer to return to the front to take our dear Lieutenant Liebetran his cross?" I step forward. The other two leave. I almost think they were running. The commandant takes me aside and tells me something that I have already known for a long time: Terempki is probably no man's land, if not already in Russian hands. I decline to take anyone with me on this death ride.

11 August: After the cross is finished, I place it over my shoulder, insert a pistol under my belt, a hand grenade in the shaft of my boots, and off I go. I take the shortest distance directly across the minefield. Damn it, the most direct path is right at the barn on the field. I don't need to mention that the other soldiers thought they were dealing with a maniac, and that the men in the observation posts thought I was crazy. And yet, my mind has become sharper over the past few days. My intuition tells me that the Russians have not yet grasped our latest directional maneuver. They are still laying their fire stubbornly onto our positions that have long since been abandoned. This time, there is no fire curtain between the village and me (rather I should say the pile of dirt where houses once stood).

Everything is going well. The closer I get to the village, the weaker the enemy fire, which eventually completely dies out. There is no one around as far as I can see. The silence is eating at my nerves. Is the Russian infantry going to begin its advance? Damn it—for the first time I am really afraid, really scared. The last thing that I need is for "Hans to push a wild boar into his pants" [*wildsau in die hose scheibt*, i.e. soiling his pants]. No, I am not going to do that.

With my hands trembling, I push the cross into the ground. I then pay him my respects, my one and only comrade, our lieutenant, at his final place of rest, and then start to cry like a child. What would you say to me now, my little lieutenant? "Sobbing is for women. Pull your shit together Hannes!"

These past few minutes of reflection have really refreshed me. No, little one, you will not see me act like a weeping boy, I am sorry. It has been a bit too much over these past few days. I then start to head back.

Unbelievable, Terempki without artillery fire. I didn't think it was possible! It is getting light out; I still have approximately two kilometers to cover. Who knows if the Russians saw me, or it was just out of coincidence, but all at once five or six shells land near me. I throw myself into the dirt and clutch the ground. To the left and right, in front and behind me, trees stand burning from the impact. The howling and crashing in the air is like yesterday, though yesterday I was not alone! Small brisang shells buzz closer. These damn things approach without much warning; they're right here—*ratsch-bumm* [German slang term used by soldiers for the Soviet SiS-3 field gun]. They explode, causing shallow craters in the ground. They explode and release thousands of shards that slice anything close by.

And then, there is a terrible hit. When I try to get up again I notice that I cannot. My right leg isn't responding. *Scheisse*, there is a large hole in my pants and blood is running out of it. My hands are also bloody. There is a strange pulling in my face and blood has just started dripping from it. Those must only be scratches, but my leg, damn leg! Man [*mensch*], you cannot lie here and fall victim to those Red bastards! There must be a way! And there is. I get a move on under tremendous pain.

Who's there at the barn (or where the barn used to be)? It is my dear Sepp, and thankfully his sidecar motorcycle. This is when I black out. When I start to wake up, he has only one word for me: *Rindviech*! [ox] This makes me really happy. I know that he said it to conceal his emotions; what a loyal soul! He places me into the sidecar and races back. He finally stops at Petschtowaja. In between the cursing and laughter, he tells me that our troop has taken leave to rest for a few days to the rear of Wassilkow. He has suggested that as a result, I will be able to recover while being with the troops. What a fool, as if we even needed to talk about that! He then digs out his last bottle of vodka from down in his sidecar. It's a real small party this morning. As an extra bonus, we get to enjoy witnessing the downing of 24 aircraft by our invincible Messerschmitts. "Sorry that we shot at you yesterday." Oh well, after that my Sepp calls me an ox and I know that we have become inseparable comrades. I am indescribably happy. For a few hours I am able to forget the fear and distress of the past few days.

12 August: We have arrived in Barachty and are joyfully greeted by our comrades. The commander shook my hand in silence, looking deeply into my eyes for a long time. The fact that he did not say anything was the best expression of gratitude for me. Afterward, I am bandaged up, which unfortunately cannot be performed without pain.

And then the moment which I have been dreading all day arrives: the field doctor has ordered my transfer to the military hospital. One of the guys winks at me and says, "Man, be happy! You get a taste of home...." I punch him in the face. The commander sees it and approaches to ask what is going on. I ask for permission to stay with my comrades. He turns briefly to speak with the doctor and then says, "I am unable to deny your request. You will remain here!" How wonderful this day is!

My stretcher stands in the shade of fruit trees in a meadow covered with flowers. The bees are buzzing and butterflies are playing their games. I am so happy and thankful that I am able to stay with my comrades. Only the hum and thundering from the front, and the pain that has now fully kicked in, reminds me of these past days.

My group has dramatically shrunk in size. We will need each and every one of them for the next campaign. We cannot count on replacements. Was it not my duty to stay with my guys under such circumstances? I think the commander understood this.

13 August: I am doing well except for the constant pain. The weather is awesome, and then there are these beautiful letters from my dear Rosel, this brave soldier's wife. The commander looks after me like a father. He gives me eggs, fresh butter, cream, and honey. I have been using this time mostly for sleeping, which helps me forget, and we have so much to forget.

14 August: Red fighter planes paid us a visit tonight and threw down a dozen or so bombs. This doesn't upset me as much after what I have lived through during these past days. One can hear the thunder emerging from the front as clearly as it was yesterday. Apparently the Russians have managed to establish a strong bridgehead on the Dnepr River. The front is very thin there, perhaps our break is over? That would be harsh, and mean my transfer to the field hospital. A civilian has informed us that a group of eight Bolsheviks dressed as German soldiers went into the village to ask for German reinforcement troops in Barachty. Because of this the strength of the night watch has been doubled. One cannot be too careful behind the front.

15 August: The entire division has gone out to battle. The brave regiments march past us on the street. You brave, remarkable lads, where are all the comrades that went shoulder to shoulder with you to the front when you were on the street the last time? One of the men approaches me on my stretcher to shake my hand. Why not? We have both bled in the drumfire of Kiev. Exhausted, he sits down next to me, drinks from my bottle, eats my ration, and has ten draws from my last cigarette. He then told me something about the final hours before they were withdrawn from the front: "Before we retreated, we laid mine-fields. The Russians somehow found out, at which point they collected the sick and disabled from the mental homes. The infantry then herded them over the minefields in front of them. It was an extraordinary picture: naked as they were when taken from their beds. They ran in lines toward our positions. Hundreds were torn apart by the mines." Only these losers could think of something so evil. And these guys are our opponent.

The numbers of dead slowly make their way to us. The 530th Infantry Regiment was almost completely annihilated, and will be filled in with the remainder of the 528th and 529th Infantry Regiments.

16 August: The pain is starting to vanish. Thank goodness things are going better!

17 August: Three PaK units move out in the morning to secure the village. We receive news that a bunch of troops and partisan fighters were found outside of Kiev. They must have been planning to go through the thin front line to attack our troops from the rear. Other special forces, paratroopers, have landed far to the rear. The village is now encircled in a defensive ring.

18 August: I am without pain for the first time, and leave my stretcher for a first attempt at walking. I witness the interrogation of partisans in the meadow. A reconnaissance unit arrested a group whom they are now questioning. There are three young girls ranging in age from 18 to 20, and one boy around 17. They say they were laborers at a textile factory who were let go due to the lack of work. Their passports are too new and the amount of money they are carrying is too great for laborers. They cave in after two hours of interrogation and confess to being partisans. Their mission is from the infamous Major Friedmann. They have the following orders: join a second group of partisans near Wassilkow during the night of August 19. The second group will bring highly sensitive explosives. The girls will find out the location of HQ here in Barachty and in Wassilkow, which are supposed to be blown up on August 20.

Wow—we are all really surprised. We were going to be attacked. We also learn something about the organization of their group. They work in mixed groups of boys and girls, mostly students, no larger than five per group. Their tasks include the destruction of fuel and ammunition depots, bridges, and roads. They also lay out aerial signals [*fliegerzeichen*]. They kill (this means butcher, since even the girls are trained to use a knife) men stationed at outposts and motorcycle messengers.

To ensure success, they have a well established and expansive communication network. When the German troops moved in, competent Red soldiers, mostly commissars, stayed behind disguised as everyday farmers in order to coordinate the work of partisan units. They are now working hand-in-hand with these terror groups. The mess that has been created behind the front will give us headaches for a long time to come.

The translator finally asks the girls how they became partisans. What I heard deeply moved me: the murderer Friedmann summoned them one day and gave them a choice to either go with these orders across German lines, or witness their parents and siblings lined up along a wall and shot. Also, if they do not return, their relatives will be killed. Nevertheless, the commander decides that the four must be executed immediately. I can see how difficult it is for him to give this order. But this is how it has to be!

The four are led away. Three young and fresh girls will die for these bloodthirsty hyenas in Kiev. A group of soldiers with rifles lines up, the girls are blindfolded. This is nothing for us old guys who are used to fighting with the devil and death. But these are three girls of great beauty for whom we feel compassion. Regardless, they are ordered to shoot iron bullets into these young bodies. I cannot witness this. I retreat to the most remote corner. Finally, after what seems like an eternity, I hear the rifle salvo.

The war against civilians is not for us "*frontschweine*" [frontline pigs]. Everybody is very quiet for the rest of the afternoon.

19 August: Russian bombers are attacking. We have dead and wounded. A group of partisans are arrested and shot after a short interrogation.

20 August: I am doing much better. My wounds have healed almost completely. It's about time, because there are rumors about our next mission.

21 August: Orders have arrived. We advance into position tonight. What am I saying, we? I have been ordered to stay behind. Does he have to give me orders? After a short back-and-forth, the commander, understanding the front line soldier, agrees to let me move forward with my guys.

"Doctor, this boy is dying of boredom here! He belongs with his men on the front!"

What a joy. Why shouldn't this be possible? The positions on the front are now fortified; the mobile attack came to a halt weeks ago.

22 August: We made the rotation to the front without any enemy fire worth mentioning. The trenches are awesome. A system of trenches and saps has been built. The line of fire is perfect. Our position holds the bridge and village of Potschtowaja. The Reds will get their heads bloodied if they tried to break through here.

The rest of the day is used to deepen the trenches and repair the barbed wire blockades. After nightfall, small troops lay out minefields. Shells are only finding their way to us sporadically. For the most part, they fall short of the target and explode in the Weta marshes.

23 August: After prepping us with heavy artillery fire during the early morning hours, the Russians attempt to storm our position. Wave after wave approaches and breaks down under our fire. Man oh man, it's like target practice! It is incredible what reserves these guys possess! It is sheer insanity to attack our fortified position. Regardless, new masses of soldiers are still coming forward. At present, they are huddled down in the depressions in the same line formations as they started. Our shells tear them apart and our machine guns mow them down. And then, I see something that as a soldier moves me deeply: for hours now, enemy soldiers have been trying to approach the bridge with great bravery. The Russians installed heavy machine guns in the houses just a few hundred meters to the rear in order to give them fire protection. Again, 18 to 20 men jump up and run toward the bridge, just to be shot to bits and pieces.

Two PaKs and half a dozen of our machine guns spread fire across the opposing riverbank. It is crazy to try and break through here. Heaps of fallen soldiers are piling up in front of the bridge. Two Russian soldiers, the remainder of the last wave, run back to the houses crazed with horror. Ten meters to the houses, their own machine guns rattle and hack them into mounds of flesh. This drama is repeated several times before the Russians are able to pull back the entire line. Can anyone understand these people? Can anyone understand that they are so much under the control of their commissars that they will not quarter these bloodthirsty hyenas? A bullet would be too precious for them. Is there anyone who understands this?

24 August: The heat is brutal and beats down on our heads. Now we get the chance to experience the other side of the coin for yesterday's target practice. Several hundred are lying dead down there in the depression and are putting out such a stench that many of us start to puke like butchers' dogs. Keeping a wet handkerchief over my face brings only little relief. I have a raging headache. I am not at all up to par.

27 August: I remember little of the past few days. A fierce fever has gotten a hold of me. I am back in Barachty. Today is the first day that I don't have a temperature. It went away as fast as it had started. The only thing remaining is the miserable weakness and my rubber knees. Yet it's not so bad; they have butter, eggs, and milk here. Everything will be *karascho* [good in Russian] within 24 hours.

After quite some time, I received mail from Rosel and my mother today. All will be better soon, and with so much joy. It must be.

Everyone is urgently needed. There are fierce battles and I need to be with my men.

The Moscow radio station has its "German hour" tonight. We, 299th Infantry Regiment, are once again their topic. It's amazing how the guy can rant: "299th

Division is a division of murderers. (He rolls his t's like an expert.) Orders have been issued to no longer take prisoners." What an honor for our division to be addressed by name from the gentlemen in Moscow. Their anger is a measure of our success. Otherwise, they would not be so angered. According to broadcasts from the very same station, we had been annihilated near Zwiahel. Yet somehow, we are now causing them huge losses. Whatever, we know what to expect!

28 August: It is my birthday. When will I be able to celebrate it in the circle of my dear folk once again? The sky shows its sunny face again after yesterday's rain. I feel a boundless yearning for Rosel and Erika and the peacefulness of my little apartment. When will I be able to sleep in a real bed again, not in a wet hole in the ground? When will I be able to cross the street again without listening for gunshots, approaching shells, or aircraft? Dreams! Dreams! When will they become reality?

As a special surprise, the long arm of the Russian railroad cannon reaches Barachty for the first time. Huge projectiles slam roaring into the ground. What a birthday salute! A third of the village lies in ruins after two hours of fire.

I hear the messages on the radio tonight: the speaker was just beginning to announce the first message when someone yelled out antifascist slurs. The German speaker's words are rebutted and denied. According to the loud yelling, the Russian station must be close by—in Kiev? What crazy ideas these guys have!

I am going back to the front tonight. I do not care what the doctor has to say!

29 August: I am back with my men. A few things have changed here. The barbed wire barriers were doubled in depth after the Russians managed to make it to the first trench and wreak havoc with their hand grenades.

There are many craters between the trenches. There are four crosses made out of birch with helmets placed on top. One of the helmets has a large hole in it. Schumacher also fell.

Our position is no longer being hit with stray fire. Walls of well positioned fire rolls over the position day after day.

30 August: Heavy nightly attacks from the Russians. They used those damn rifle grenades for the first time. No longer are they causing just small injuries. The first firewall tosses shrapnel around our heads early in the morning. Two dead, six wounded. Our morale has reached a low point. Someone has brought news from the rear that there is a 1,000man replacement column marching toward us. We do not like that at all. We had hoped that after the fall of Kiev, we would be sent back to Germany to regroup. According to rumors, that has been the common practice in the past. *Scheisse*! The *milk beards* [*milchbarten*] are coming!

Even I believed the rumors! I could slap myself for this! Any hopes of getting out of this witch's cauldron are put to rest. It is becoming increasingly difficult for me to sound optimistic and positive in my letters to Rosel, but it has to be this way; I know how important my letters are to keep her dear soul in balance. She will be happy and joyful, and will not know about our dejected spirits.

31 August: Nothing new on the Weta! Artillery and shell firing, attacks, and crashing detonations. The dull droning of the bombs; the "Hurrahs" roaring from the Red devils.

1 September: [XXIX Corps commander Hans von] Obstfelder received the Knight's Cross. [He received the award on 27 July.]

2 September: Extensive manuevers apparently are closing in toward Kiev similar to those at Sedan in the west. Once again we serve as the pincer of the encircling arms. We are called out to shed some blood during the weeklong trench battles.

3 September: Always waiting, waiting! We are not allowed to attack, but have to hold the line against increasing pressure from the Russians.

4 September: The Red artillery has been hammering our positions with calibers of all sizes for hours now. I hope we make it. Pressed flat on the floors of our holes, we await attack orders or the end to all this suffering—a nice direct hit. *Scheisse*, it's all *scheisse*!

5 September: Today is again a big day for the Soviet air force, which comes somewhat as a change. Budenny's swallows arrive in flocks from Kiev. Out of politeness, they initially hand us their business cards in the form of thousands of pamphlets. Eventually, dozens of large, long, tin drums drop from the sky.

My first thought is, "Firebombs!" But since they released their bombs right over our heads, there is no immediate threat for us. We look curiously above the hedges and down into the valley, where these damned things crash down. Strange, there are no detonations. The tin drums just burst open. Hundreds of small bearings fly through the air; they are shimmering like tin cans. About ten minutes later, the valley is in flames. Small yellowish violet flames are everywhere. An observer from B-position comes to us shortly after. His group witnessed the whole spectacle in close proximity. The 6-to 8-meter-long cylinders were filled with small cans. After the cylinders exploded, the cans inside swirled about and burst open. Flames were everywhere a few minutes later. Phosphorus bombs—another evil trick!

Despite this, we should be thankful to the Red devils. They have transformed the valley and its heaps of dead bodies into a crematorium. No stench of decay will turn our stomachs upside down tomorrow. What would have happened if Budenny's swallows had aimed better?

"Ribs, Kassel style" [Kassel, a city in Germany], well smoked as someone has remarked.

6 September: Changing guard at B-position at 0300 hours. Six men move into the lonely position. It is quiet despite our expectations. Well, at least what we call quiet: sporadic shell fire and the rattling of a single machine gun. Wet fog hangs over our positions, it is abysmally cold. At least it provides good cover; the enemy is unable to see us walking through the barbed wire barriers as we carefully and slowly crawl through the minefield. Thirty minutes later we reach the forward trenches of B-position. The fog lies in thick banks in the valley. The enemy might attempt to breach our position's front line under the cover of this fog. We are the eyes of our division and as such, we see the first waves of enemy fighters approach within half an hour.

Our protective artillery fire lands well and eliminates the first two waves, but more masses are clashing against our section of the front. If it continues like this, we may have to retreat to the primary position. No one says this aloud, however; German soldiers do not retreat that quickly. Our observation post is quickly altered into a defensive position. The camouflage tarp is removed and a step is dug into the wall in order to bring the machine gun into place. Hand grenades are lined up, ready to be used. The bayonet is attached to the rifle to prepare for one-on-one battle.

The Reds have managed to break through to the right of our position. Quite a few are torn apart by the mines, but the Red devils don't mind a few hundred casualties. The Bolsheviks have understood the importance of our defensive position and bring more and more reinforcement troops. Their masses attack non-stop. Their artillery fires without a break, and from a great distance, directly into our trenches.

The fog is long gone. The sun is beating down on us and driving us crazy. Terrible one-on-one fights have erupted in several sections around us. It means nothing to ask for heroic individual actions. Everyone is a hero here; everyone simply fulfills his duty to the best of his ability.

The Bolsheviks are finally pushed back and retreat around noon. The Russian artillery takes its angry revenge. One fire attack after another rains down on us. The wall of enemy shellfire lies approximately 100 meters to our rear by about 1700 hours, and moves slowly toward us. Explosions are coming closer and closer to us. Just now it almost got us. Loud sounds similar to an organ approach above our heads, three times, four times.... At once we throw ourselves onto the floor of the trench. Again, there is a crashing as if the world itself were exploding. Dirt is flying around our ears and rains down on our helmets.

A fist-sized chunk of shell slams into the ground no further than a meter from me. What good luck! Luck is what one needs in a war! Casualties appear small when measured against the successes. Piles of dead Russian soldiers are lying in front of our section and in the most forward trenches. The worst thing is that we will be sick to our stomachs tomorrow from the stench of the decaying bodies. Once again, we will be running around like nurses with our handkerchiefs over our faces. But there is an unexpected change of events: we receive orders to be replaced in the evening. No one can understand what this message does to the emotions of a soldier on the front. There were probably some guys who even cried … it's an issue of nerves.

The messenger, the bearer of good news, is celebrated like a demigod. He receives our last cigarettes and alcohol. The exchange is done at midnight, without any major incident. We reach the supply troops in Barachty in the early hours of the morning. Now it is about sleeping, sleeping, and more sleeping.

7 September: The heat is unbearable. The moist, hot air makes every move torturous. Flies, thousands of fat flies, make our lives a living hell. Day and night, they are everywhere. In thick masses, they land on anything edible. I lose my appetite every time I think about where these flies started … on the piles of dead flesh and in the latrines. A part of the occasionally severe consequences of this situation are the gastrointestinal and stomach illnesses.

There can be no talk of rest or sleep. Since partisan movement has increased behind the front, thus making the area unsafe, the dreaded watch patrols are implemented, which are meant to bring back partisans and defectors captured near the front. This time they are not young and fresh girls, but fanatical Bolsheviks. They look at us with their empty faces and smile. A body search discovers many interesting things: Russian maps, thousands of Rubles, and brand new passports. Since we are already tense and irritable from the brutal heat, their stupid smiles push us over the edge.

The interrogations are appropriately stormy and "effective" [the original *schlagkraeftig* is a play on words. *Schlag* means heating, and *schlagkraeftig* means effective, forceful, or punchy]. One of the partisans has a pistol aimed at his head and just says with a smile "*karasho!*" After this, they leave him to the translator, who beats him black and blue. The boy is now moaning on the ground and confesses everything: he lists the orders and the people who gave them. We learn from this that one can threaten a Russian with taking his life; put a rope around his neck and he will simply smile in your face. However, if you beat them up, you will be able to see the fear in their eyes and they will confess whatever you want to know.

8 September: It started to rain lightly during the night, and is now raining cats and dogs. The ground turns into black mud within hours. What were once roads and streets yesterday have turned into creeks of mud today. Muddy water shoots through the gulches into the valley. Within hours the bottom of the valley has been transformed into a lake. You can't get anywhere by vehicle, not even a kilometer. Our boots act like filters, though unfortunately in the opposite direction—mud goes in, water goes out, and the dirt stays inside.

I think of the brave comrades in their trenches and holes on the front. These poor *schweine*! They will not have a single dry thread on their bodies in this weather. Their holes will be half-filled with dirty water. Nevertheless, the artillery is barking today. Damn, when will this terrible trench war be over!

9 September: Rain and still more rain. I hope it won't continue like this for the next 14 days; otherwise, the attack on Kiev is down the drain.

10 September: The same gray soup. We will be going to the front again tomorrow. Everything is even gray and dull inside of me. The past few days have not brought us the rest that we so well deserve. We are even more tired and jaded than before, and we are ordered back to the front, into the dreadful muddy holes and in all this miserable weather.

We receive final orders at noon. We have a difficult task ahead of us: infantry support in the Saporoshje. Of all sectors, we are ordered to this terrible one. This part of the front has tasted even more blood than the Potschtowaja sector. It is one of the most complex sectors of the entire western Kiev front. The area is covered in thick woods, expansive swamps, and is very difficult to oversee, which allows the Russians to pull all kinds of dirty tricks. Well, we'll see. I'm not at all happy about this entire situation. At least we have one joy today—the rain has stopped. Thank God!

11 September: The sun hangs hot and bright in the sky. One is surprised by how fast the roads and paths dry out. Where does all this mud soup come from? Nevertheless, the heavy vehicles get stuck more than once or twice. They are stuck in the mud up to their frames. Hurray! With much effort and sweat they have been pulled out.

The way to Saporoshje indicates to us how important the tasks are at the edge of the front. There is nothing, absolutely nothing for approximately 20 kilometers to the rear of the units fighting on the front. It is unbelievable that this thick line extends for some thousand kilometers, withstands the pressure, and eats its way east. This is different than France. There, the military units were organized five kilometers deep. First there were the combat units, next the regiments for rotation and replacement, then the reserves (the marching battalions), and finally a division for emergencies.

Yes, dear gentlemen at home, every little shooter-ass here is a hero. Everyone, even the weakest guy, needs to be a real man on the Eastern Front, otherwise he will encounter misfortune. Then the Russians will break through and there will be nobody behind us to stop them.

It is nice to hear the special announcements. Father Krause smiles silently (well, well, how was it back there at *Chemin des Dames*?) [Reference to the three Battles of the Aisne in World War I France.] Dear Father Krause, let it be told, we have already gone through a dozen or more "*Chemin de Dames*," and who knows how many "Doumamonts" are still in front of us. Father Krause, it has always been the same guys who have been giving their blood on the front lines since 22 June! And Mother Krause is also happy, but in a different way. Where is my boy? Is he still alive? Is he healthy or…. Even if he gave his life for the victory, the mourning mother's heart would still feel joy for the victory and glory of the German flag. She would be proud of her boy who is lying somewhere in the vast lands of Russia, with his eyes wide open. Oh you wives and mothers back in the homeland, we are aware of your bravery. We are no longer your sons and husbands, but your comrade fighters. In our own way, every one of us gives his or her all.

We reach Saporoshje in the afternoon and prepare for the replacements at night. We are replacing a group from Knight's Cross recipient Major [Albrecht] Lanz's [396th Infantry Regiment]. They fought bravely. I envy the men under this wonderful leader and person. He's a man who has intelligence written all over his tanned face, which is full of humor. He has a kind word or a joke for everyone.

Here is the task our infantry has received: form reconnaissance troops and complete an aggressive investigation of the area up to Kiev. It is typical for this campaign that soldiers from all branches take on infantry duties as needed. There are no designated headquarters anymore. The higher ranks are no longer giving orders from secure locations. Now, everyone, officer or secretary, carries a weapon at all times, and uses it at least a dozen times a day.

12 September: The Russians must have noticed something. The replacement turns out to be an evil undertaking with many casualties. They hammer us with spiral mines [*spiralminen*], insidious hand grenades, and artillery shells of considerable caliber.

It quiets down around noon. The Russians did not use their opportunity for an attack; it would have created chaos and cost many casualties. A scout troop with two prisoners returns in the morning. An especially tough and fanatic enemy lies on the opposite side—handpicked members of the Bolshevik Party, like a "Red SS."

There is heavy shellfire all day. If the Russians only knew how small their opponent's unit actually was. Yes, if…. It is good that they often do not have an overall understanding of the situation. We are beating them at their own game: we build bogus positions with large oven pipes pointed skyward, and work on the fortifications all day.

13 September: Russian scouts are patrolling the front line. Breitung and little Horung are taken by surprise and mutilated by hand grenades and bayonets. I move forward with a few men to free them from their miserable situation. The Russians are throwing egg grenades [*Flaschen Eisminenzünder (Fl.Es.Mi.Z.)*)] at our feet on our way back; it is a shitty situation if you are transporting seriously wounded men. We take cover in a bomb crater, as a two hundred kilo shell approaches with a roar and slams right in between us. I think every single hair on my body stood straight up at that moment. The glowing hot projectile is sticking out of the mud no more than a meter from me. A dud! This is a rare occasion for the otherwise good Russian ammunition. I don't need to mention that we had never before left a cover faster than that before. Boy oh boy [*junge, junge*], if that grenade had actually worked, a tin would have sufficed for an official funeral of our ten-man group.

We are leaving our trenches for a very risky reconnaissance task in the evening. According to intelligence, the Russians placed a high-voltage barbed wire barrier into operation yesterday. Our assignment is to discover its path and locate the power station. This time, however, we are unable to fulfill our task, because the Russians commence a heavy surprise attack. It all goes so fast that we do not have time to retreat behind our lines. We are in a terrible situation. We lie in the deep ditch of a small creek no more than 80 meters in front of the enemy lines. We see the Bolsheviks storming left and right, sometimes so close we could touch them. We hear the commissars giving their orders. We are lucky that it is a dark night. We would meet our end if they were to detect us. German and Russian tracers are crisscrossing over our ditch. Minutes weigh like years. The Russians flood back after about an hour. We immediately offer flank protection; our machine gun rattles until the barrel overheats. And then, our comrades arrive and everything is good again.

14 September: A terrible crashing raises us from our uneasy sleep. The Bolsheviks are placing heavy artillery on our sector. Except for the combat positions, everyone takes cover in the bunker, because shells exploding in the trees is not to everyone's liking. I am on guard in the most forward trench near the woods. There are explosions, one after another, in the swampy meadows. A majestic beech tree stands approximately 100 meters from me. The other guys have named it the "blood-beech." This is the only dry spot and is surrounded by swamps. The Red dogs continuously attempt to break through this location. The tree will be blown up tomorrow, for it is assumed that it is used by Russian artillery as a marker on the landscape. What a pity for such a beautifully grown tree.

It is crazy—one is lying here under fire and observes a tree, the sunlight, and anything that plays in the light. Man, Hannes, doesn't this make you long for your beloved forest in the Taunus [German mountain range], and beautiful

Sunday walks with Rosel? Instead, you should be thinking about the shells that are slamming into the ground in front of you.

A few large calibers start to arrive at this moment. It is ridiculous to use such large calibers that are shot from a long distance on a position like this! Damn it! What is that? Where is our beech tree? A cloud of menacing black smoke has engulfed it. As the smoke rises, the tree starts to tilt, at first slowly, then faster and faster, until it slams to the ground. The first thing I hear is the thunder of the impact and then the crashing of the tree branches hitting the ground. Now you see, Hannes, your dreams about your Taunus forest are really not well suited here.

Lunch does not taste too good today because we are too nervous. An ass approaches us with news, which is now being hotly discussed in the trenches. First, there is the replacement order; we will get out of here today. But when it rains it pours—we are going back to our old positions in Potschtowaja-Weta. This is the horrible sector where we lost our best! Second, the general attack on Kiev will start in two days. Finally, finally! One could shed tears of joy. This terrible trench war will be over. It is unbelievable; I finally get to know why we had to be engaged in this nasty trench war for weeks. [Colonel General Heinz] Guderian from the north, and [Field Marshal Ewald von] Kleist from the south, have encircled a large area. An enormous encirclement has been achieved which is unprecedented in the history of war.

There will be a battle of encirclement and annihilation that people will probably still be talking about in a hundred years. Man, imagine that; when, in a couple of years, you're helping your kids with their history homework, and the topic for the next lesson will be the "annihilating battle of Kiev." You can then tell your kids all the things that are not mentioned in the history books—your experiences! Man, Paul, you, myself, and the rest of us, we're all part of this! No matter what has happened so far, is it not amazing that we are allowed to participate in this? Who's thinking about the fact we have not yet ended it and that the next few hours could bring death to anyone of us! But today, today.... Tomorrow we are going to roll and who knows, the day after tomorrow we might attack. Which one of us "*frontschweine*" [frontline pigs] is thinking about death? We wouldn't be able to fight with all of this thinking going on.

15 September: This time the replacement was without hassle, and the weather is great! Everybody is in an excellent mood. There are no grumpy faces anywhere. The news has trickled through: the attack will start tomorrow. We now hate the city that has been lying before us for weeks without permission to enter. But just wait, Kiev, proud city full of weapons. Things are going to change soon! Our mouths hang open in amazement during our march; a lot of work has been done during these past three days.

Heavy mortars and long-barrel cannons have been put into position and covered with camouflage netting. And there are shells, lots of shells. We have never seen that many in such a large pile.

We reach Wassilkow in the afternoon. There, the first thing we do is have a feast and drink some alcohol. After that there is some thorough grooming. Only when you are clean-shaven and washed do you qualify for one of these precious corner lots in the mass grave. Meanwhile, we desperately wait for our attack orders.

16 September: The attack has been rolling since 0500 hours. The main goal is to establish a good attack position for the general attack. A raiding patrol to Gatnoje, which had already incurred bloody casualties six weeks ago, delivers important intelligence. It appears that the Russians almost abandoned their most forward line. Did they retreat to a better fortified line?

Gatnoje is taken by storm. During the course of the afternoon, Potschtowaja is run over and we are back to our previous front line. With this we accomplish the requirements necessary for the general attack. We dig in, which turns out to be a good idea, for the Russian fire curtain begins soon after we are finished. Our own ordnance returns the fire. Some hundred cannons fire in order to make use of the remaining daylight to zoom in on the targets. Only a few large calibers arrive from positions far behind our lines. However, wherever these stinking sweaty *schweine* are, there is death!

17 September: We are still in our initial position for the general attack. The neighboring division is only making slow progress. Despite heavy Russian artillery fire, we experienced frontline soldiers are able to get some rest. Our well-honed instincts tell us that the Russians are preparing for a defensive posture and will not attack.

Budenny's swallows appear by surprise around noon. However, the situation is different than the last time in Terempki. FlaKs, calibers of 8.8 and 2cm, have been arranged in masses to maintain the attack. The scenes that follow are awesome.

The Bolsheviks perform two laps of honor. Our FlaKs don't fire a single shot. Great! The Russians, who were unable to see our camouflaged anti-aircraft cannons, feel like they own the sky. They return with just as much force as they did during the initial days of August. And then it starts: the tack-tack-tack of the 2cm FlaKs and the tinny sounds of the 8.8cms. Eighteen Martin bombers crash to the ground in flames within the next 20 minutes. Well, now it's really serious, Father Budenny!

18 September: Our 21 and 30.5cm cannons have been firing onto the Russian defense lines around the outskirts of the city for the last 24 hours. There are rolling attacks from our Stukas. A dark, black cloud hangs over the city after a few hours. These guys deliver precision work. According to orders, the residential neighborhoods of the city are not to be attacked. They are to attack the fortress, the train stations, ammunition depots, and the Dneipr bridges. Orders for the general attack arrive in the afternoon. Tomorrow is the day. Guys, prepare for the mass grave! You can live out your hatred against this city that has been right in front of your faces for weeks, though as of yet unattainable. Tomorrow—finally, finally!!!!

Hans Roth with his comrades in front of a Sd.Kfz. 232 *Schwerer Panzerspähwagen. (Photo courtesy Christine Alexander and Mason Kunze)*

March to the East and the Winter of 1941–42

HANS ROTH

Editors' Note:

Unknown to Hans Roth, while his infantry division had waged a bloody confrontational combat before Kiev, a huge debate had raged among the German high command that would have profound consequences for Operation Barbarossa as well as the entire course of World War II.

By early August von Kleist's First Panzer Group of Army Group South had advanced 150km east of Kiev along the lower Dniepr, while Guderian's Second Panzer Group of Army Group Center had reached a similar point to the north. Budenny's million-man Southwest Front now looked like a salient, capable of being bitten off should the two panzer groups advance toward each other behind the Soviet concentration. However, to strip Guderian from Army Group Center would mean calling a temporary halt to its drive on Moscow.

Hitler was the main champion of eliminating the Kiev salient, since he believed that by erasing the main Soviet grouping in the south it would gain him the Donetz industrial region as well as the Caucasus oil fields. He may have also had an instinctive reluctance to follow the path of Napoleon, who had marched straight for the Russian capital, only to find himself holding a worthless prize with the true strength of Russia swarming on his flanks.

The chief of the German General Staff, as well as all the generals of Army Group Center, argued that Moscow had to remain the *Schwerpunkt* of the offensive, since for political, economic, and communications reasons it was far more important in 1941 than it had been in 1812, and that Stalin's war effort could not survive its loss.

Hitler won the argument, and in late August the Second Panzer Group peeled off from Army Group Center to drive south. A few days later the First Panzer Group drove north, and on September 14 the two forces met at Romny, east of Kiev. When German tanks marked with "G" (Guderian) met tanks marked with "K" (Kleist) it meant that Budenny's Southwest Front holding the capital of the Ukraine was doomed. It turned out to be the largest single victory in the history of land warfare, with 665,000 prisoners taken, and the entire south of the Soviet Union apparently laid open for further advances.

In his contemporaneous journal Hans Roth appears unaware of the strategic machinations, only seeing that Soviet resistance during his final attack on Kiev (his division was one of the first to enter the city) seemed to have evaporated. In fact, Budenny had begun to evacuate the salient as soon as he learned of the movements of the panzer groups behind him, but Stalin had countermanded his orders and demanded that he hold fast. Budenny was relieved of command and his successor was killed in the pocket.

Sixth Army's von Reichenau, though doubtless an excellent commander, was also the most "Nazified" of all the senior German generals in the East at this time, and issued orders to his troops to be ruthless with the civilian population.

During his time in Kiev, Roth's journal describes him witnessing, with horror, an *Einsatzkommando* action, which may well have been Babi Yar.

After the reduction of Kiev, Army Group Center retrieved its Second Panzer Group (the Third had been dispatched north to assist around Leningrad) and resumed its drive on Moscow in early October. At first huge victories were won, at Vyazma and Bryansk, but then the Soviets were able to call on their strongest ally—which Roth well describes in person—General Winter.

Now deep into Russia across a front of a thousand miles, the Germans found the late-autumn roads behind them collapsing into mud. Supplies and ammunition could no longer reach the frontline troops. When the ground froze the vehicles could move again, but then it turned out to be the earliest and most severe winter in memory, rendering German *Soldaten*—still in their summer uniforms—almost helpless against frostbite, with many of their weapons useless in the bitter cold. The worst development was that the Soviets appeared to possess unlimited reserves, including entire divisions of Siberian troops, well clothed and equipped for winter warfare. Stalin commenced a counteroffensive all along the front.

During this period when German troops were obviously at the end of their tether, Hitler sacked a number of generals who demanded to withdraw to more defensible lines. Among these were Guderian and von Rundstedt, commander of Army Group South, the latter replaced by von Reichenau, Hitler's most fanatic general, though he quickly realized that his predecessor had been correct. (Reichenau himself died of a heart attack within weeks.)

Hans Roth's *Panzerjäger* unit appears to act as a "fire brigade" during the winter of 1941–42, dispatched from crisis to crises, though his main battles take place at Oboyan (Obojan), near the crucial rail link between Kursk and Kharkov (Charkow) at the apex of Sixth Army's advance.

Somehow surviving the winter, he seems both mystified and relieved when fresh German reinforcements come pouring into the front with the advent of spring, though he concludes this journal with simply wishing to see his wife and young child again.

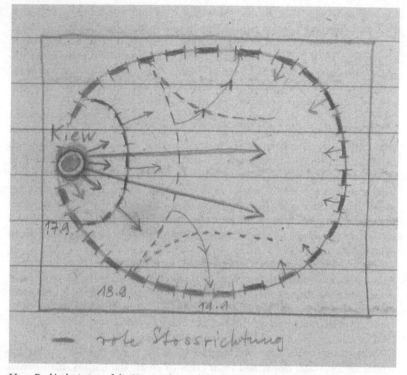

Hans Roth's depiction of the Kiev pocket and the Red Army's attempts to break through the German encirclement, September 17–19, 1941.

23 September: Heavy fighting is to our rear. Early on September 19 we penetrated the heavily armed outer ring of the city. The enemy, by far not as strong as we had assumed, was defeated in a bloody, close combat, and by 0900 hours we had already reached the western part of the city. The Reds have quit their attempts at heavy street fighting. At the same time, strong assault parties attacked the citadel from the direction of Lysa-Hora, and by 1100 hours Nazi swastikas were raised there.

By noon we are in the center of the city, no shots are heard; the wide streets and squares are abandoned. It is eerie. The silence is making us nervous, for it is hardly believable that such a large city has fallen into our hands in such a short amount of time. Is this a ruse? Is the city a trap covered in mines? Are we standing on a volcano?

These are the questions that everyone is currently asking. Today we have an answer to all of these questions. In order to lure the occupying armies out of the city, which was to be spared at all costs from combat, a German offensive was simulated east of Kiev back on September 17, with huge artillery preparations. Budenny issued orders for a devastating counteroffensive, which in doing so removed troops from the well-equipped defense circle, and in turn nearly completely exposed the city. Approximately 120km east of the thin German line, the location of the mock operation, is the supposed outflanking army. Made drunk by victory—as they hardly encountered any resistance—Budenny's troops chase the "fleeing" Germans. They advance farther and farther east, and by September 19, are many, many kilometers away from Kiev. At this moment, the fate of several hundred thousand of Budenny's Bolsheviks is sealed. What irony of fate! Budenny, who up until now, intoxicated from his victory, believes that he is herding before him a panic-stricken, fleeing German army, pushes with tremendous pressure, though only into nothingness, for the enemy has vanished overnight. Only against one flank corps is there a minor exchange. Regardless, he believes he has cut the enemy to pieces (bad lines of communication were perhaps the main reason for his devastating defeat).

An irony of fate: in these days of victory celebrations, Stalin, who believes Budenny to still be in Kiev, gives orders to prepare the city for a winter defensive. And then, that afternoon, it hits HQ like the crack of a whip: Kiev is in German hands. Lost, everything lost! The drama has begun!

What does this western defense line, which Budenny depended upon just like the French did with the Maginot Line, look like? It's not a common line of bunkers; no, it is a collection of diabolical resources, which can only be conceived by the brain of a paranoiac. I will try and describe some of these horrific death zones that we passed through while intensely fighting on September 17, 18, and 19:

> To the rear of Gatnoje, there are fields of cooperatives, vast vegetable farms. They lie there harmlessly in the sun. Who would believe that hiding among those plants is the most horrific death: a high voltage current!

Atop the vegetation is a webbing of fine caliber wire the length of several kilometers. This rests on thin, isolated metal poles, which are all painted green; a deadly net of high voltage current, which is run by a power plant in a bunker. It is so well camouflaged that we recognize it unfortunately much too late, only after the continued accumulation of losses.

Then there are the devil's ditches, lined up in great depth, several hundred meters long. They are mined, and when a single land mine is tripped, entire fields, which are connected underground by detonation channels, explode. At the same time, water pipes explode and rapidly flood the area two meters deep.

There are even a few more goodies that happen to be just lying on the ground, seemingly random objects that are interesting to every soldier: watches, packs of cigarettes, pieces of soap, etc. Each of these objects is connected to a hidden detonator. If the soldier picks any of these objects up, he starts the ignition and detonates a mine or an entire minefield.

In this category also belong well-hidden trip wires, which cause contact mines to explode. These monsters jump up ¾ of a meter and explode, showering burning oil everywhere. There are other areas where hidden among trip wires are thousands of knife-sharp steel spikes, which are poisoned and cause the injured to die a horrible death ten minutes later. All of the defensive belts are littered with automatic flame-throwers, which are activated by pressure.

Well—just imagine, among all these devilish things there are still the normal battle installations: two-story bunkers, automatic weapons stands, ditches, tank ditches, kilometers of barbed wire, tank barriers, in addition to the average mined streets and paths. Add to that infantry mines, booby traps, ban mines, vehicle mines. And now, just imagine this whole hellish apparatus during combat; this is their defense against our attack.

Initially there is the usual shell fire. The infantry is firing their weapons, tank artillery, anti-aircraft artillery, mortars, and trench mortars. Then there is the 7.7 bunker artillery, the field guns, the 122mm long barrel artillery, the heavy artillery from 15 to 22cm, and finally, the artillery mounted on railroad cars and the heavy mortar battalions in the Kiev fortress.

As for the infantry combat, first the expected: gun and machine gun fire; then the Bolsheviks' dum-dum bullets, fire grenades, Molotov cocktails, air mines, and mine dogs. I have more to tell about these exquisite Bolshevik contraptions: we are familiar with the dummy shells from the West; I don't need to talk about them. As for the fire grenades—we call them that—in reality they have nothing in common with grenades. From the outside, it looks like a normal infantry missile with tracer. Once the phosphorus has burned out, the missile explodes into several splinters. Those who have seen the injuries caused by these monsters will never take any prisoners over them. These devilish projectiles are supposed to be banned by the Geneva Convention, as if these Red *schweine* waste a thought on this!

Molotov cocktails are essentially burning bottles which are thrown like hand grenades during trench combat. The effect is the following: upon impact the bottle explodes, the liquid inside ignites in the air and burns with a bright flame; a temperature of 800 to 100 degrees Celsius is reached and white smoke develops in large quantities. Imagine how nicely such a flame would burn your uniform jacket! The second application is firing them from normal infantry guns. With the aid of a middle piece, a shooting cup is mounted. The pressure of the powdered gases throws the fire bottles up to 200 meters. And by the way, they also shoot egg-sized hand grenades in this manner.

Mine dogs: we shot about a dozen of these German shepherds alone near Schuljany. The animals carry a device with explosives on their back. According to a prisoner who has trained these dogs, they are made to attack tanks and other vehicles with their load of 3 kilos of ammunition. By means of a wooden lever on the device, the load explodes after two safety latches are removed. According to other sources, these dogs are also trained to viciously attack people, and have caused serious damage to marching troops.

At various locations along the Potschtowaja front, the Reds are dropping air mines. This mine has wings and a propeller, and is attached to a red balloon half a meter in radius which detaches once it touches ground. Those dirty buggers [*dreckdingen*] rip holes into the earth that reach as far down as the water table.

This was only a small sampling, a very small one. What is this though, compared to the atrocities which the criminal gang in Kiev have themselves concocted, and of which only very little is known so far? Supposedly all public buildings are rigged with mines. Already two days after the conquest, three barracks have exploded, one of which was occupied by German soldiers. From then on, nearly hourly explosions have been ripping through the air; factory after factory, warehouses, hospitals, and schools, all exploding in huge jets of flames.

The civilians are starting to come out of their homes and are slowly becoming more trusting. There are many gorgeous people among the Ukrainians. Touching scenes play out on the street: surrounded by them, we are caressed, kissed, and all this, with a tremendous amount of crying. These poor people must have truly suffered a great deal under the Bolshevik reign of terror. Through their tears they stammer, trying to talk. Many of them speak broken German, and so we learn of many devastating fates. They are thankful for each bite of bread. Many of them have not eaten for days, the Reds having systematically destroyed all provisions in the city. At noon, the streets are as busy as they would be in peacetime. On the motorway, vehicle after vehicle rolls eastward. Supply lines, small echelons, and tanks: Kiev has never seen so much life on its streets. The sidewalks are black with curious onlookers.

Suddenly the unspeakable happens: a terrible explosion, and at three different places on the main road there are flames higher than a house. Huge rocks and ripped iron beams are flying through the air; and then, nothing but stench and smoke fills the street. Cries and moans, in a wild panic the mass retreats. Many are crushed against the walls of buildings or stampeded to death on the asphalt. With weapons in hand, we finally manage to force the headless crowd to a side street. What happened?

After the smoke dissipates, we see the horrible results: the wide street has been ripped open over a length of 100 meters. Once where there was a monument to Lenin there is now nothing but a gaping, deep crater; the walls of the 4-story houses on both sides of the street are caved in. Under the smoking debris, there must be hundreds of people.

The peace and quiet is over! A few hours later, two full divisions are given orders to immediately start forming special command units. One receives orders to search the city following a precise plan, which was left behind by the Red Army, for dangerous elements and terror groups. The other is transformed, along with the *Sturmpionieren*, into a search unit. It is their task to find mine clusters and remote detonation devices. In particular, the GFP and the special SS commands are working feverishly. That same afternoon, round-ups of the Jews start to occur. More about this later, and in greater detail.

Interrogation and investigation show the following: 1). The remote detonation device which caused the terrible explosion at noon was installed inside the Lenin monument. 2). There are more remote devices in the center of town. Despite drastic measures, we do not learn more about the where and how. Most likely, the Ukrainian *Landesmuseum* appears to have been compromised. We search this monumental building throughout the evening. Although the large rooms are pleasantly cool, we are sweating like *schweine*. Damn, it sure is shitty to crawl through such a giant building, with fear always breathing down your neck, thinking that you might blow up with the whole thing at any minute.

Then finally, in the basement, in a small side room, we hear the clear ticking of a clock. The noise is coming through the walls; no wire, no conductor, nothing is visible. This is scary! What do we do? We continue searching for another half hour—an eternity for us—to find this device from hell. We then get orders to evacuate the building immediately. The entire neighborhood is cleared and barricaded. What a dramatic affair. How is it that we still have our wits about us?

At exactly 2230 hours, the giant building blows up. Five or six blocks burn through the morning hours. And not only here; there are many places in the city where jet flames are rising up into the sky. Huge explosions are thundering; a blood-red cloud hovers over Kiev.

September 24: In the early hours of the morning field units receive orders to clear the city. Only local command, administration, and security staff are to remain, thank God! We did not close an eye tonight; explosion after explosion, not a single windowpane was left intact in our area. The walls of the houses have gaping cracks in them.

We move into the suburb of Mikolska-Bortschtschagowka. We are so comfortable in these beautiful houses—God only knows that we aren't spoiled at all. Boy, they still have chickens here. The famous Primus [paraffin burner] is started and soon a cloud of tempting barbeque smells hovers over the barracks. For hours, the whole war can kiss our asses, and then some. But such a favor is not granted. Don't get caught with egg on your face.

Shortly before midnight there is a terrible explosion. Stucco runs down the walls, the air pressure slams the door, windows rattle, the food is stuck in the back of our throats, we throw everything down and run outside. A huge mushroom cloud of smoke hangs over the city. Something terrible must have happened. All of a sudden the food does not taste good anymore, the tempting roasted chicken thighs remain untouched. A heavy pressure lies on everybody.

We are waiting and waiting for the news about what has happened. In the evening we know more. The local command station housed in the largest hotel in Kiev blew up and with it more large administrative buildings. A whole quarter of the city is burning, and under the debris there are several thousand civilians. High officers and many soldiers lost their lives as well. Somebody reports that the fully occupied soldiers casino blew up.

It is horrible. For the first time in a long while those brave front soldiers are watching a movie, are laughing and are happy, and seconds later they are ripped to shreds by the hell machinery of this band of bandits. There will be a terrible atonement....

September 25: Early this morning I drove with three other guys to Terempki. It was a most sensitive undertaking. The whole area is still full of landmines partly contaminated with loess. Even now, days after the fighting, the empty positions reach out for our lives. Eerily quiet is the "field of death," treacherous still, because many thousand kilos of dynamite are lying in the earth, waiting for a wrong step to rise up roaring in a shrill daring flame.

The responsibility is a heavy pressure. I should go alone and at my own risk. Now through their pleas the other three have worn me down and I have taken them with me.

Everything here is sinister, still fresh the traces of the terrible battle but there is no shrieking or whistling in the air here, or thunders of detonations.

Potschtowaja—space without drumfire, walking upright close to the field; who would have thought something like this a few days ago?

My God, what a sight!

Along the total length of the high forest of Terempki, friend and enemy are still lying there, exactly how they died 6 weeks ago. Yes, this Terempki forest, which once was a magnificent forest, but now there are only ripped tree trunks and in between the horror assaults you! Damned me, a soldier should not stroll as a pedestrian on those battlefields which have not completely absorbed all the blood, where within the barbed wires there are hanging things, which were worn by soldiers once during battle, but which after the battle—no no! Then we reach a huge pile of rubble: Terempki.

All around us a landscape of moon craters. These were our battle positions. Then we are standing at the spot where we buried the dead comrades. The earth has been tilted many times. Nothing is discernable anymore; there, where we laid them to their final rest, are now huge funnels at the bottom of which we can see murky ground water. How fortunate that the young women, mothers and brides know nothing about all this!

These were indeed our positions. Many thousands of shells have mutilated them; one can only imagine how the ditches and passages ran, and cannot fathom that once you were crouched in there for 48 hours at a time. It is incomprehensible that a few men were able to flee this hell.

We are driving back, nobody is speaking, silently each on his own with his thoughts. Farewell from Terempki, from all these dear comrades. The memory of this piece of earth is heavy. How can anybody in his lifetime forget these zones of horror?

We are homeward bound, towards the huge plumes of smoke, back to the burning Kiev. Poor city! We spared you, more than was good for us, and now gigantic fires are glowing inside you, your body convulses under the beatings of terrible explosions—not your own sons but the sons of Judah are ripping these mortal wounds, mangling your beautiful body past recognition.

When will this horrible war find its end. Everybody is telling me I am seeing the world all black in an alarmist way—no comrades, to the contrary, I see white, I am seeing white snowy areas and many many of you all dead.

Don't think Hannes, for heaven's sake, don't think!

September 26: Many kilometers wide the center of the city is one ocean of flames, further and further the fire eats away at it. Two more urban districts have been evacuated this morning, approximately 20,000 people are homeless; half of them are occupying with all their belongings the adjacent streets and plazas.

What a pitiful sight!

This morning pioneers blew up the roads close by; it just had to be done. The SS special command is extremely busy. Interrogations and executions non-stop. Somewhat suspicious individuals are simply shot in the street and their bodies remain right there where they fell down. Men, women and children are walking by, talking and laughing: "*nitschewo*," this is nothing special, a dead person, not much!

The soles of the shoes are stepping in the fresh puddles of blood; the wide sidewalk is full of red traces.

You Russians, who will ever understand you?!

The *Einsatzkommandos* of the Waffen SS are very busy as well. All Jews without exception have until noon of the 25th to report. Sure, only half of them show up, but nobody will evade us, for a tight belt of outposts surrounds the city. That very day the revenge for our comrades who lost their lives in the mine attacks is beginning. Now, 24 hours later, already 2000 Hebrews have been sent to Jehovah!

I have a long conversation with a young SS soldiers of this "kill commando." They "freed" all the larger cities which were touched by our advance of the Jewish population. They understand their butcher job well; these boys are experienced killers, I am astonished. We soldiers in the first attack wave have never thought about the stuff that happens behind us in the cities we leave, as we're chasing further after the enemy.

The perspective of the front soldiers is forward, towards the enemy. He tells me about the holocaust of Zhitomir. "At that time we were bloody beginners," says the 19-year-old (with an emphasis on "bloody"). "For two days they had to dig 50-meter-long trenches;, each trench was calculated for 250 Jews. We killed a total of 1800 Jews in Zhitomir, 5000 somehow died before.

"Then, on the third day the trenches are ready, everybody, from baby to oldest senior had to strip naked. The first 250 have to step to the edge of the ditch, the throaty barking of two machine guns—the next ones are herded forward, they have to climb into the ditch and position the dead bodies nicely next to each other, no room must be wasted—the larger spaces are nicely fitted with the dead children—forward forward, more than 1500 must fit! Then the machine guns rip the air again, here and there somebody moans, a short re-shooting of the machine guns: next! and this continues through the evening. We have so little time, too many Jews inhabit this country!"

First I cannot speak at all. This young man talks about it as if he was on a casual pheasant hunt.

I cannot believe all this and tell him so. He laughs and says I should have a look.

We are riding our bikes to the outskirts of the city, to a steep gorge. I will cut this short; the food in my stomach is curiously loose. What I see there is terrible, this horrible picture I will never forget in my entire life. At the edge of the gorge there are Jews standing, the machine guns are whipping into them, they fall over the edge, 50 meters.

Whatever stays at the edge is "swept" down. When the one thousand quota is filled, the heap of dead bodies is detonated and closed up.

"Well, isn't that a great idea, the detonation?" asks the blond with the smiling boy-face.

My God, my God. Without a word I turn and run more than walk back to the city.

This boy is 19 years old! All this does not only leave traces on the clothes; what will happen when these people return into the homeland, back to their brides and women?

September 27: The huge fire in the city center continues. New explosions, new fire breakouts, stored ammunition explodes.

September 29: On the road once more! After a 24-hour forced march we reach Priluki tonight. We drive through the countryside; here and there we encounter a few gunshots by a few nuts in lost positions who will be defeated shortly. The destruction of the 5 surrounded Russian armies is complete, cautious estimates speak of 650,000 prisoners in our hands. Their endless rows pass us; maybe they are the same guys who fought opposite us for weeks. For days now they stood though on a lost position. We encircled them; closer and closer we drew the ring.

Hour-long gunfire destroyed mercilessly those who were trapped, it was insanity not to surrender.

The long line of Soviets passes. What kind of people are they?

In their eyes and in their demeanor is something strange, something dull, completely un-European, even un-human. Bolshevism has destroyed their soul and de-humanized them to an animal level; therefore they fight out of instinct like animals in a herd. It is not the personal braveness of the individual who is called to sacrifice his life for a greater idea but the instinctual defense against danger.

Bolshevism has consciously destroyed everything soulful, everything individual and private that also makes up the character and the value of a human being. What is left is the animal in the Bolshevik, who, however, does not have its finer instincts. Humans in the state of animals are much lower than the actual animal. That is why the animal Bolshevik is so hard and bloodthirsty, cruel and stubborn against the enemy and against himself. This is how to understand the demeanor of the Soviet in this war. What looks like bravery is brutality!

September 30: We will be staying a few days in Priluki, in order to cleanse the surrounding forests of single Bolsheviks. For Russian conditions my lodgings are pretty passable. While most of the people swarm out I stay behind as important map entries and tactical drawings have to be made.

First I wash myself thoroughly and shave and then I sleep for a few hours. For lunch there is a generous helping from the soup kitchen of which the Russian families devour the most part hungrily as so often is the case.

These poor starved people! It is always the same; a piece of dry bread makes them happy and content for hours. I am sure these people have seen better days many years ago at the time of the czar. Again and again I have to ask myself how it is possible that here in the midst of the richest region of Russia, in the wheat silo of Europe, people are starving and have to lead the life of a dog. Unscrupulously these Bolshevik criminals have sacrificed the life and happiness of their people for an armament which in its scope is without parallel.

If our motto was "first cannons, then butter," the Soviet Union's was "No butter, no housing, just the bare necessities in clothing. No culture, only cannons!" The Bolsheviks have succeeded in deceiving the entire world about the extent of their armament. They had imagined that one day, their army of millions, equipped with unimaginable weapons, would start to march westward and trample down all of Europe. Is there a single soldier who doubts that such a march would have led to a world catastrophe of unknown proportions for all peoples? Does anyone doubt that in Germany no stone would have been left unturned? Well, something else has come to pass! And you comrade, and even myself, we have given it our all, given all our blood for this. We all underestimated though, the leadership as well as the smallest soldier—the Russian himself and the huge degree of his armament. The loot of weapons is much larger than we expected the entirety of the arms of the Russian Army to be, not to mention the aircraft, tanks, and automatic weapons. And as for the Red Army soldier himself, he is the toughest enemy, the grimmest fighter that we have encountered up until now.

The six weeks of trench warfare outside of Kiev has demonstrated better than ever his strength, as well as his weakness. The strength of the Red Army soldier lies in the defense. His natural inclinations enable him to masterfully utilize all advantages in the terrain. The most distinguishing trait of the Russian soldier is his stoic holding out until the end, often out of fear of the commissars. The enemy has proven to be nimble at delaying tactics, and well-planned organized retreats, in addition to camouflaging his withdrawals. The mining of the abandoned terrain is always fresh and always updated with new techniques. Most of the time they use timed fuses with an unknown life expectancy. The evacuation of Kiev was a masterpiece in this regard, for among other things we eliminated over these past few days were mines with a life span of 165 days.

The Russian has proven to be a master in the construction of mock installations; their field positions are unsurpassed. Their attacks are predominantly executed in stoic, mass advances; if they do not succeed, they simply repeat them until they do. Almost always, a recurring characteristic of their attack is prepping the field with intensive artillery fire supported by tanks. The time of attack is

Typical Panje hut in the village of Aksariskaya near the River Don, Russia. *(Photograph courtesy of Håkan Henriksson)*

most often at dusk or during the night. The infantry leads the advance in tight formations, often upright in a strict march. Their digging in after reaching a certain position is fast and skilled.

The Russian favors guerrilla warfare; here he is the champion through his cunning methods of fighting. The partisan war has been well planned, prepared, and executed by the Red leadership.

Let's not forget to mention the artillery, those God damned Bolshevik batteries which are considerably greater in strength than we ever imagined. Their weapons of all calibers seem infinite; we encounter them even on the smallest of stages. The Russian's arsenal of weapons includes, besides his own brands, nearly all the brands from other nations, including French, English, American, and even German (Krupp). Single batteries with missiles are occasionally encountered. Ammunition is available in good quantity and quality.

A special place is occupied by the fire grenades, which I have encountered in several varieties, like phosphorus grenades and thermite grenades with horribly surprising firepower. Ammunition is always used abundantly. The destructive fire of the Red batteries is often aimed at a single point for days on end. (We encountered that all too often at Terempki.) In times of light combat activity, even the smallest target, like a single rider or messenger, is attacked with a disproportionate amount of ammunition.

Radio and wireless operations: here lies their huge investment. The Russian works here with a bunch of cunning methods as well, but this is not the decisive factor, for he conducts deceptive radio traffic; upon retreat, long after the departure of the commands, radio transmitters are left at the old location. But so what! Between the Red Army general staff and the divisions there exists usually only a single radio wire; between the divisions and the regiments and battalions, there are only messengers. The failure of the Russian radio service came home to them bitterly, and the defeat of the Red leadership can be primarily attributed to it.

4 October: Much faster than expected, we leave Priluki on the morning of the first. By way of a 24-hour forced march, we are supposed to reach the heavily threatened part of the front near Olchana. In Romny, during a crazy mix up in the pitch-black night, I become separated from our troops. Together with brave Sepp, we wander on the badly destroyed terrain between the fronts for days without finding the division. At the Putiwi bridgehead we stumble upon Guderian's panzer units.

This morning we finally rediscover our troops 112 kilometers to the south. The experiences of this adventurous journey alone could fill all the pages of this diary.

5 October: Once again we receive an important yet risky order. Until the arrival of the division in four or five days, the location of Olchana is to be defended by the mobile panzer division against overwhelming enemy fire.

Before leaving this morning, a few combat vehicles of the 9th Panzer Division threw the enemy back a few kilometers to give us time to dig in. In haste, only those positions of bare necessity are dug up. Boy oh boy, there's something in the air! "You've been abandoned, small troop!"

We are the very front line, and the second and sixth wave all together, no infantry, no artillery—nothing, absolutely nothing! What a mess!

Just like during the Terempki days, swarms of Red fighters and bombers are glued to us. Hut after hut is destroyed by fire. In the evening, the Red *schweine* attack with a loud "hurrah" our position, running right into our machine gun fire. It is obvious that these are poorly trained troops. During the night there is crazy activity over there. A spy unit brings the reconnaissance; the Reds send out another set of troops.

6 October: In the light of early dawn, the Reds attack again. However, this time these are not the amateurs who storm us, but experienced rabbits who force the sweat from our pores despite the coolness of the morning. In a careful counterattack—we cannot take risks with the few men that we have—we succeed in throwing back the Reds; we even take a few prisoners. Since tonight we have encountered the famous "Moscow Proletarian Guard," and Asians, lots of Asians, who, as demonstrated by the attack, fight with utmost determination and devilish cunning. We unfortunately suffer losses, among whom are two of our best: Lieutenants Forester and Kohl. It's a shame, such a shame; such wonderful men!

For the first time, we are visited this afternoon by American bombers, who incinerate the last of the huts with their on-board cannons. A little later, those dogs attack again; we have to evacuate the position and retreat toward the hills in the northeast, all while fighting. Only by giving it our all are we able to keep the fanatical howling horde at bay. These are no longer human beings! Damn! Have we stumbled into a cowboys and Indians war like in Karl May novels?! Like agile cats, they climb into the trees; shots whip over us from impossible angles. Just like the niggers during our time in La Berlières [France], they grip their long knives between their teeth. What a treacherous Asian mob. Damn! Gentlemen, it looks like we'll be burying corpses!

Just when our despair is at its greatest, the "Olchana miracle" occurs! Reinforcements arrive! All of a sudden, there they are, our brave comrades from the infantry; nobody saw them coming during the heat of the battle. More and more of them arrive, and group after group files into our defensive position.

That same evening, the Bolsheviks are thrown far back by our counterattack. Unfortunately, we lose sight of the enemy in the darkness. We retake our old village position; the infantry provides strong protective fire, allowing us to get some sleep. This is the frontline brotherhood! Soon, we are all snoring deeply and dreamlessly in our dirty holes.

7 October: The weather is changing; an icy northern wind whips over the vast plains. Slowly but surely the cold is seeping through the thin cloth of our shabby coats. Our hands are numb and stiff. Olchana lies in shambles, there is not a single room to be found far and wide that could offer us some warmth. And slowly, a premonition comes over me: it is gradually becoming clear to even the most incorrigible optimist that the hardest part is still before us; the second merciless enemy is advancing—the Russian winter.

There is no Russian attack this evening; the night passes by quietly.

8 October: It has become lousy cold; heavy snowfall with ice storms from the north. Operations of any kind are impossible in this shitty weather. Nevertheless, we must move forward in our assault detachment during the evening hours.

The roads are rivers of mud; man and machine each give it their best. Without any significant enemy contact, we press on to Nidregaylow. Lying on the roads are dead horses, abandoned cars, burned out tanks, uniforms that have been ripped to shreds, ammunition scattered all over the roads and fields, harvests that have been destroyed and trampled over. Shortly after Nidregaylow, we cross paths with the marching 165th Infantry Division, which has commenced its attack on the neighboring area, and whose open flank we are supposed to protect.

When night falls, we form igloos and await an attack from the Bolsheviks. But nothing happens; the enemy must have retreated even further.

9 October: Chasing the retreating enemy in the direction of Sumy.

10 October: Relentless snow showers mixed with rain make any further progress impossible. Yesterday evening we arrived in Krawino. The rain has transformed the trenches into lakes all around us; we are trapped pitifully in our nests. On the radio we heard news of the victorious encirclement battle near Vyazma and Bryansk.

The Eastern campaign has been practically decided. The remnants of the Red Army are one step away from annihilation; the Bolshevik leaders have fled from Moscow. Is the end in sight for the East? We hear this and even more over the loudspeakers; surely this will be the headline in the daily papers at home. I grab my head; how is this possible, has our leadership gone mad overnight? All of this is not true, it cannot be true; all of us here see too clearly what is going on. Do these gentlemen have blindfolds over their eyes!?!

What is the homeland supposed to think? Our wives, mothers, and brides will go crazy with happiness when they hear this news; they will cry tears of joy that the horrible bloodshed will be over in a few days, and will expect their men and sons home by Christmas at the latest.

For heaven's sake, the reality is totally different. The eastern armies are encountering the ultimate test of nerves. We Germans are not used to winter combat in freezing temperatures and all of this mud. Is it really necessary to employ such devices, such poisonous stuff? At home, there will be a terrible awakening from these happy illusions. In a few weeks the newspapers will be full of black crosses like never before.

11 October: Again, a powerful snowstorm. All of a sudden there is a deep freeze, 7° C below zero! The roads are frozen solid. We would be able to advance if, yes if, there was any fuel! Gas and supply trucks are still far behind, somewhere hopelessly sunk into the mud. About 60% of the cars are somewhere stuck in the mud. That's right; this is what a victorious march forward looks like! And the muddy season has only just begun, and already after two days of rain we have these losses. All of this does not fit quite well with yesterday's victory fanfare!

26 October: For the first time in several days I am without a fever today; a smelly hut and some straw was my hospital bed. This treacherous Russian fever held me in its remarkably strong grip this time. How utterly abandoned I felt in that half-dark deserted room!

27 October: It is always the same: a dreary leaden sky driven by strong winds and alternating snow and rain showers. The roads and fields are the same: far and wide nothing but mud and muck, sometimes up to a meter in depth. The question of supply has become a huge problem. This shouldn't imply that we do not have anything to eat; thank God there are plenty of geese and ducks here. But we are missing tobacco, sugar, coffee, and all those wonderful things which have to be supplied to us from behind the lines. This is why Sergeant Roth made for himself today a makeshift cigarette from newspaper and German tea. It actually didn't taste that bad, and was copied a few times. The craziest of mixtures are tested. Some groups spend their time on producing sugar, others on distilling schnapps from dry bread, which gives them an extract of a pure, dry alcohol. All of this happens inside stinky, small huts. Anyone who does not absolutely have to go outside during this shitty weather stays inside these pathetic shacks, choosing to endure all the repulsiveness of these pig sties.

What does it look like inside one of these huts, which obviously only have a single living space which we share with a family of seven?

> In the center of it all is a tremendous stove, which takes up about a third of the whole room; the house is more or less built around it. The wooden cots built right next to it represent the bedroom for the entire family. Underneath the cots, and in the many niches around the stove is storage for their valuables. There are pigs squealing, chickens roosting, and potatoes in storage, along with other supplies.

> Hooks have been placed in the ceiling here and there, from which a cradle is suspended; a wooden bowl with a small child hangs by a rope from the ceiling. The *babushka* spends many hours of the day keeping the cradle in perpetual motion by never abandoning the sling tied around her foot, which is also connected to the cradle. She only moves from this spot to sit with the rest of the clan for the never-ending potato suppers. Anyone who is able to hold a spoon sits around a huge pot, and amidst the loud smacking and slurping they "dine" until they are full and burping. All of this only increases the feeling of a prehistoric atmosphere, which one would expect in the huts from early civilization.

> Possession of paper indicates education and wealth. Those who have even a small amount to be able to decorate their walls are well aware of this luxury. In our hut as well, there are torn newspaper scraps, pages from old school books, invoices, children's drawings, and doodling as "decoration" on the walls.

> Out of admiration for the children's paintings, and with all due respect for the attachment to the newspaper and its multiple uses, one is overcome with horror at seeing these "furnished" walls. Not only because of the dirt, smoke, soot and soil, and yellowed paper scraps, no, it's mainly because

of the existence of the small house pets that live their infinite lives behind this paper. We move the benches away from the wall, but at night, when we hear a small creaking and rustling inside the paper, we know that the bell is ringing for them to come out.

There are no handles or locks on the doors, which are nothing more than planks mounted on hinges used to close up a hole in the wall. In some places, so many old rags and pieces of felt have been nailed on top of each other that the planks become jammed. The plank itself is protected from drafts by way of a thick tapestry of straw, old clothes, and other stuff. The tiny windows are completely sealed during winter; however, they do not open in the summer either. The broken panes have been replaced by the *babushka* with wads of rags and small sacks of straw.

All of our senses have suffered greatly during the war. We have listened to screams and moans; we have witnessed many who have suffered brutal pain, so many images about which we will be silent forever. Our noses have fared quite badly too: the smell of smoke, the stench of corpses in the summer heat, and much more. But one memory will remain permanently in our minds: the heavy, grim atmosphere inside our living quarters.

Just imagine the following: local people of various ages, surrounded by many children, who altogether have not washed themselves for years, other than taking a sip of water into their mouths, spitting this onto their hands, taking another sip, and wetting their faces with it. (How often have we had to fight before we got a decent amount of water with which to clean ourselves? They only put a single cup of it in front of you, not out of malice, but because they don't know any better.)

And so this is it: indigenous people, with their many small children, pigs under the stove, sheep skins which have not been removed from the stove for generations, gummed up windows, barricaded doors. Add to this fifteen soldiers with their weapons, all joined together for supper around a flickering petroleum lamp. Afterwards, they smoke heavily, countering the smelly haze of the *Machorka* [Russian tobacco smoked by peasants] against the even worse one of the German tea. If this isn't a recipe for stale air, compound this with the jolly warm stench of bodies! And it is inside this room where twenty-five humans sleep in the narrowest of quarters.

A unique aspect of this atmosphere is the lamp. In the division offices we have generators which produce electricity for the lights, as the officers need to work for hours at night, unlike the common soldier, who uses the darkness mainly for fighting or sleeping. If he wants to carve out a little circle of the darkness for his own business, like I want to do right now, he will sometimes have a carbon lamp or even a candle. He has to rely on the light source of the particular country he is in; here, it is a petroleum lamp in all its glorious perfection.

Without question, the simplest contraptions are the small vodka bottles, suspended from the ceiling by a wire. Suspended in oil dangles a piece of twine, rag, or felt; in especially lucky circumstances there is even a wick. These squeeze through the opening of the bottle and burn at the top with a sooty, flickering, small flame. Such a "smoking candle" is in front of me right now as I am writing these lines.

A step above this is the oil lamp without its protective glass cylinder. The wear and tear of time and its continual movement by the soldiers destroyed the glass long ago. Despite this, it provides enough light for one's surrounding space and to write one loving letter after another to the folks back home. Croesus [King Croesus of Lydia, 560–546 B.C.] was a man who was able to distribute a beam of light from an oil lamp, with or without its protective glass cylinder.

And where do we currently sleep? I should first mention that the main preoccupation during these days of no combat is sleeping. God knows we have lots to catch up on. Therefore, those who are not writing, eating, or frisking themselves for lice (when searching the seams of our shirts for lice, all "killings" are happily reported), are sleeping. We sleep all over the place. Is there anyone who still asks for a blanket? A wooden bench, the floor, a large table—ultimate bliss is straw! Our sleep is deep and dreamless, but at the same time light, alert for any danger, which holds back the nightmares. We dream just as much of normal sleep with deep, quiet breathing, without any itching lice, as we do of a bed with white sheets and pajamas. But we will have to relearn all that, just as we will have to relearn to undress at night.

Indeed, that is a wonderful image. The most beautiful, however, the most cherished dream, is home, our home. Those who look at photographs of their children, worn out from constant handling, the light eyes of the women and girls in the photos, whom we look at with a quiet smile, know this: out here we only have the strength to endure the hardships and exhausting tasks because of the love from home that embraces us. The dream of a white tablecloth, of a tender kiss, this is the source of our strength. The dream of a good life, the war-drives through France, which have taken on an image of sun and wine here in the East, is the last adventurer's dream. Yet that adventure no longer has any allure for us. Rather, the quiet of home is the secret sun in all of our hearts. The longed for, blessed army postal service is its messenger.

For fourteen more days we are stuck in Krawino, and then finally the muddy season is over, and on November 10, a strong freeze suddenly sets in. The thermometer falls almost overnight to 12 degrees below zero.

November 15: It is finally here; the ground is frozen solid. We can start.

November 16: Sumy falls after a hard battle. The losses are huge. Officer Lader, who went out on a reconnaissance mission with his group, did not return; all are dead.

November 18: We reach Lebedyn. These past three days have disturbed the division quite a bit. Only 50% of the weapons and vehicles are operational. The division therefore receives orders to vacate Lebedyn until further notice, and to repair the artillery and vehicles as quickly as possible.

Lebedyn, by Russian standards, is a pretty country town and paradise for us after the lice-infested Panje huts of Krawino. The Soviets have erected here large, administrative buildings; on the outskirts of the town are airfields and barracks. Nothing but Potemkin villages! [Reference to an urban legend that originated during the time of Grigory Potemkin, minister to Empress Catherine II. The legend states that facades of villages were constructed along the banks of the Dnepr River in order to impress the empress during her travels of conquest.] From afar they are imposing, with their whitewashed chalk facades. But what a great disappointment when you're standing right in front of them, or when you even enter them. Meter-long cracks in the ceilings and walls, doors that hang crooked on their hinges, which neither open nor close; staircases that are bent out of shape, swollen window frames, and uneven floors are the least of the problems, all of which astonish us.

None of the buildings is older than five or six years. One thing strikes me here again: nowhere in this workers' paradise have we encountered an electrical line under the stucco ceilings! The wiring is always done in the form of a twisted extension cord along the wall and the ceiling. They are not even familiar with insulated lead pipes, which are mandatory in our country. It is always the same; even in the cities we find shocking primitivism and poverty.

But what about the wages in this workers' paradise, how high are the prices for life's essentials? Here are a few examples—but it must first be mentioned though, that the Ruble, prior to the war breaking out, was set at the exchange rate of 1 to .82 RM [Reichs Mark].

Average wages (monthly):

Skilled specialist*	300	Rubles
Red Army soldier	7	Rubles
Officer	210	Rubles

*Here there is no difference between an accountant, lawyer, or doctor versus a skilled laborer.

The amount of rent is determined by income, on average, 80 Rubles.

A good suit	1500 to 2000 Rubles
A pair of shoes	200 to 300 Rubles
A winter coat made from plain fabric	2000 to 3000 Rubles
A goose	120 Rubles
Eggs and butter	25 Rubles

Immediately within the first few days, a militia was formed of trustworthy Ukrainians who have proven themselves to be faithful and brave comrades during these crucial hours over the upcoming weeks.

A partisan group of 2000 men has been reported. We deploy our men and encounter initial exchanges with these well-armed gangs. They possess machine guns, mortars, PaKs, and even infantry weapons. As these *schweine* are beginning to seriously threaten Lebedyn, we acquire reinforcements from Achtyrka. At one point, we even have to flee, leaving our dead and injured men behind, whom we later find mutilated like animals. In the town itself, insecurity is mounting. A petty officer is mugged; the culprit is hanged from the gallows on the very same day. The next evening I was attacked by two thugs. It was pitch dark out, and they were both able to escape into the labyrinth of housing nearby. One of them must have been badly injured, for during our sweep of the area the next morning we notice traces of blood all over the place. Nevertheless, we have not been able to apprehend the perpetrators.

During the afternoon, ten hostages were shot dead. We are now acting with an iron fist; the gallows in the town square is always busy. Executions are the daily norm. It has to be this way.

We receive bad news from the front: on November 21, the part of the division that had a chance to recuperate has left in a rush in order to meet up with Petersdorf Group, which is in charge of the extremely dangerous Obojan sector of the front.

Meanwhile, it has become terribly cold, rarely above -25° to -30° C. The majority of us are still lacking winter clothes and we encounter our first cases of frostbite.

12 December: The largest part of the division leaves Lebedyn. In a "sleeper car," i.e. mainly by railroad tracks, we reach Obojan on the 19th.

22 December: The division is divided into individual security groups which are now under the command of different units. The front here is very thin, and not at all without breaks. Near Rshawa, the demarcation line to the neighboring army, there is a 40km length of the front line that is unoccupied. What we encounter here at the front is not at all encouraging. This is supposed to be our winter position. Are we not supposed to halt the onslaught of the Reds here?

You just want to cry; a few holes have been blasted into the frozen solid ground, a little bit of barbed wire, that's all! The men who we relieve have boney, pale faces; there is a strange glimmer in their eyes. They shake our hands in silence and slowly make their way to the rear. An hour later, a direct hit brings us two deaths and several wounded.

Tonight is the first mass attack from the Bolsheviks. With the support of tanks, fast ski battalions come over us like a tornado. An icy eastern wind forces snow into our faces; our eyes are swollen shut, our weapons refuse to operate. We have a visibility of no more than ten steps in front of us. Here and there, a Red tank appears out of the snow, like a ghost, often only meters away. The muffled roars of hand grenades, wild screams, horrific hand-to-hand combat is happening all around us. Two cannons are overrun.

There is no more holding on—everyone for himself!

In Kolchos, two kilometers behind the front line, our group gathers back together. We wait and wait, for half of our unit is still missing—no one else appears.... The drama has begun....

23 December: We receive reinforcements during the night, but the men are so exhausted they're on the verge of collapsing. They have done the unimaginable, marching 30 kilometers in knee-deep snow during an ice storm, even bringing with them two cannons. Under these circumstances, a counterattack is senseless, yet tomorrow it will be too late.

We do not understand why the Reds have not followed through.

Under strong tank attacks new holes are blasted, and the Panje huts and potato bins are transformed into bunkers.

24 December: There is increased reconnaissance activity on both sides during the day. It has gotten even colder, -30° C, someone says. As we are already lacking ammunition, along with two men, I take a small Panje sleigh and we start to move toward the battalion command post. The small, emaciated Russian horse trots with small steps. In front of its mouth is a cloud of steam; its matted hair is crusted over with ice.

It's so cold our breath wants to freeze. All of us have pulled up the collars of our coats; ice hangs from our caps and our beards, even though we are hiding our heads down around our shoulders. Our legs are wrapped with sheepskin. Without mercy, the storm blows the snow like sand over the small path, which has been frozen over by glass-like ice.

Our horse stumbles along. The cold reigns relentlessly over this vast landscape which we try, in vain, to shut out. No one says a word, for it seems as if each word, once uttered, will freeze. The miserable huts stand frozen solid like glass in the snow. Beneath our hard steps, the snow crunches loudly as we hurriedly try to shorten the distance, for the cold aches like an open wound.

Finally, after two hours of exhausting stomping in the snow, a small hill appears. Alongside the hill you can see the exposed, tall birch trees, but as you approach, you are able to recognize that there are caves within the earth, in front of which are squeaking lids intended as doors. This is the entrance to the battalion command post, which is under fire every day.

The interior of the room is dominated by a stove made of clay and dirt, with the chimney being nothing more than tin cans stacked on top of each other. A meager light provides just enough illumination to study maps and write orders. Four officers are sitting inside with their legs crossed; all non-essential items have been stacked outside. Above the stove there is bread and meat on a wooden plank; it was frozen and had to be thawed. Just like all the other food items, it freezes during the short distance it takes to get from the field kitchen to the bunker and has to once again be thawed.

Suddenly a heavy fire attack races over the hill. We seek protection in the soldiers' dugouts, which are of course the same as ours, meaning nothing but a hole in the ground, 1.7 meters wide and 50cm high, without any light or warmth, and intended to accommodate two men. These days, quite a few holes have lost their owners, and so we find refuge easily.

Thirty minutes later and the firestorm has passed. With stiff bones, we crawl into the daylight only to see that our good little "Kunny," along with our most valuable sleigh, has been beaten to pieces, lying in a pool of red broth. I am so angry that the curses I try to shout are stuck in my throat. How are we supposed to bring the precious ammunition up to the front, to our frontline brothers?

A short while later, a group of ten men with heavy sacks and ammunition on their backs, leaves the battalion. In silence and frostbitten hands, each of them steps grimly into the footprints of the man in front of him.

Oh how our thoughts are so different. Today is Christmas Eve, and at this time everyone will be lighting the Christmas tree at home; little Erika's eyes beaming, Rosel standing there next to her smiling quietly. Her mother's heart will be heavy; all her thoughts will be far away, here with me. One burning wish will be with all: God, let him return safely to us! Just don't think, don't become soft, wipe away the ice from under your eyes!

Our comrades are waiting desperately for the grenades, because today the Reds, who hold nothing sacred in this world, will begin their storm! Someone is moaning, his feet frozen, he can hardly walk anymore. His load is distributed among us and we march on. Just hurry up, hurry!

It is already dark when we arrive half-dead from exhaustion at our group. We receive official orders to get some sleep in one of the holes. Ridiculous! Who is able to sleep when upstairs there is thundering and howling, and every man is needed? So out of these ditches we go!

Our shells tear into the rows of storming Reds, shredding large holes into the Asian pack. These guys fear shells like the plague, since there are no tanks to back them up as they retreat shortly thereafter.

Oh holy night!

Twice they return tonight, and twice we herd them back with their heads bloodied.

Oh holy night!

The candle burns all night long in the earthen bunker of the medical orderly; moans and screams can be heard from there. Near the morning hours it quiets down; our battalion does not have to suffer anymore.

25 December: We are huddled outside in the firing hole with our machine guns. We handle our weapons carefully and cautiously; we cannot repeat what happened on December 22. Not a drop of oil can touch the steel, for it will freeze immediately.

We look over to where the enemy is lying, he who would love to form an alliance with winter and who tries again and again to break through our positions. We have learned quite a few things from him already: we wear our shirts over our coats now, and as we have no white paint, each morning we quickly piss on the steel door, then spread snow over it, and there is your camouflage.

Soviet fighters approach, howling, in low altitude flights. The whole mess is now starting up again. We grab our ammunition clips. The enemy's artillery is revving up; we are lucky to have such deep snow, for on the rock-hard frozen ground, the effects of the detonations are so much stronger. We hear the tanks rattling closer, and we know that there will be no rest for many hours.

Over on the other side, the enemy's snowshoe units are emerging silently from the forest in their white coats. Our machine guns are barking, our hand grenades are ready; our comrades inside the bunkers have been alerted and are firing while standing behind the trees, as the icy and crusty earth offers no cover. And as so often has been the case within the last few days, the hard fight begins, man against man, with their own weapons becoming a dangerous liability, because their hands freeze to them if they touch the metal with bare fingers.

Machine gun bursts shred the white bark off the trees. The air is humming with them. We can hear the heavy ones way ahead of time, and everyone breathes a sigh of relief once they pass by us. All of a sudden, flames jump out of the forest; an enemy tank has been destroyed. The fighting dies down, artillery and guns are quiet. We look at the fire and think that over there, there is warmth, lots of warmth…. The fighting has moved to a neighboring area. We are mesmerized by the fire and are compelled against our will to fantasize about a large stove, a deep chair, or a soft bed in which one could sleep for an entire night without wearing these clothes that are stiff from dirt, or without being tortured by pests, or without having to have our weapons within arm's reach.

26 December: The front is thin. At night, we receive orders to distance ourselves from the enemy. To the south, the Bolsheviks have succeeded at breaking deep into the front; our right flank has been seriously threatened. Overnight, the Reds took Dmitrijeskoje.

Our group is supposed to retreat to Troizkoje. One squad—our squad—remains behind for protection. The enemy tries to push after us. All day long, the rattling of machine guns does not stop; all day long, the squad huddles in their holes and defends themselves against the enemy.

Only on the following night is our squad able to meet up with the battalion, find our way through the snow desert with the help of a compass, and take a new position near Troizkoje, which the *Sturmpionieren* have blasted into the icy ground.

27 December: Gray clouds cover the skies; mighty untamed storms drive icy needles into our faces. Up in the black trees crows are cawing. This time, though, we fare better, taking turns so that we can warm ourselves inside the dilapidated huts. There, we sit and stare into the open fire. Each of us is occupied in his own thoughts. There is great unrest inside me; I feel that some sort of enormous atrocity is brewing against us. As my comrades all of a sudden cling blindly to my predictions, good or bad, I must not show my feelings. The crackling wood also allows our thoughts to wander down pleasant paths. We are thinking of home.

"The devil knows what kind of winter it would have been...," someone says, not having to finish his sentence—we all know what he means: if this barrel would have started rolling, which was hit so hard near Bialystok and Minsk, near Gomel and Kiev, and near Bryansk or Vyazma—what kind of winter would it have been back in Germany. These days, we think about this often.

28 December: After intensive preparation work by the artillery, the Russians attack in the early morning hours, and what an attack it is! The fight is hopeless! New and more masses flood toward us; within a short time, and backed up by tanks, they succeed at driving deep wedges into the line on both sides of Troizkoje. By noon we are already encircled. Unit I/JR 214, which is rushing to our aid, is completely decimated by the Reds, save fourteen men, who push their way through to us. (Later, we found the horribly mutilated corpses lying in heaps.) Poor boys! They had come fresh from the west, from Biawitz. What were they to know about these Caucasian monsters and their methods of fighting!

The situation is becoming more and more desperate. We wire to Obojan: "Group Petersdorf is trapped, send support!" At 1910 hours, we receive the answer: "Break through the encirclement, rush to Obojan!"

A 22cm bull's eye could not have been any more devastating than this cable—for heaven's sake, is it really that bad? Is Obojan already being threatened? Are the neighboring battalions in retreat? These are the questions buzzing from one person to the next among us.

The shooting has decreased. It appears as if they are boozing it up on the other side; a victory celebration, the storm carries their yelling and wailing. Their drunkenness brings us luck. Their cannons are blown up; vehicles and provisions burned.

Shortly after midnight the breakthrough succeeds amidst terrible losses; at 0600 hours, the remainder of Group Petersdorf reaches Obojan.

The details of what happened on this march could never be described in words—fleeing in 35° freezing temperatures and 75cm of snow from a superior force that is ten times larger! Only the healthy are able to make it with their last bit of strength; the injured, heavily or lightly, are lost in the snow, lying down and freezing to death or butchered by the Reds. We now know that most of them spared themselves this fate by a final bullet.

29 December: Obojan is put on defensive alert. In the morning, a rare spectacle of nature: the sun rises three times. It looks quite bizarre; this strange phenomenon is most likely caused by light deflection in the icy air, which is over saturated with snow crystals. We do not have the time to stand for long and witness this; it is difficult to explode trenches into the ground which is frozen solid.

The Russian population has a different experience. They are standing together in hordes and staring open-mouthed into the winter sky. Many throw themselves onto the hard ground, crying and screaming; the *babushkas* are on their knees—a sign from heaven! Death and destruction is going to come over the city! We already know this, even without an omen from the sky; within two days, life and death will be decided here, a few thousand Russians with strong tank forces are closing in on the city with only minimal resistance.

The God damned 40km gap in the front line. It had to happen this way!

30 December: Heinz Stichel has returned from Germany. He tells lots of beautiful stories from back home, but also brings news of the horrible famine in the Ukraine. They had a two-day layover in Kiev. Here it is the worst. Hundreds are starving to death each day. PaKs have been put into position on the streets and squares in order to extinguish right away any possible uprisings. One single, small, frozen potato now costs .45RM, a loaf of bread 25RM! The city's population treks in masses far outside the town, often 30 kilometers away, to fields frozen solid in order to dig for potatoes with iron crowbars and axes.

On both sides of the supply roads are figures clothed in rags, waiting for one of the small Panje horse to keel over from exhaustion. Like vultures, they scramble over the dying animal. Its body still warm and twitching, they cut into it and greedily take large chunks of meat, which never happens without any thrashing. Dear homeland, be content with the few meat coupons you have!

At noon, Russian bombers appear out of the blue, circling for an hour over the city. One after another unloads its explosive cargo. Many houses burst into flames. At the end, pamphlets are dropped in huge quantities. They are directed at the civilian population. The contents: "Comrades! Leave Obojan, we are going to raze the city to the ground!"

Hey, not so fast, what about us, we are still here after all!

Nevertheless, a large portion of the population leaves the city with all of their belongings in hand, which is not a mistake—this way we at least have some space.

In the evening we receive the bad news that a large supply and medical echelon was attacked and destroyed 25km from here, near Jakoblewo. This comes as a heavy blow. The railway to Bjelgorod-Charkow is the lifeline for 300km of the fighting front line; its destruction by the enemy means the following: no ammunition, no reinforcements, no provisions. During the night we receive orders to form two reconnaissance units, which are to be deployed in the direction of Jakoblewo.

31 December: After heavy bombardment during the night, we leave the city at dawn. At around 0900 hours, we reach the location of the attack. The wreckage of a large truck is still smoking. In the streets and ditches lie the horribly mutilated bodies of our comrades. The chest of a lieutenant has been ripped open; intestines are lying in blood-soaked snow, only the heart is missing. We know from the events of the last few days that these savages, this Asian tundra scum, have eaten the hearts of the brutally slaughtered officers. Think of Karl May's *Indian Wars*.

The driver's cabin of an ambulance is painted red with blood from the injured that have been massacred. Mail is scattered in the snow. Photographs of wives and children, the nicest Christmas present for loved ones on the front, are now soiled with blood. I read a small card with two small pictures attached to it: "Dear Dad, this is me, your Inge, and dear Mama. I have grown so big, when are you coming home?" Little Inge, he will never come home, your dad. Damn, tears are welling up in my eyes.

We leave this place of horror; one of the reconnaissance units under Lieutenant Simons branches off to the right of the street, I myself, and my ten men and two machine guns, take off to the east.

After a good hour of burdensome marching in high snow, we reach a miserable little village—no trace of the enemy. The locals are interrogated with pistols drawn against them. During the night, the Reds supposedly left this place and are lying in wait with a force of 500 men in the neighboring village. There are approximately 800 meters between them and us, and even more important is the fact that there is a gorge in between. It would be insanity to try and penetrate this with my men. This much I know I must do: very carefully I bring our two machine guns to the ridge of the gorge and place them into position. I am lying with my binoculars on a hill overlooking the ridge. Upon my signal, the machine guns suddenly bark out several rounds of ammunition.

First, there is nothing to be seen—but then, they come running out of their huts, all scrambling; the officers are cursing and screaming, it is total chaos. My boys are shooting well, and considering the great distance, an astonishing number are hit and collapse. But then it whistles back at us from the other side. It is high time to clear out. Two hours later we meet up at the pre-arranged location with the other group which did not have any enemy contact. Tomorrow we will come back and smoke out this gang of *schweine*. We do not know yet, but how will this play out differently?

Half frozen, we reach Obojan in the evening. On our way, we were attacked by Ratas; unfortunately two men were injured. In our quarters, there is lots of partying, for the supply office has given out suspiciously large amounts of liquor, the finest French cognac, "Hennessy." Someone says, "The Defense Ministry is having a sale, gentlemen, it stinks!" A little later we will all know just how right he was.

Oh *Scheisse*! Today is New Year's Eve, and we are all buying ourselves one hell of a hangover; maybe it will be the last one we have in this lifetime! In that case, "Cheers, comrades!"

This night is turning out very badly; chains of Red bombers arrive without let-up. By morning, entire streets have been reduced to rubble. The mission to raze the city to the ground has begun.

1 January, 1942, Obojan: We are getting news that the supply lines have been ambushed. The enemy is now advancing on the streets of Nikolskoje. With my reconnaissance unit, I am also able to determine that there are strong enemy forces near Pselezkoje whom we encounter on the front lines. Krasnikowa is also seriously threatened.

The division gives orders to commence our defense of the city. The only units that we have at our disposal are weak, and only a very small number of them are experienced frontline units. These include the men from the bakery, butcher, and supply units, along with their staffs—all less than 1,000 men.

In mid-afternoon, Russian bombers appear. They release countless bombs in rolling attacks through 0500 hours the next morning. Because most houses have well-constructed basements, there are only a few losses.

2 January: Near Dmitrijewskoje, Group Bargmann is defending itself desperately against a superior enemy force. Here, just like everywhere else, everyone is giving his all in order to protect Obojan. If the city falls, there will be a gap in the front for hundreds of kilometers, and no longer a connection between Charkow and

Kursk; access to the well-built railroad would thus be lost. It is very unfortunate that the Bargmann battalion is missing its supply of shells.

Fourteen trucks have been loaded with ammunition. The protection of the crews is taken over by Neckam and me, along with two groups.

We are attacked near Kriwzowo by strong tank forces. Those 52ton tanks squash our vehicles like they were toy trucks and the ammunition carried inside them explodes. The tracks of the armored vehicles make pulp of the injured.

With a heavy anti-tank rifle we shoot and ignite a medium tank just 10 meters away. Then they roll at us and we are running half crazy with horror for 20 meters. The bullets are whistling behind us. Damn! I throw myself into the deep snow, hitting my head on a tree stump, bleeding like a pig. My God! The lungs are rattling, the eyes are caked with blood, I am at the end of my strength! Still, up again, running, only running. If I could just reach the forest over there! Where on earth are the others? Again, bullets are scraping my ears, from the right side there are ten or more Red Army soldiers running at me. This is the end! Then suddenly there comes the thought. It is the last shot at saving this little life, this straw of consciousness: I run some few steps more, again the bullets are coming at me—then I throw my arms into the air, turn around on my own axis, and then I let myself fall down!

The Reds arrive, step on my chest and stomach, they see the blood on the face and on the uniform. I can discern the words "krowj" (blood), "mjortwuj" (dead) and "soldatmushij" (simple soldier). They are just about to empty my pockets or undress me when there is loud screaming and cursing from the tanks; it must be orders directed at these guys. Dusk is falling and they probably want to get lost. They let go of me, a kick with the foot for a farewell and they are gone.

I am saved, damn it, indeed saved! These pigs took with them my machine gun and my field hat,

Luck must be with the simple soldier! I have been saved by my missing braids and EK band and the blood on my face. Carefully I move into a shallow fold in the ground, which stretches all the way to the forest. Under the protection of the first trees it is over and it grips me, the crying of the nerves. Chest and stomach are hurting from the kicks of the Reds.

Nevertheless, further on, just move on! It is terribly cold and I cannot stay put here, hypothermia comes quickly. I take my socks off and wrap them around my head in order to protect it against the cutting ice air. The night is moonlit, and by detour I reach Krasnikowa. Toward the direction of Obojan the sky is blood red; the low thunder of the detonating bombs can be heard clearly.

Where are the others; how many could escape the slaughter? These are the thoughts that keep going through my head and will not allow me any rest.

January 3: The marching group has been cut to pieces. Neckam and myself are in Obojan, supposedly there are still three men on their way here; we are the only survivors. Now I have been admitted into the club of the "corpses." Eight men who were yesterday in the same situation as I was carry the honorary title of "corpse." Now I am the ninth one. These are men who I will gladly take along on reconnaissance and front-line missions.

Again the chains of enemy bombers arrive; it is the beginning of events to come.

The daily order of the general who is with us and remains here with his staff is read: "Obojan will hold out until the last man has died; a general joins the defense line with his weapon in his hand...." A "hail" to the Führer and the men take up their positions.

The main access roads are secured against tanks by mines; we form veils of shooters as well as advanced posts, which are now all occupied. Every available man has to lend a hand.

The first alarming news arrives, only 4km southeast of the city the Reds are advancing with strong troops and tanks. Group Bargmann retreats, bitterly fighting back to Obojan. Also in the north, near field watch 2, strong tank noises. From a different position comes the news of Russians advancing by trucks.

With senses and nerves on high alert, the defenders of the city await the attack in an area of 2 square km. Heavy tanks put their feelers out here and there, but remain outside shooting range. Towards the evening we have been completely surrounded.

Shortly before 22.00, in complete darkness, there is the first attack in the south and east. In the south it is met and rejected with bloody close combat. In the east, however, the enemy is successful in making deep progress. Ear-shattering explosions are ringing through the streets, the Reds fire into the city from all sides, the noise of the exploding and detonating bullets is amplified a thousand-fold, and from all sides tracer fire is crossing. Tank grenades shred into the houses; burning roof timbers and rafters smash into the street. The air is full of singing and chirping, nobody knows where the shots are coming from. Across the street the Bolsheviks are sitting in the gardens. The "corpses" go on another spying mission. The quarter is barricaded and the Reds are thrown out in a counterattack.

But again and again they are running at us from the south and the east.

January 4: In the south the attack of the Reds stops immediately in front of our lines. Field watch west reports that the enemy is moving closer and closer to the city. Here a deep valley traverses the terrain from west to northwest, which separates the city from the suburban villages. In this valley lies our most important water source. All day long there is heavy field fire right here. Fetching water alone is paid by numerous losses. A brave raiding party finally gets us some air. Late in the afternoon enemy tanks are closing in on the city. Equipped with "Molotov cocktails" and gasoline canisters we man our defensive position;

sufficient hand grenades are kept ready and close by, and the flame-throwers are put on alert. The colossal beasts are nearing, firing wildly, until they are in reach of our outmost position which has the order to let them pass through. But angrily we have to recognize that they dare not enter.

After a short while they disappear behind a ground elevation and attack the city from there, firing directly without pause.

With the setting of dusk all hell breaks loose again. The 7.5 shells of the tanks are ripping huge holes in the rows of defenders, the huge pears of the heavy mortars arrive gurgling in the air.

Bombers destroy with 200-pound bombs whole street quarters, the city is burning at every corner. The losses are enormous. I have been on my legs now for many days and nights. I follow my orders feverishly, do reconnaissance, operate the machine guns, the artillery, throw hand grenades.

Every single man fights unimaginably. 25 times the Russians attacked today with tank support.

Many times tonight the pig has infiltrated the city for a short time, in our counterattacks we threw him back each time. We men are standing like iron in the defense despite terrible losses and terrible temperatures (-42 degrees C), for a large part with frostbitten hands and feet. Being sick is not an option; we are fighting for our bare life.

January 5: We receive the order to burn all files and boxes, personal, paper and map material. The trucks with luggage and equipment are being prepared for detonation. The pressure of the Reds is huge. If that is not enough, now ammunition and provisions are becoming scarce.

In the morning a heavy tank is blown up by 8.8cm flak artillery, the infiltrating enemy is destroyed. Among other things they have incinerated our provision storage; there are dead bodies lying in the snow, army bread tucked under their arms. At noon, air raid alarm. With muffled roars they are approaching—but what is that? A squadron of our heavy bombers!

Finally!! They circle, push deeper and deeper, three times, four times they fly over us at close height. The bomb shoots open … there, in the middle of the city the rows of bombs are falling, parachutes are opening: deployment of ammunition!

The Russians are shooting like there is no tomorrow, it sounds strangely close in the clear winter air. A heavy load is lifted off our chests when we see the floating parachutes come down. Finally there is help from the leadership! On one of the ammunition shells somebody wrote with chalk; "Hold on! We are coming!"

You bet we will hold on!

Ammunition is at hand again and roasted cats and roasted dogs do not taste that bad either. The mood barometer points to "Nice weather."

We have to succeed!

January 6: In the south there is loud fighting to be heard. Group Postler is supposed to attack there in order to bring relief to the occupation of Obojan.

Right now we sense nothing of the sort. To the contrary, in the northern part of the city the enemy succeeds in infiltrating with a battalion. The fire of their mortars lies heavy on the spot of the breakthrough. This time the situation is very grave because the attack is supported directly with tanks.

In the evening the heavy battle is still raging in full force. Our quarter is again barricaded. Tank shells, flares and explosives are whistling through the street. One block of houses bursts up in flames. In its eerie glow we see the Reds jumping their short steps, a good target for our machine guns. At midnight, 2cm anti-aircraft artillery is put in position—and that cleans it up. In the hardest fighting, man against man, the Bolsheviks are thrown back.

A small scene should illustrate what kind of tough enemy we are dealing with: While advancing with my group we are cleaning a garden. In a foxhole we discover a wounded Russian officer. I yell out to him, "Rukij war!" (Raise your hands) His answer given with a smile goes "Njet!" (No)

A hand grenade thrown in his hole rips him to pieces.

At a hedge close to the end of the garden there is a badly injured Red. Shell splinters have ripped the fingers off his hands; the legs seem to be smashed as well. We are five steps away; brightly he lies in the light of a burning house. When he sees us approaching he makes a lightning fast move and rips off a hand grenade with his teeth and lies his head on it. "Lie down!" and already the hand grenade explodes with a hollow thud. Vogel, who is slow on the pick-up, did not make it to the ground, a dozen splinters ram through his body. (He dies within the following hour.) During the course of the night the most beautiful news of these hard days arrives from the division: A battalion, I.R. 217, stands with its spearhead 8km south of Obojan. A patrol immediately makes contact. This time the "corpses" are spared from this mission. During the early morning hours the brave infantrymen succeed in breaking though the pincer movement.

It is high time that they arrive, because our losses already amount to 1/3.

January 7: A raiding party of the enemy makes it to the city center. We catch them at the field post office. Lying behind the filled sacks of mail—we have erected a considerable barricade out of them—we are firing like mad at them, then we attack with hand grenades and at the point of the bayonet, for the danger is extreme, 20 steps further there lies the general and his staff. Those gentlemen also open fire from all the windows of the staff quarters. And then an image which I will never forget, free standing on a balcony, our best comrade, a white haired officer, our general Neuling. Without a care about the whistling of the bullet bursts he is unloading his machine gun into the rows of the attackers.

Suddenly, to the surprise of friend and enemy, there is loud rattling and hissing, and two or three times a terrible burst of fire comes from a cellar window to the right onto the street. Flamethrowers!

The effect is terrible. Corpses burned beyond recognition are lying in black lumps on the street. The remaining Bolsheviks are fleeing in horror. But our machine gun bursts reach the fleeing; the enemy patrol is destroyed completely.

A little bit later a heavy attack supported by tanks calls us to the northeastern part of the city. The Red hordes arrive, screaming a shrill "Hurrah."

Mortars and tank shells transform our defensive position, the Kolchose yard, within the shortest time into rubble. Half of the defenders are dead or wounded. Our artillery fires at a 52-ton caterpillar. But not one shell penetrates the thick armor plating. We want to despair. Now our second machine gun gives out due to a direct hit. Officer Nold is dead, the other two, who armed it, are heavily wounded. We demand reinforcement but they cannot come through because there is heavy fighting in the west as well as in the east.

Finally, after 30 horrible minutes, a tank and an assault gun arrive, and the latter shoots down a Charkow tank. We are advancing our counterattack, and what a miracle: the Reds are retreating.

With the fall off dusk we pick up chores, which we had missed, the whole area in the front is mined by our pioneers despite very dense combat fire of the enemy.

The mess of noon today will not be repeated soon. Our losses today are damn high!

During the night, heavy attacks of Red bombers in rolling waves, strong mortar fire, some infantry attacks. All in all it is quieter than during the last few nights, nearly too quiet. We are suspecting something devilish. The large cupola of the north church—an extraordinarily beautiful building, seat of the important B position—is fired at and ignites, in a bursting rain of embers the tower collapses. Bright as daylight the fire illuminates the northern position, every man, every single gun is clearly visible from above. Like hawks the bombers bear down on our trenches. Their bombs brings us many losses.

But the airplanes are bathed in red light as well, and our machine guns and the 2cm anti-aircraft artillery take aim like wild at the good targets—God knows, they succeed: a heavy bomber is hit and crashes burning into a field. Great is the jubilation, more even as the others are scurrying away.

January 8: There is absolute quiet in the direction of Strelezkaja, not a single shot fired from over there. The eternal attacks probably will have also tired out the enemy; they will be asleep over there—as they can, because they determine the pace of the action, not us. Maybe they assemble their powers for a counterattack? Who knows? But we have to find out. A reconnaissance troop goes out. With utmost care the men are stalking toward the village. There is utter quiet in Strelezkaja, few posts are standing around, bored and freezing. Without them

Kharkov town center prior to German occupation. *(Photo courtesy of www.wwii-photos-maps.com)*

noticing we return at 5.00 a.m. to Obojan. In a hurry we assemble a strong raiding party with two PaKs, even assault guns are included.

At 5.30 a.m. we penetrate Strelezkaja. The surprise of the sleeping Russians is one hundred percent successful. Most of them do not even get the chance to get up. Without mercy everything and everybody is gunned down or clubbed to death on their sleeping cots. The whole nightmare lasts about a half hour. Strelezkaja burns down to the ground, in every hut there are 20 to 30 dead Russians; the houses become places of cremation. (Today we know that more than 360 Russians fell victim during the bloodbath.)

Well, you Asian pack, you certainly did not dream of that!

At 7.00 a.m. we have already taken up our positions again in the line of defense. The heavy mortars beat into the city, machine gun salvos are whipping through the streets, the usual!

At noon again, a resuplly of ammunition and provisions.

Otherwise nothing unusual. It is calm, alarmingly calm. At 15.00 hours there is suddenly the heaviest shooting.

Now we are in the know.

The Reds are ready for the counterattack! At the same hour an order arrives from headquarters: tomorrow morning at 9.00 a.m. an attack maneuver is to be undertaken. Group Dostler pressures from the south, the occupying forces will we trapped within the shortest time in this scissor formation, if they do not get possession of Obojan this very night.

Tonight our fate will be determined.

At 20.00 hours the concentrated storm on the city begins.

At different locations the enemy succeeds in breaking through; in bloody close combat he is beaten, breaks through again at different places, infiltrates the field hospital and causes a horrific bloodbath among the wounded. With limitless fury we force him back again, not being in control of our senses, we are shooting, stabbing and beating around us like in the throws of madness. On a ward in a side wing of the hospital there has been a horrible struggle. The Reds do not have any more hand grenades; with long sticks the Caucasians beat at us, with our rifles we force them towards the windows and throw them hand over feet out the windows into the yard. I look terrible, the hands are bleeding, the uniform is ripped, soiled with brain matter and dirt. A tank shell rips howling through the outer wall, a hand-sized fragment rips the head off the body of my companion, nothing happens to me. Damned, am I immune?

Up until the early morning hours there is bitter fighting in all street quarters. With the breaking of dawn the attack has finally been defeated.

January 9: The pressure of group Dostler, approaching from the south, onto the deep open flank of the enemy is definitely discernable.

Around 10.00 a.m. the enemy attempts another breakthrough in the north, but with the aide of our two storm cannons this undertaking is stopped and squashed right in its inception.

Outside the heavy firing, the day passes in relative calm. The hour has arrived when we, together with our infantry, assemble for the counterattack. At around 21.00 hours our own intelligence reports that the enemy is retreating toward the northwest while leaving a rearguard. He must retreat because he is forced to do so from the outside.

January 10: The connection with group Dostler stands. The retreating enemy is nearly completely destroyed; the remaining troops are forced eastward.

January 11: The small brave fighting group of Obojan takes a roll call at the main city center where there remains not one building standing. The general, who was awarded the Knight's Cross the day before, thanks his men. He reads a thank-you telegram from the Führer, which makes us all very proud. (Only once before during this war has the Führer issued a similar personal telegram: This was to general Dietl at Narvik.)

We can hardly believe it: Obojan is free again, and free is the connection to the rear areas in Kursk and Charkow. Finally there is something to eat and finally we can sleep in. Unimaginable hard days lie behind us, bitter fighting at temperatures of -45 degrees Celsius. But despite everything we held on to Obojan, thus honoring our dead comrades. They will not have died in vain!

The heavy casualties of these fights are demonstrated by the following numbers:

Dead are 195 men

Missing in action: 18 men

Wounded: 327 men, 65 of whom are suffering from exposure of the severest degree.

540 brave men gave their blood, 540 of 1,130 defenders. I believe numbers speak louder than words.

What the Russians had planned and their overwhelming manpower is demonstrated in the following order which we intercepted from a captured lieutenant; it refers to the large scale attack of January 8th and 9th:

> O. must be taken under all circumstances during the night of 1/8 – 1/9. Available are: 16 battalions [assuming 500 men per battalion we were looking at at 8,000 men] and heavy weaponry. From 17.00 hours until 20.30 hours O. is to be attacked with all available artillery and tanks in order to be stormed. At 20.30 hours the battalion Potowka will break through the German outpost in the north, will battle through the outer city fortification and will march in spearhead formation towards the south of the city. After successfully reuniting with our own troops stationed in the south the city is to be annexed according to plan.
>
> In order to prevent the enemy from escaping from Obojan, the Samonew, Timansko, and Lachiwirkow battalions will form a blockade to the northeast and east; an additional regiment will take care of the south (Omsk).
>
> Battalions "Maxim Gorki" 2 and 3 will traverse from the north to the northeast, thereby regaining the connection to those stationed in the south. Again, please refer to the special command of 12/17/41. This special command, issued by Stalin, which we have known about since Christmas, states this among other things: "In the future, the only Germans I want to see are dead Germans!"

Oh well, those horrible days are over, and the Bolsheviks have had to reckon without their host. We too seldom take prisoners now.

12 January: Sleeping, sleeping, and more sleeping.

13 January: A strong, agile raid party is formed under the leadership of Colonel Hackle. At various locations to the east of Obojan, there continues to be heavy fighting.

The Reds succeeded on January 1, just at the eleventh hour, in leading two regiments through the gap near Rshawa, who were to provide reinforcements to the occupiers. We would have fared really badly had they been able to advance more quickly. The two regiments rejoined those who were flooding back, forcing the combat to continue near Werch-Dunajez.

14 January: In a forced march, our assault detachment is thrown there. The fighting and the cold over the last few weeks have worn us out badly. My men are only skin and bones, and the "corpses" now truly have a deathly pallor about them. Ever since the early morning hours, we have been laboring through the goddamn snow. For hours now, the storm has been blowing across the land. It eats through our coat and any protective clothing; it curdles the blood and petrifies our bones so much so that the freezing temperatures feel like a biting pain in all our nerves. By now, only the long poles, which are standing in the snowdrifts on the sides of the roads, show us the way. Darkness is falling upon us. The long nights now stand over this land where a relentless wind from the tundra rushes over the solemn, white distances, cold as a knife under the merciless, blinking stars. At -40° C, our weapons speak a terrible language. Who has not, during these winter days, and indeed, how many times, been called to the utmost limits of his strength!

After a short rest in a run-down hut (no one is allowed to sleep, although we are dog tired, and just about at the end of our strength), we carry on. At daybreak we reach Werch-Dunajez.

15 January: The enemy is sitting before us at Saikin and Plotawo. Our infantry comrades, whose ranks we now join, tell us about the Reds over there. These are new forces which have been brought over from the Soviet Far East; reserves whom the Soviet leadership believes will change their luck in this war to their favor this winter.

Yesterday, our infantry took Werch-Dunajez; the rubble is still smoldering. They are a crazy bunch, those Caucasians, Kyrgyzsians, and Mongols; stoically, they stay put in their snow dugouts when resistance is hopeless. Perhaps they are hoping to go undetected. But their hope is in vain, as our eyes are now accustomed to the snow.

In the dark night, Soviet forces, the strength of one battalion, march toward our positions. Their actions are unfathomable. Our outposts detect them, and within 100 meters, they are smashed to a pulp by the combined fire of our vigilant company. They cover the bottom of the basin in a wildly gruesome pile, at the point where death met them while fleeing or marching.

We press forward toward Saikin and Plotawo. In the villages, the sight after our attack is not any different. Corpses—nothing but corpses. The penetrating Soviet forces suffer immeasurable blood sacrifices. The immense Red losses give too easily the wrong impression that our fight here in the East is not that difficult. To the contrary; the true picture of the enemy goes like this: tough, stubborn, and malicious.

It will never be possible to describe in words the deprivation and exertion that we have suffered during these defensive fights led by our brave infantry comrades.

16 January: A deep layer of snow covers the ground, and we have to fight for each step that we take. The icy cold temperature freezes our limbs solid, and our fingers would stick to metal if we were to touch it with our bare hands.

In front of us Gotschegurowka is burning; it still has to be captured today. The Red defense is tough, and for some of us, this is the hour in which our life becomes fulfilled. In this burning village, where there is not a single house that remains standing, our company will spend the night. Where? Next to a smoldering beam, in a snow hole, in a wind-sheltered corner of a remnant of a house that still stands? The only thing we know is that we will indeed spend the night here, despite the cold, despite the privation. Will the supply trucks follow us, or will we have to set up camp where there is no camp, and with our stomachs growling? Will we awake after a freezing night, with frost-bitten limbs, and sense nothing like a warm tea, a warm meal until—if the attack does not continue—supplies have reached us? Maybe we will just chew on the hard *zwieback* of our iron rations, and try to thaw the frozen meat in tin cans.

17 January: Orders take us to Jekaterinowka, to secure the Rshawa battery. Approaching from the south, two regiments, who are relying on Group Dostler, are moving into the 40km gap. But the Russians have also been able to bring in strong forces. Bitter fighting takes place, the outcome of which is of absolute importance to Charkow and Kursk. Our own tanks are rolling behind us; Stukas successfully enter the combat. In a tough wrestling match, our regiments succeed in pushing the enemy slowly to the east.

We are marching straight through the embattled area. The field of corpses that is left behind in the occupied villages is wretched. The black dots that cover the distant snowfields cannot find any graves. Who is supposed to dig into this ground, which is frozen solid two meters deep? Who is supposed to collect the innumerable Soviets? We are the only ones digging graves for our own comrades. An explosive charge pushes up the hard earth, and a cross in the snow, forged by the men's hard fists, pays witness to the fact that somebody here has given his life in this never-ending battle in the East.

And so, the victorious battle rages on, as the Soviet reserves bleed to death. We know that the resistance is not as strong everywhere else as it is in this particular area, where the Soviets want to force them to break through with all of their might. We are standing at the focal point of the Eastern Front. But at least we know that at this particular point, there will be no decisive success by the Soviets.

18 January: On the road at -40° C, 1.5 meters of snow, and an ice storm.

19 January: Toward the evening, we reach Jekaterinowka. As we are frozen solid to the bone, we set up camp as quickly as possible. Camping in the village—now that sounds cozy. A warm lamp and a crackling fire, a solid bed, a soothing drink, bacon and eggs—France, you are so far away! This is the reality: you push open the door and immediately have to duck, because otherwise, you would smash your head into a wooden beam. If you are lucky enough to pick your quarters, a hot stench assaults you, rests on your suffocating lungs and chest, and a sluggish cow, which has been lying on warm, soaked straw, raises her head. Only then will you enter through another door into the actual living room, where now a briny odor surrounds you. But your nose has long since been dulled against all these smells, and even if it were only just months ago, you had thought it impossible to endure such emanations for even half an hour, you see quite realistically now that the stove is burning and there is enough space for you and your comrades.

In the flickering light of a candlestick there is the familiar picture: sprawled above the stove a farmer is in hibernation next to the chickens and a *malenki* (a small pig). Now between these rags and the rubbish on the stove bench, there are a few children's heads moving, staring at you with large eyes; and even the children, too, appear to you like strange animals, dirty, crawling and slithering, but under no condition human.

God, if these were the only living creatures living in this house! The candle dies down, and now the house pets start to emerge from every corner. Bugs, fleas, and lice, the hours become torturous and suffering; not a thought of getting some refreshing forty winks, as now they are all stuck to your clothes. Day after day you go lice hunting; forty, fifty, and even three times more is the daily loot. And how disgusting is the scurrying of the mice, which the winter forces from the fields into the houses, and who are now racing and whisking with their thin whistle all over your body and face as soon as you lie down. On this particular night, the mice chew fist-sized holes into the pockets of my coat, which I wear while I sleep. There were small remnants of *zwieback* in the pockets—pieces of my iron ration.

The next morning, you get up, only to be confronted once again with the reality of how soiled and dirty this quarter is, how all the tools are covered in goop and full of dung, how disgustingly greasy the table is, how gummed up the benches are—and yet, you are still grateful to have encountered such good quarters.

In the villages on the front, there where our last security forces lie, the picture is a completely different one. There, misery resides in every hut; there is no straw to be found, and at night, you put your coat on the cracking, ice-cold ground, or you pack yourself onto a hard, wooden table. And yes, the bugs have taken refuge from the cold in the cracks of the planks; in their place, however, the mice and rats hunt through the living room unafraid, and in broad daylight, which allows you to club down ten or even twenty of them. This doesn't matter and makes little difference. You can also see lice taking a walk in the broad daylight; they crawl upon you and you are unable to defend yourself. And here on the front you must also be prepared at any hour for a hailstorm of fire to come over you, or for a sudden attack from the Reds in the middle of the cold-stiff night, or to be aroused from the urgently needed sleep because perhaps a few houses down there might appear out of the blue an enemy reconnaissance patrol.

20 January: During the afternoon our units clear out. Tomorrow morning we will march back to Obojan, where new tasks await us.

We use the few hours of quiet to finally write a letter home. Who knows when these few lines will reach our loved ones back home? Snow drifts several meters high have made it impossible for the vehicles to pass through the roads.

Watch patrol at midnight. Billions of stars hang in the ice-cold winter sky. Once in awhile a shooting star falls in a glimmering path. Wish for something, foot soldier, if that spark of an old childhood dream is even still alive in you. With lightning speed, a thought of the holidays crosses my mind. But that silly dream is nothing but a memory. Those days were already over when the shooting star announced coming happiness. This war silences all such hope.

Far in the distance, bright fire illuminates the sky. It returns often, and a few seconds later, the muffled sounds of the artillery rumbles over us. Over there, our comrades are confronting the enemy; at this very moment they are probably ducking into a snow hole to avoid the howling song of the enemy's shells, or their bodies will rise like shadows out of the ground, storming forward to attack.

21 January: Departure for Obojan. Strong snowstorm!

22 January: We are supposed to have two days of rest, since on the 24th we are supposed to take our position with Lieutenant Hegner in Woroschilowa.

Not much needs to be logged during these days. Weapons and equipment are inspected and we catch up on a lot of sleep. When the mail comes through on the 23rd, there is overwhelming joy. At night, there is hardly any sleep because the heavy 100-pound bombs are thundering down on the city until the early hours of the morning.

24 January: On our way to Woroschilowa. Attacks from Russian fighters and bombers. At night we set up camp in a piss-poor, godforsaken village. Exhausted to death, and half frozen, we wrap ourselves in blankets.

Sleeping, just sleeping! A telegram rips us from our uneasy slumber. God damn it! Is there no rest at all to be had by us?!

Strong enemy forces threaten the area around Woroschilowa; we have to march tonight. Again, out into the cold—fighting over and over—fighting, is there anything else for us?

Thank God the road is good and there are only small snowdrifts; the *Sturmpionieren* have been able to hold them open for the ammunition and supply convoys. These brave men too, achieve the impossible here. We will never forget these quiet, faithful helpers and pathfinders in the truest sense of the word.

Despite the brightness of the moon, we are unable to discern anything around us. The many dark spots along the side of the road—are they piles of sand which have been hauled in here from afar by the *Sturmpionieren* during the day and stored there, or are they dead horses? One really doesn't look there anymore, as everybody is occupied with himself, and we have all seen enough horse cadavers—thankfully frozen—slashed by the sharp beaks of birds which now line the streets in the East.

One hardly looks out over the vast plain, where on the horizon, between the forest and the icy river gorges, where the enemy's gun flashes, as well as our own, light up the sky—a distant fire display toward which we are moving in a silent march.

"Still 5km to Woroschilowa!" We know that when they say five, they mean ten. Misleading us is the trump card of these forced marches. We listen to shot after shot; in between the sometimes loud and sometimes quiet strikes, we drift off into our thoughts.

We make it through an area of forest. We are wishing that we were finally at the front in our ditches and dugouts! Not only because the temperature has fallen below -35° C. No, much more so because we know that the enemy is directly in front of us over there. Here on the road, he is everywhere, lying in snow holes and bushes waiting to ambush us; shooting from his traps and burying wooden mines along his way.

25 January: Woroschilowa—a heap of rubble amongst a pathetic trench system—our new position. The daily assault from the shells does not allow the snow to stay on the ground for long. As our comrades tell us, this can also be considered a "frontline" position because every day something burns down here, the flames at least giving us some much needed warmth. Besides the shelling and the artillery fire, nothing much happens today. On the other side, as well as here, men are resting from yesterday's major offensive.

26 January: There is an incident during the afternoon, unimportant as such, but one that nevertheless leaves us in a state of unrest. An enemy patrol has succeeded in approaching very near to our position; we observe them unknowingly for a while until they throw a few hand grenades, fleeing before we are able to recognize them and fire. Far in the distance we notice a few figures in snow coats disappear and vanish. Nothing can be done to them anymore. The dry sputtering of a machine gun is much too late; the snow splashes up high from the impact of the bullets and dissolves into the sunlight, but the patrol has long since disappeared behind a depression in the ground.

Us *Frontschweine* indeed possess a sixth sense by now, and it is telling us that very soon all hell is going to break loose, and this mess is going to start all over. In the neighboring area close to the *Sturmpionieren*, who are holding the position up to the road, the anxiety is obvious. And when the food service arrives with the evening soup, the machine guns next door are wildly sputtering again. We are in the middle of filling our plates, but are still keeping our ears alert.

Anti-aircraft fire now enters the developing battle. And shortly after, when the infantry rifles come alive and the first listening post returns with the news that something is happening over there, everybody drops their spoons, grabs their weapons and helmets, and goes over to the post, where the men there eye sharply the encroaching darkness of night. In the meantime, the artillery too, has heard that something is happening up on the front.

Heavy shells are shuffling through the air and crashing down among the enemy's trenches. There is a hellish uproar when, to the left of the road, anti-aircraft artillery, which has taken position there, starts sending their lightning missiles hammering and roaring toward the enemy.

Now everybody knows. And because a breakthrough with heavy tanks, even to a small extent, concerns us all, there is a sudden widespread and silent abandonment of the evening soup.

The company does not need to wait much longer for the hard work to begin. It must begin!

How is it that our fingers become stiff at the trigger and will not curve through at the decisive moment? Yes, so much so that some even lower their weapon or machine gun, confused, only to stare ahead, not knowing what is happening to them! Damn! Is this possible? These troops are *feldgrau* groups, companies who flood through the enemy ditches, waving and calling in their German helmets.

Is this possible? Are we being fooled by a nightly spook?! But we are all fully alert. A lieutenant colonel, the leader of the infantry, jumps out of the trench. "Stop! What is the password, which regiment!" In the meantime, we have to adjust our scopes with trembling fingers: 200– 150–100. But nobody from the other side gives an answer, which results in a rush of men who are storming, waving, and calling! It's at that moment that the leader of the company jumps back into the trench and gives orders to fire with thin lips.

We are shooting with clammy fingers, shooting faster and faster with the fixed sight—in a second, the mirage is over: the calls and orders from over there sound blurry and strange all of a sudden. These aren't German men, or German commandos; no German infantryman jumps like that! Finally a united, defensive fire hammers into the advancing masses, despite the *feldgrau* uniform and helmets. We shoot into them with intense and rabid bitterness.

If only no more new masses, who are no longer in German uniforms would swell over the wide field of snow. Hundreds of Soviets scurry at us, clumped together, and then break apart, to be shot down. With new ones continually breaking away from their positions, these are no longer companies, these are battalions and regiments. How long will we be able to hold out? Is there enough ammunition; how is our supply of hand grenades should it come to the bitter end? But don't dwell on unnecessary thoughts, stay calm and hold out.

All through the night the fighting continues. Their reserves seem to be invincible. Only this morning brings some calm along with reinforcements. A rifle company arrives and, despite their exhausting march, immediately takes position on our thin line.

27 January: Strong patrol activity on both sides. The Reds are preparing for new attacks. Heavy losses from the low altitude attacks of the Bolshevik fighteres and bombers.

Late in the afternoon more reinforcements arrive: infantry and 2cm anti-aircraft artillery.

28 January: After the attacks during the night, which were quite strong indeed, it is now calm. The Reds must have suffered tremendous losses; corpses are lying in heaps in front of our positions. Our 8.8 anti-tank cannons destroyed three tanks; one of them was an extra heavy one.

Reconnaissance units return and bring news that the enemy's tanks, along with their infantry units, are retreating to the northeast. A counterattack is ordered for tonight. At the same time, we receive orders to march to a different sector. *Scheisse!* It is always the same: when the danger is over, we are no longer needed! It is always the same fool's story.

I am curious which fire we have to put out now.

"*Schisjojedno!!*"

30 January: Never before have I been so aware of the unimaginable vastness of the Russian countryside than now, when the forests and fields are covered by a huge white shroud. For the first time in a long while, the ice cold whistling is quiet today; it isn't snowing, and thus for the first time we are able to see the incredible vastness of this space. The eye reaches the horizon without being able to stop at one point. A seemingly endless white plain stretches ahead, without interruption—or so it seems—for the deep gorges that cut through the land are hidden by the snow.

The Reds have secret hiding places. Here, hidden from the naked eye, right in the villages, is the enemy's line. Here along the upper Donetz is Grjasnoje, a small nondescript village, over which we fought for weeks. The Bolsheviks nearly succeeded in bringing the village into their possession, but at the decisive moment, the sheer will and bravery of the German soldier ensured victory.

But now, it is all quiet here; this time we have not been called in to be the "fire brigade." Medium artillery attacks, a few visits from aircraft, every other night a light attack—that is all! And it's a good thing, because the last few weeks have treated us badly.

Completely on their own, here as well as in innumerable other places on the Eastern Front, which stretches for thousands of kilometers, the occupying army fights their daily battles. The village, with its sad huts, is our chateau, which we defend together with a company of infantrymen.

1 February: Last night we had to defend against a particularly vicious attack from the Reds. There was bitter close-range combat, and two good comrades were killed in action.

The company leader of the infantrymen, a World War I veteran, and an old fighter of the Eastern Front, tells us about the old times. The present war is much more brutal than the Great War 25 years ago, for we are now encountering a fanatical enemy over there on the other side.

No one surrenders; both sides will fight until the last bullet. More than anything though, is us being overcome right at this moment—due to the vastness of the space—by a feeling of utter abandonment; confidence in our own power is the only thing that gives us hope for victory. We can hardly count on help or support from our neighbors. We only possess the villages, while the fields in between them, where night after night, day after day, tough battles are fought, are a no-man's land.

There is no well defined positioning system like there once was during the Great War, because the ground was already hard as stone when the German advance was halted.

Due to the lack of a contiguous front line, it is possible for the enemy to circumvent individual positions and attack us from the rear or from our flanks. To this, add the difficulty of the terrain, which is traversed by numerous gorges, offering favorable circumstances for the attackers.

All of this causes our nerves to be strained to their limits, as every night we experience numerous house battles and ambushes. Much too often, just like here in Grasnoje, we have to refrain from using barbed wire barriers because the villages are so spread out. Relentless is the battle to seize each individual house, since those pathetic huts are the only protection from the cold. This is also why such dwellings are equipped on their sides with firing ports, so that as soon as the enemy attempts to infiltrate the village, our fierce fire is able to assault them from all sides.

3 February: Two days and nights of utter peace lie behind us. Only then and now does an egg grenade stumble over into our territory, or we hear the short bellowing of a machine gun or the whistling of a fireball, then all is quiet again. This is a great position to be in; we sure could spend a few weeks in this Grasnoje hamlet.

It would have been so nice, but it wasn't meant to be! During the afternoon the guard replacements arrive and with them orders: "Security detachment is to leave Grasnoje, Lieutenant Hegner to report February 5 for orientation in Jakoblewo."

Krach! [Bang!] What *scheisse*! Once again, this is sure looking like another inferno! Oh well, cursing is of no help. The P.299 [299th *Panzerjäger* Battalion], the good old midwife, has to jump in.

Our clothes are all packed, we deploy early tomorrow morning.

4 February: Strenuous march amidst a strong blizzard. On the road, partisan fire. Because we are *Frontschweine*, and not the young nobility of the supply lines, we make short work of the situation. The closest village bursts into flames—the fireworks feel warm in this damned cold.

5 February: By midday we arrive in Jakoblewo. A few hours earlier, strong Red aircraft carpeted the place with bombs. Every corner of the place is still on fire. Thank God they did not hit our ammunition or supply facilities. Lieutenant Hegner brings new orders: we are to immediately march on and take up position tonight near Leski. You notice anything, soldier? Take up positions at night? Boys, that stinks!

I am carrying a few worn out, dirty guys to Leski. Their faces turn serious. "Listen to this." A low rumbling and thundering drifts over from the east. That is the drumfire from Leski.

6 February: Everything went well, without any losses, and we move into the trenches and holes. Together with my group, we squat inside a potato cellar. Upstairs, we can hear the thundering crashes; sometimes close, sometimes far away, hissing shells of all calibers are driving into the ground, plowing into the hard, frozen ground, as chunks of earth the size of a table are catapulted meters away. The old Leski vererans know all too well what this hellish concert means.

A little later, the Red masses will advance again, and as so often is the case these days, will get stuck in our defensive fire. Day after day, and night after night, the Reds keep storming us. The strongest artillery fire is between Charkow and Kursk, potentially the most favorable breakthrough point to our supply line; only here is it possible to start deploying the planned grip against Charkow.

Taking this hill along with the ruins of Leski is a decisive action for capturing the thruway, the road to Bjelgorod-Charkow, as well as Kursk. The amount of blood that has been shed for this dirt heap is incredible, and there will be more!

7 February: For hours now, the earth has been splitting open under terrible drumfire from the Reds. Chains of Russian Martin bombers crash their loads into the heap of ruins that is Leski. After two storming attacks during the night, and three during the morning, we are now expecting a fourth wave.

By 1300 hours, B-position in the west is able to count 1,600 impacts from the heaviest calibers on the hill. Battle headquarters suffers a direct hit; the whole crew has been buried under the rubble. The Wessendorf artillery suffers a direct blow; Klemmer's dead body is recovered from the rubble.

In the evening, the fourth attack of the day has been withstood. Meanwhile, the mortars have destroyed our foxhole. The fuel stored there for the close-range fighting of the tanks has ignited; all our belongings have been burnt. The poor pig who has no more blanket in -35° C temperatures, is now also lacking his water bottle and cooking utensils. "Hold out, boys! We cannot falter!"

Goddamn this hell!

8–14 February: There is not a single day or night without three or four vicious storm attacks from the Reds. Four hours on end, their racing drumfire battles our meager covers. We fear this relentless hammering from the Bolshevik armies; the mass attacks of the Red infantry do not scare us as much. These are mostly poorly and hastily trained men, who walk upright and stoically into our defensive fire.

The extremely heavy tanks that accompany the attack are much more dangerous. Our defense, including artillery as well as tank fire, is virtually powerless against these rolling monsters. Tank shells in addition to special ammunition are deflected without effect from the heavy armor. Without obstruction, the Red fighting vehicles crisscross over rubble and our positions. On deck at the very top are eleven to twelve boys, who have in their pockets tins of our "Schoko-Ka-Kola" [chocolate provided to German soldiers], and in their fists hand grenades which they are throwing into our defensive lines. At first we did not take them seriously, these hoodlums, but soon we come to know better. Tough and agile like cats, they make us suffer considerable losses. They have a whole company of these dangerous children, the "Proletariat Young Guard," over there.

I struggle to describe in detail the horror of the hand-to-hand fighting with these children. Anyone who has not been here will never be able to understand what unfolds here. Grown men, many of whom have sons who are the same age, have had to engage in brutal, bloody fights with the children! I will not be able to forget these horrible scenes for a long time.

Parallel to the northern position, there runs a gorge into which our guns are only able to fire with difficulty. This is a most favorable deployment area for the Red Army. When the wind is favorable, we can hear from the frontline trenches the screaming and cursing of the commissars, and shortly thereafter, two, three gun shots, then the screams of the victims, and finally the silence of the grave.

A few minutes later, they rise in white masses out of the gorge and run by the hundreds, driven by the mad force of their *politniks*, right into our deadly machine gun fire. Prisoners and deserters tell us about the terrible losses suffered over there. The commissars' pistols, the fear of a bullet to the neck, drives this herd forward again and again. When the enemy attack collapses on February 11, their own grenades are thrown into the masses who are flooding back.

We are not afraid of such a crowd, which is forced, out of its own fear, to attack us. If only the murderous artillery fire, which rips just about everything on our side to shreds, would come to an end. If only we had weapons that could crush the tanks playing this murderous game with us.

On February 12, our last two cannons are run over by 52-ton tanks. Supported by a number of aircraft, the Reds attempt a large-scale offensive around noon. For a day and a night, there is bitter fighting over the higher elevation positions. Our losses are exceptionally high; the average company size is now only about 30 men!

Slowly, very slowly, despair creeps into the hearts of our men. We group leaders have to use all our power to keep the men alert and ready to fight and defend. A difficult task indeed! Our words sound utterly unconvincing, as we ourselves no longer believe that we will make it out of here alive. Mass grave Leski!

15 February: At the same time that the Reds commenced their large scale offensive on February 12, a 40km wide, 70km deep breach into the front line was achieved by three Bolshevik tank divisions to the south of Charkow. At this time, we know that over there Guderian [*sic*] is at the counterattack. But we also know that both breakthrough operations, here and over there near Charkow, were directly connected, which was part of the large-scale Bolshevik plan to encircle Charkow, thus isolating the northern part of 6th Army. Only through our brave and tough resistance was this undertaking successful.

16 February: We can hardly believe it: reinforcements have arrived. The boys bring good news with them: tanks are expected to roll in soon, and even today assault guns will be deployed and used right here. My mood barometer climbs back to "nice weather." We will hold onto our coffin, come what may!

17 February: In the early morning hours, thirty German attack planes suddenly arrive. Like sparrow hawks, they dive into the damned battery positions near Schochowo. All over the place, dirt and metal spew upward in high fountains. For today, though, all is quiet; at night everybody gets a few hours sleep for the first time in a long while.

18 February: Yesterday's air raid not only destroyed several of the enemy's guns and cannons, it also squashed the Red's preparations for the attack that was to follow. Today, too, our air comrades appear around noon; in three waves of ten, they plunge, howling into the enemy position. Thick yellow-black smoke stands for minutes above the gorge on the other side.

19 February: At dawn, completely to our surprise, heavy tank forces suddenly attack. Accompanied by two battalions of Caucasian sharpshooters, they succeed in breaking through on the right and left flanks of the "coffin"; by 1300 hours, Leski has been hopelessly encircled. The Morse code from our signals unit is never silent. SOS calls go out to the north and the south, to the division and the corps. We receive the same answer from both sides: "Reinforcements have left 3576 (Jakoblewo) on 2-18 in the direction of L."

Damn it, they should have been here long ago! What are we to know about the fact that somewhere between Jakoblewo and here, a decorated soldier has fought his first and last fight? Why we are not informed about such events will forever be a mystery to us. Men marching in their battalion, 180 comrades bound for Leski, who have never encountered active battle, were massacred like

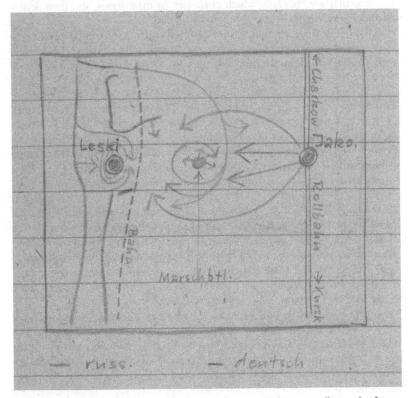

A sketch of the Luftwaffe attack on February 18 that pounded Soviet artillery and infaantry positions. "*Jabo*" was German slang for *Jagdbomber (fighter bomber)*.

animals by the Reds last night! But what do we know about that! The night turns awful! Without pause, the Asians run up our hill. Again and again, we encounter murderous close-range fighting. For how long will we be able to hold out? Where are our replacements? We have very little ammunition left. Well then, shoot slowly and don't forget to save the very last bullet! At dawn, Oles dies, the fifth and last man of my group, from bayonet wounds to the chest. We are all slowly facing the end. Too bad, living has been so beautiful!

20 February: Despite the snowstorm, which has picked back up, we are able to hear very faint artillery fire in the west. Could this be our savior? The attacks from Leski are becoming weaker and weaker by the hour, and end completely by around noon.

Suddenly, several bombers appear. We take cover with lightning speed. But this time they are Heinkels, which circle two or three times, and then deploy the much sought after ammunition and supplies.

A few of our tanks and shooters are approaching from the west! Replacements and guard changes! I see quite a few guys, strong as bears, with tears in their eyes. During the night a reconnaissance patrol makes contact with the relief troops arriving from the west.

21 February: The Reds are retreating and flee to the east. At 0900 hours, German tank forces reach Leski! The reception is indescribable. Full of deep joy and gratitude, we embrace our "black brothers," our saviors. After a short break they begin to storm the enemy's position. We cannot allow the Reds any room to breathe; we have to clean up over there finally, once and for all.

The afternoon passes with the orientation of the new replacements.

22 February: Relieved! A small number of dirty, dilapidated soldiers pass the area where our dead comrades lie. Half of them will remain here; here on top of the "coffin," these brave men have found their final resting place. We have dug three large mass graves. The Red shells have done their dirty work here as well. The ground has been ploughed from strong explosions, the contents of the graves scattered, ripped apart for the second or third time. An even more gruesome one will soon replace this horrible picture.

After a four-hour march, we reach the location where the Reds butchered the 180 men of the marching battalion. These animals, these sub-humans, even had the time to mutilate the naked bodies of the dead soldiers and pile them up in large heaps. According to information from prisoners, these *schweine* even took a dozen photos of this place of horror. (Four weeks later, on March 25, hundreds of thousands of leaflets with reproductions of these pictures are dropped over Charkow-Bjelgorod.)

Physically and emotionally exhausted, our small group reaches Jakoblewo at dusk. Although everyone here knows the sorry sight of the Leski relief unit, this time someone turns his head around to look. We all resemble mad men: full beards cover our pale faces. Some of us are wearing Russian caps, while others are wearing the yellow-brown Red Army coats, sheep pelts, and sacks wrapped around their boots. Besides our weapons, we no longer have any gear left—no blankets, no bread bags, no water bottles or cooking utensils; everything, and I mean everything, has been completely destroyed for a third time on February 20. Now, two sleds are sufficient enough to pull away the last two machine guns. Our three cannons are lying shredded and overrun at the "coffin."

23 February: Back in Obojan. Those days in Leski have affected us deeply on the outside as well as on the inside. Some are suffering from a bad case of nerve fever, others from severe frostbite. Rheumatism is also rampant. My leg hurts badly, probably from the last wound. But shit, we are soldiers and not old wives! And if any one of us has a nervous breakdown out here, so be it—later, at home, the love and patience of our wives will heal many surface and inner wounds.

24–28 February: On all sides of the front, heavy defensive battles are being fought. The winter that the Reds have placed all their hopes on is coming to an end. It is still terribly cold, icy blizzards are still whipping over the vast plains. "Now or never" is the motto which Stalin uses to force hundreds of thousands to run and bleed to death. We have reached the climax of the winter battle. Everybody performs like a super hero these days.

All sections of the unit, with their last reserves, take part on the defensive line. Defense means to ward off the enemy. Warding off does not imply waiting until the enemy arrives, until he takes the initiative and determines the outline of the battle. Warding off also demands counterattacks and engaging in reconnaissance patrols to find out the enemy's intentions in order to beat him while his strategies and plans of action are taking shape. Warding off means conducting small skirmishes to acquire favorable positions. It not only means being consistently on guard, standing one's ground in murderous artillery fire, holding out during attacks from the air, but also standing up to the power of tanks. It demands being prepared day and night. Warding off also means not being tired for a single second, always having your hands on your weapon. This eats at your nerves and takes its toll on the depleted strength of your body and soul.

At home, they will never be able to have even a remotely accurate picture of the demands that this defensive fight in the East requires of us: exhaustion, mobilization of will power, and personal sacrifice! Up front are the infantrymen, then us, the tank hunters, their eternal companions and most faithful friends! We are the front line, closest to the danger. During these months, we have seen nothing but snow, enemies, and desolate vastness; we experience nothing but danger and the battle of man versus nature.

For days, our boots do not come off our legs, and the warmth of a stove is far away. The cold temperatures and snowstorms shake us through and through, and even when we eat, one hand is always on our gun. One ear is always trained to the outside, listening for the enemy—even during those hours when combat has died down.

Doubling one's own commitment and strength is required to compensate for the holes that death rips into our lines; the unwritten law of brotherhood and the moment's necessities demand nothing less. I could give hundreds of gut-wrenching examples and incidents of such selfless comradeship among us *frontschweine*.

What makes these defensive battles here in the east so hard and filled with deprivation is the sheer mass of men and material that the enemy throws at our front ruthlessly and relentlessly. It is the battle against the snow, cold, and ice. These are the difficult hours, when ammunition becomes scarce and when from the other side, more and new waves of men are thrown at us. These are the difficult hours when the soldier at the front line is waiting in vain for food and drink, because the supply truck is stuck in a snowstorm. This is what it was like in Leski, when the superior force appears to be suffocating. These are also the trying hours for the leaders who are often confronted with the decision, "Shall we hold out any longer? Haven't we already done everything humanly possible?" And still, none of us complains, we, who hold watch in the lonely foxholes of the East. None of us thinks of giving up hope just because a meal is missing. None of us thinks of cursing because our bodies have not felt the warmth of a stove for so long. We know that all of this is asked of us because the greater purpose of the war demands it of us.

The winter battle during these months has become the Second World War for us. We have been forced in this defensive battle to encounter war in its harshest form, further amplified by the brutality of the enemy.

Poland and France cannot be compared to the years of the Great War. Even we young soldiers know this from our own experience. The Eastern campaign, however, and especially the weeks spent here, would stand up to any comparison with the intensity of the Great War. And this means in all aspects!

It is trial by fire for the German Army, for each and every one of us. And we are up to the test a hundredfold, with a degree of duty and devotion which can truly only be appreciated by the direct leadership and the Führer himself; this man, who as an old frontline soldier, understands the thousands of horrors on the front line. We do not at all feel like "heroes"; we only want simple acknowledgment for our performance.

We do not want to be pitied for our hard life; we only want the pride and trust of our homeland. It is one of the more bitter experiences for us fighters on the front, during one of the most brutal wars ever, when someone, who does not know about all the misery and fighting in the trenches, already believes and talks about a lost battle, or furthermore, when for tactical reasons, a village or section of land is surrendered back to the enemy. Those who speak like this trample on all the blood spilled while fighting for the ideal, and on the superhuman efforts which we take on with the last bit of our strength. What does it all amount to, such words like fighting, and exertion? What can the words snow, bitter cold, ice, loneliness, mental burden, blizzard, freezing, and poor roads, possibly mean compared to the reality? With those words, we connect a meaning from our European life which is not valid here in the East. Here they mean the exaggeration of the unbearable. Nature alone is presently throwing something into the battle, which can only be described as a gigantic intensification of the European winter. What Bolshevism throws into the field is completely opposite to any concept of true soldierly spirit; it is inhumane cruelty to the highest degree.

Again and again, the Reds deploy a combination of artillery, tanks, aircraft, and infantry. Pure mass is the god to whom these infidels seem to pray and serve. They believe that the number is of decisive importance. We know all too well that this is dangerous. These days, however, it is becoming particularly apparent that the person, the individual soldier, can be more effective than sheer numbers and mass. More than ever, the burden of battle lies on our shoulders.

Due to the snowdrifts and the icing of the roads, tanks and vehicles are stifled in their mobility and denied their utility. Sorry, but the little Panje sleighs have taken their place. Engines and machine guns suffer terribly in the cold. They may break down, but the human, we cannot, otherwise the front would collapse.

It is becoming apparent in this battle what a decisive role the mental acuity of each and every comrade plays. Here, we stand, live, and suffer everything that humans are capable of enduring, from terrible cruelties to great atrocities. Who could possibly name all the acts that are perpetrated hourly out here on the front? Just like during the Great War, trench warfare, hand grenades, and the bayonet receive the highest of honors. Hand-to-hand combat is the horrible daily reality; drumfire is the accompanying music to death. And despite everything, we stand like an insurmountable wall against the Red witch's brew; may God give us strength to hold out during these most difficult days of winter.

10 March: They have moved us from north to south and back again, from Prochorowka via Solnzewo and Baharow, always to where a fire needs to be put out. Tuesday we encountered a large-scale offensive from the Reds, which started on February 23, the anniversary of the founding of the Red Army. With huge mass deployments on the southern part of the front, this was the last great test of endurance for our forces. They were broken by our defenses, fighting with all the strength we could mobilize. Surely the Bolsheviks will try more than a dozen times to break through our lines from now until the spring offensive; but their attacks will never regain such a dangerous reach. We know that we have lived through the most difficult part and in only a short while spring will have sprung.

11 March: There is still heavy pain in my leg. They have advised me to transfer to a field hospital. But I will hear none of this. There will be no way to pry me from here! So now I am lying flat on my back. Next to me there is a folding closet; day and night I am on communication duty with the command posts. It is a task full of responsibility, and I am happy to be of some use.

12 March: It is relatively quiet here except for the aircraft visits, which occur with strange frequency. These guys have learned that this location is crammed with staff from every branch of service. Day and night there are alternating rounds of bombers which snot on the houses. But this is not of great importance, as the damage is only minor.

13–14 March: Over night there was an air raid warning. Orders to go on high alert were given. Three heavy transport aircraft have flown in from the direction of Bjelgorod. Airborne units have attacked the general staff office in the army division the day before yesterday and caused a lot of damage. Guards are doubled and patrols are sent into action.

During the early morning hours there is a raid. But their attempts at breaking through here are in vain, for the well positioned fire of our batteries destroys the enemy's strength before they are able to prepare themselves.

The evening passes quietly; except for the guards and the outposts, everybody huddles in the huts, which are badly damaged by bullet fire. A candlestick is burning on top of a wobbly table, around which my men have congregated. Some of them are writing letters, others are engaged in heated discussions. I belong to the latter. Again, there is talk of vacation, home, relief, and the many slackers. When the words "behind the lines service" and "supply units" are mentioned, an incensed howling erupts. All of us were very angry this morning at the supply line servants and kitchen bulls. Those guys squander their days with a warm ass, while we on the front hold down our positions all winter long in the snow and freezing temperatures. I know very well what the conditions are like for these "fine" comrades to the rear of the front line, in Sumy and Lebedyn, and also know through numerous letters how much our frontline sacrifices are met with complete bewilderment by many at home.

Here on the front, we who proudly bear the name "*Frontschweine*" have become an inseparable brotherhood of men who have been hardened, who have been welded together by death and blood into a close community. And all that these guys, full of dirt and lice, have to hold on to in order to persevere is one thing: love—the depth of which nobody at home can ever imagine—a boundless love and adoration for everything that says "home." I truly believe that only those who encounter death breathing down their neck every day—be it in hand-tohand combat or in the heaviest drumfire—are capable of such an unconditional love. Each and every one of us would gladly sacrifice his life for you at home. These are the troops who bear the brunt of it all, who stand at the very front line—this is what we think.

To our rear are the supply and provisions units who already think much differently. Their fear of being deployed to the front line, along with their fear of us, becomes all encompassing. And by the way, these are the guys who will be celebrated as "heroes" later at home, thanks to the bloody tales they tell. This I mention only in passing, since for the true soldier of the front, all of this posturing and pretence are totally inappropriate, as loud and boasting words do not fit our memories of the dear guys whom we've lost.

Even further to the rear are the occupying troops, whose "problems" are with the whores and other womenfolk. These are the ones who are shown in the photos at home, who are wrapped in thick fur coats, grouped together in the snow and ice to form a nice picture. ("Oh those poor guys, what a terrible Russian winter!") Is there anyone at home who knows that these are the very fur coats that are sorely missed here on the front, is there anyone who knows they are drinking with these women the very schnapps that would give us the gift of warmth and an hour of forgetfulness?

And then, to the very rear, are the anti-aircraft crews at home. They aren't even aware that there is a war anymore, except for the fact that there is a higher percentage of women per anti-aircraft soldier. Come join us, you livingroom warriors, relieve your comrades manning the 2cm and 8.8cm FlaKs; they deserve it, those dear brave guys!

The supply department for these three groups are the three big "supply filters" (a filter permits the "thin" to go through, but traps the "thick"). Soldier, do you notice anything? We, the Eastern fighters, are not allowed to carry a weapon back in the homeland! Why? Yes, why indeed....

22 March: The Reds are already deploying strong aircraft forces before noon. What is all this compared to Leski! The day ends amidst weak attacks. During the night there is a surprise attack from strong Bolshevik forces supported by tanks, which is brought to a halt, however, after a two-hour battle from the defensive fire of our batteries. A few prisoners and deserters are being interrogated. The prisoners are part of a Russian raiding party. It does not seem to look particularly rosy over there. Provisions and ammunition are supposedly bad and insufficient. It is the job of the Reds' raiding party to take prisoners and acquire automatic weapons.

23 March: Today is relatively quiet as well; only light harassing fire reaches us from the other side. Wonderfully warm, the sun is suspended in a marvelous blue sky. The ground has begun to thaw, the muddy season has begun. In a few weeks, the ground will be dry again, ready for the spring offensive.

24 March: Tomorrow we will be relieved. This time we are not looking forward to it. The days have been quiet, quiet for our standards; only medium shell fire during the day, and at night, occasionally a few weak attacks—what's that to us? We are used to a completely different set of circumstances from this winter. Too bad that we are leaving; it has been a great group here!

25 March: The relief is accomplished smoothly. At noon, Russian fighters surprise us during our march. One man is slightly wounded by air fire. Without any further incident, we reach Obojan during the evening hours.

Today I had the opportunity to read an interesting enemy news bulletin, which listed several numbers from the battles near Leski. During the period between February 17–24, during which the Reds repeatedly focused their attack on the area of Oserow-Leski, the enemy lost in 75th Infantry Division's sector alone a total of 20,000 men, among whom were 9,000 dead. These are, measured by the current fighting strength, approximately the size of 4–5 divisions. Add to this the number of prisoners and deserters. On other parts of the front, the circumstances are no different. From numerous prisoner reports, we learn that entire companies have been reduced to 20 or even 14 men. This indicates that things are not at all rosy over there.

The incredible blood sacrifices that the Bolsheviks have made during these past winter months will also have a very negative effect on the approaching spring offensive for the Reds. Nevertheless, exaggerated optimism is not appropriate here. We know that the Soviets have not let this winter pass idly. Further to the rear, reinforced lines have been put in place; the industrial centers in the Urals have churned out a series of new and improved T-34 tanks.

27–28 March: Every now and then, we are paid a visit by a few Soviet aircraft. They arrive humming, passing narrowly above our heads, and blanket us with their on-board fire; there is buzzing all around us, which means that we have to take full cover! And quickly! Those who are unable to find a hole in the ground climb into or rush under a truck and wait for this "blessing" to pass. Here and there, bombs are also dropped.

29 March: A clear and cloudless sky—perfect weather for flying. Suddenly, in the middle of dinnertime, our brave anti-aircraft fire starts barking. And while high above those small, dangerous, black clouds develop, we start to hear a low hum and see three Soviet bombers pass over us. The anti-aircraft fire turns wild. We are all standing there observing excitedly, just as if this was a thrilling boxing match, the position of the shots. There—that was a hit! A cheer composed of multiple voices erupts when one of the bombers starts to trail, becomes unstable, sways, and then slides down vertically over one wing, trailing a long, dark smoke cloud behind it. Even before we are able to hear the dull explosion of the crashing bomber we see back there along the forest edge the mighty mushroom cloud of smoke.

The two other bombers have calmly continued their flight. There—one of us saw it first and is pointing with an outstretched right hand toward a miniscule point in the sky, which quickly grows larger, and takes a straight course toward the bombers flying east. A *jäger*! A German fighter! Now the suspense starts to build! Long forgotten is the split pea soup. Split pea soup will be there another time! But you don't get to witness every day an air fight like this.

As the fighter approached close to the bomber, at high speed, it suddenly pulls upward, floating directly above one of them, and then plunges from above in a steep angle toward the bomber, sending burst after burst into it. One appears, then another one. Always short, well aimed bursts. He then turns away without paying any more attention to the enemy. Initially, we are a little bit disappointed, but we then realize what is happening. Coming from an initially narrow, thin trail of smoke which the bomber seems to pull behind it, grows thick black smoke, a jet of flame, and then it plunges downward. At the last minute, the pilot ejects in order to save himself. But his parachute only floats in the air for an instant before it is pulled into the abyss by his own crashing machine.

The fight lasted no longer than two minutes, by the time the fighter had already disappeared. The sky is blue and cloudless, just as peaceful as it was before. Even the split pea soup in our bowls stayed warm—that's how quickly it happened.

30 March: Totally unexpected, the weather has changed overnight. A blizzard rages with a strength that we have not encountered all winter. I pity the sleigh units who were surprised by it in the open field. Our eyes are unable to penetrate more than two meters into this crazy flurry. In front of us are two enroute sleigh units; we are very worried about them, as they are several hours late. Only by the evening does one of the vehicles arrive; there is no trace of the second one.

31 March: The storm has subsided. The sun hangs in the sky peacefully, as if nothing has happened. And yet, a lot has happened overnight. In yesterday's blizzard, the second sleigh unit missed the road and fell into a deep gorge; our comrades froze to death during the night. And something else, even more serious, has happened: with the heavy eastern storm to their backs, the Reds have once again succeeded in blocking the highway near Drosty. In order to boost the counterattack, we reach the breakthrough point by around noon.

The enemy's power has already been broken; there is not much more for us to do here. Our artillery has wreaked havoc in Drosty, which had been occupied by the Reds for a few hours. The beaten enemy had to leave hundreds of dead people behind. It is looking particularly gruesome on one of the village streets. Someone calls it the "avenue of death." Others pick up the phrase, write it on a board, and attach it to a pole on the side of the road—Avenue of Death! Until the war ends, this part of Kursker Street will be named this.

To the left, in a ditch, lies a dead female gunner; the artillery has mutilated her badly. One half of her still young face is completely missing. Her long, blond hair is hardly able to cover the terrible wound. If her grey-brown shirt had not been ripped open across her chest, I would not have known that a woman's fate had ended here.

It is a strange sight for a soldier, who is only used to fighting against men, then to suddenly be confronted with the dead body of a woman. Occasionally there is a woman among the prisoners. Among them are bad, ugly bitches whose thirst for blood and brutality does not fall short compared to those of their male counterparts in the Soviet Army. Mostly women and young girls, who have been pushed by Bolshevik pressure and instigation, leave a final reminder of their female dignity behind and dabble in the craft of men, with a gun in their hand.

1 April: A security mission calls us to Medwewskoje. This is also the temporary gathering point for what remains of the 299th Infantry Division and other units, which had been assigned to different groups. In terms of formation, we are commencing the "cleansing" of the front. Within a few weeks we will track to the north in the direction of Kursk and will be once again be under the trusted leadership of General Moser. Spring cleaning has also arrived on the front!

Mid-April: It's the muddy season!

Roads and streets, which were frozen solid only a few days prior, have now thawed and become bogs which threaten both men and animals with drowning. In many sections of our position there is nothing but dirty ice water for kilometers; during these weeks, on nearly a daily basis, we have to wade up to our chests through icy water in order to reach the staging ground of our attack with the enemy.

By the end of the month, I am ordered to undertake an important courier mission to Orel and Charkow. It would fill every page of this book alone to retell what we encountered there enroute with the partisans and the dangers on the roads, which are mostly submerged in water.

In Charkow, we happen to get caught in a tank battle, and in Bjelgorod, a heavy Russian attack blows up our store of ammunition—it's a miracle that we have come out alive. Before Kursk, we are hunted down by Ratas, and my sidecar is riddled with machine gun fire; near Ponyri, a group of partisans try to capture us. In other words, we are glad as hell to be able to return to our group twelve days later.

By the end of April, the division is pulled from combat. We reach Kursk via an overland march, as the roads are impassable. We continue to the north, and two days later reach the main railroad hub of Ponyri. We take up quarters in Beresowiz. We are in the area of 2nd Panzer Army, and after the odyssey of the past winter months, we are finally able to return to Group Moser. Those wonderful days of rest suddenly come to an end on May 15. In a rapid forced march, we are thrown to the southeast of Orel, into the very dangerous Liwny sector.

25 May: Forgotten are the winter and the muddy season—a stifling heat now hangs over our positions. Summer, with its scorching temperatures, has arrived almost overnight. Both the weather and the fighting are hot in this goddamned sector. Let's hope that these are the final weeks of trench warfare, and that soon we will move forward again.

These brief summer months will soon be over and then, yes, perhaps then, there will be for us an unfathomable event—a reunion with wife and child, with father and mother.

May God grant us the chance to see our home once again.

Frontline Warfare and the Retreat
After Stalingrad

Editors' Note:

As Hans Roth's third journal begins he's in the Livny (Liwny) sector, east of Orel, at nearly the farthest reach of the German front in Russia. Here he experiences trench warfare, as each side trades attacks and bombardments, and the Soviets attempt mining operations beneath the German fortifications.

In the meantime the great German summer offensive of 1942 commences, with drives on Stalingrad and the Caucasus. At first the offensive is highly successful, conquering hundreds of kilometers of additional territory. Roth goes on leave during August, but by the time he returns to Russia the German momentum has stalled. In fact, the Soviets are launching counterattacks all across the front. Woronesh (Voronezh), one of the first German objectives of the campaign, becomes the scene of bloody urban fighting.

On November 19, the Soviets launch a gigantic counteroffensive that caves in the German-allied fronts on either side of Stalingrad, isolating Sixth Army. Roth's unit, which is outside the pocket, is dispatched to help bolster the Italian-held sector of the front along the Don River, but is helpless to prevent its utter collapse.

Roth's battalion is then dispatched to Kursk, only to find Soviets closing in on the town and the Germans preparing to abandon it. City after city falls to the Soviet advance, and Roth finds himself marching halfway back to Kiev. Reflecting the fact that his *Panzerjäger* unit was once again employed as a mobile fire brigade, Roth not only expresses homesickness for his family but for the rest of the 299th Division, saying, "We heard that they fought gallantly." During this period the journal largely foregoes exact dates, and when his unit is transferred to Orel aboard flatcars in mid-winter, his description is only of "endless misery."

Despite intense combat around Orel, which is now part of a German salient bulging into Soviet territory, Roth manages to survive his second winter in Russia—one in which Sixth Army is utterly destroyed—and witness a new build-up of German forces. In the war to date, the Soviets had succeeded in the winter, whereas they had not yet been able to stop the Germans during good weather. The summer of 1943 would put this system to one last test.

June: Before me is a vast Russian plain, massive gorges cut treacherously deep into the black earth, like cracks in a windowpane. Forever humid and swampy, they are a threatening breeding ground for malaria and other feverish epidemics which are yet to be named. The HKL [*Hauptkampflinie*—main line of battle] extends here along a thin strip of woods and sparse huts. The ground has been scarred and the grass scorched by thousands of impacts from the months of dug-in fighting. A tropical heat hovers over the badly torn up trenches. On the other side in this flickering heat can be found the Russian bunkers. It's very difficult to keep your eyes open, for the heat is heavy and our limbs are like lead.

The half hour before noon, with its tempting calmness, is the most critical moment of the entire day. We wait for the meal service as we doze off, only a breath away from falling asleep. Then, all of a sudden, a hissing comes across from the other side, crashing with a thunder beyond our cover. The same thing occurs every day at noon. Regardless, we're still startled from our dreams every time. The images of home and all our longing thoughts are abruptly torn apart....

The hissing, rolling, and thundering last for one to two hours. Here and on the other side, the relentless wind mixes the stinking plumes of smoke from the explosions, these waves of fumes in all colors, with the blinding white shrapnel clouds, into a dirty grey mass. The firewall begins to die down slowly.

The nights are damp and cold, and full of restlessness. After the artillery fireworks every evening to honor the departing day, the action increases on the front. The heavy artillery has been put to rest, and now it's time for the small guns, for the PaKs, MGs, and carbines. On the front line, late-arriving troops fumble through the darkness. Glaring white flares hiss in the night sky. Like startled hens, *maxims*

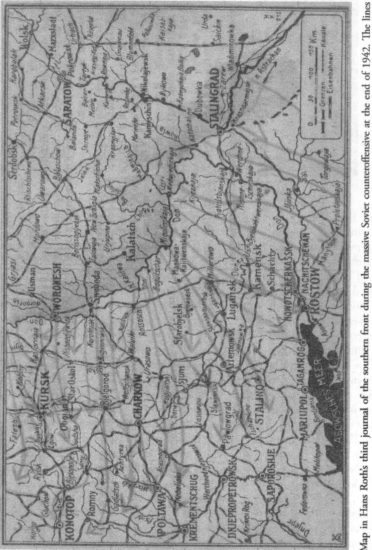

Map in Hans Roth's third journal of the southern front during the massive Soviet counteroffensive at the end of 1942. The lines drawn in pencil apparently indicate the multiple enemy thrusts that cut behind Sixth Army, which found itself isolated in Stalingrad.

[automatic machine guns] are firing off somewhere in the distance. We respond by adding more machine guns, and within a few minutes, the whole chicken coop is in a great flurry, a hellish racket throughout the sector. It often takes hours before friend and enemy calm down; most of the time the night is over by then, and once again you have to forget about getting any sleep.

The air raids during these starry nights in the Liwny sector are unforgettable. An overwhelming calm after the evening's infernal noise of dueling artilleries, a few quiet minutes when you can write a letter in the trench, then, all of a sudden, a fine singing in the air: the *Ivans* [German slang for Russian soldiers] are coming!

The light singing transforms into a rattling howl, which now fills the air for hours. Each night is the same awe-inspiring picture; hundreds of lightning flashes burst into the air. Shades of white, green, and red splatter the sky; long yellow-orange streaks shoot into the air, and are accompanied by the hard knocking of 2cm anti-aircraft artillery. Glaring white magnesium flashes then fall from above. Red flames from a fire sizzling on the ground jump out 50 to 60 meters, and then appear as yellow-white ornaments on a burning Christmas tree, which is what we call the American tracer shells—only there are no gifts under it, but rather infantrymen.

We try to conceal our movements in order not to reveal any more to the Russians than they can already see, for dawn is encroaching over our sap trenches and ditches. Next a slurping and gurgling come from above, which turns into a booming hissing, then a huge bang; the earth trembles, a shower of shiny glowing splinters cut through the air ... once ... twice, and once more. Planes then hurtle by over our heads. In the neighboring trenches, flames now shoot into the sky until there are no more bombs. Flashes of light come from above; he is shooting at us with his on-board weapons. From below, we attack the multi-colored bursts with our machine guns and 2cm artillery. There is a crashing and thundering all around us. What a tremendous spectacle, just like judgment day! Whoever is calm enough to take this wild, frenetic picture in, will keep these nights in Liwny—in spite of everything—in good memory.

What difficult days! The Russians, knowing full well the importance of the Kunesch sector, throw reinforcements into the trenches day after day, along with pulling out more heavy guns and their damn Stalin's Organs, which they position across the front.

There is a fine drizzle of rain in the oppressive heat—this feverish air is as warm as piss! A considerable number of men stumble about, sick with malaria. The roads are bottomless pits of mud, the trenches one big swamp. Damn this trench warfare! My hole is about to drown, there's not a dry speck anywhere!

The sun is again shining, and the Reds, who probably just like us have been suffering like dogs during these periods of rain, are becoming utterly and ferociously aggressive. By night, with the support of their tanks, they break through to our most forward trenches; by day we strike back. This is how it goes for three days, when we, full of righteous wrath, finally bring a small section of forest, where they commenced their attack, into our possession through a bitter close-range attack. At dawn, when the whole affair starts to look more precarious than ever, the excellent *DO-Geräte* [otherwise known as *Nebelwerfer*: a multiple rocket launcher] comes to our aid. We sit on the other side with this terribly rutted forest thoroughly in our hands; no force in the world would be able to expel us from here!

We have been sitting here for a week now; a burned out Russian tank is used to construct our B-position, and the forest is packed with our most modern weapons. The Reds approach a few times a day, but only to get their heads bloodied. The position is ideal and almost impossible to capture. The Russians also seem to understand this, and over the next few days and nights hardly bother us. This, however, doesn't seem right either, for personally I am suspicious of this calm.

Our leadership doesn't appear to be too trusting of this quietness either, for our sound locating devices and surveillance posts are doubled. After two more days, everybody up here knows that the Reds are planning something devilish for us. On day three this becomes clear, and on day four, the entire combat position, including our important B-position, explodes under Russian tanks.

I want to tell the story of how this all played out in detail, and how it was reported to the corps:

30 June: A Russian officer is visible in front of our positions, apparently scrutinizing our tanks and taking photographs.

6–7 July: Conspicuous expansion of berms along the entire length of the enemy trench facing us.

7 July: A deserter divulges that a mine tunnel is being built at this position, which lacks only 20 meters before completion.

12 July: Fifteen meters from our own barbed wire barrier a metal post sticking out of the ground is observed. At the same time, Russians are sizing up our tanks from their trenches. Based on these initial observations, it is assumed that the Russians could be advancing with their tunnel toward our tanks. Therefore, a screening trench three meters deep is dug and manned with a sound locater. Based on the deserter's testimony from July 10, a counterattack with nine heavy T mines [T.Mi.Z.35] is attempted, which despite being executed along ten meters, does not bring any results. An examination of the craters does not provide any evidence of a tunnel. Three more counter-blasts don't bring any results, and a fourth one is being prepared for the evening of July 14. Our artillery and heavy weaponry are conspicuously organized along the front line. Spanish riders [*spanische reiter*, X-shaped sharpened poles tied together to form a barrier] and S rolls [*S-Rollen*, a particular gauge of barbed wire] are laid out as a precaution.

It is a terrible feeling to sit here and wait for the havoc to commence, which could rage upon us at any moment. Abandoning the position is out of the question, therefore, it's time to write your will and wait with your frazzled nerves for the volcano to erupt. What a terrible situation! Hours turn into minutes, and minutes into hours; time is now crawling by. It's making us crazy! I could scream, fume, and howl out of rage. Dirty jokes and cursing do not help in this case; the men just stare into nothingness, numb and catatonic while they wait for the catastrophe.

14 July: 1900 hours. There is a sudden explosion about 25 to 30 steps to the right ahead of our tank line. A few moments later, a second, even bigger detonation in the same spot occurs, followed by two more about 80 steps from our panzers. The battalion leader on the spot and a few men are thrown over from the force of the explosion; the troops in the frontline trenches are buried alive. The support trenches [*grabenbesatzung*], however, did not cave in; the main pressure from the explosion passes without doing much damage up front. Except for a few scratches, it did nothing to me or my men.

With the sudden onset of artillery fire, an assault unit attempts to break through our position. Everything is turned upside down with hand grenades and carbines; our small and large machine guns that were buried under the collapsed berms are not functional, and are useless in the close-range combat.

We are even able to take in a few prisoners while all of this is occurring. They will tell interesting things later on when they are interrogated. Besides a dozen wounded and three dead, we escaped with nothing more than a black eye this time. Fixed position combat to mine combat! Now we're there! The only thing I am missing now is fuel.

From the attack we also discover the following: the origin of the tunnel was located in the very first trench across from our position. Large numbers of storm units were deployed for the construction of the tunnel, which on the 14th was 170 meters long. In the tunnel, twenty men worked at a time, and the work itself was accomplished with an earth cutter the shape of a horseradish cutter. Because of the soft clay, they were able to accomplish the work in almost complete silence. At the end of the tunnel, in the actual explosive chamber, there was, according to the prisoner's account, a 1,000 kilo bomb, which was detonated on the 14th. This incident can be counted as one of the most devious forms of combat on the part of the Reds. Hardly a day passes during this singularly brutal campaign that the Reds do not bring us losses through one devilish plan or another.

The following is just a small sampling of this:

> Wired balloons and phosphorus grenades are not new anymore, as we already made their acquaintance last winter along with about fifty different

kinds of mines. On the other hand, however, are the mine traps. The especially cunning Bolsheviks cross German lines at night and at different points put up signs with the following written in German: "Attention! Mine! Trucks must drive to the right!" The right side of the road is of course mined, and the truck meets its destiny.

Other examples: the sign "This is a mine-free passage!" is placed in the middle of a mine field, or in a mine-infested crater you will see a cardboard sign reading, "collection station for grenade shells—'Remember comrade, the home front needs raw materials to be able to provide you with new grenades!'" Many conscientious infantrymen fell victim to this malicious trick before being warned from above.

That nothing is sacred to the Red *schweine* can be demonstrated by the following: in the back-and-forth of positional warfare, dead comrades have to very often be left behind in enemy territory. It is expected that a counterattack on the following day will bring the lost sections back into our hands. The Reds know that this is the minimal duty of the honorable German soldier to at least bury his fallen comrades. They know that we do this with the peace and devotion that frontline soldiers owe to their fallen comrades. Precisely because of this, they do something that is unimaginably devilish and cruel: they connect the stiff arms or the shattered limbs of the fallen with a mine, which blasts our comrades who want to put them to rest into smithereens. Again and again, I stand aghast before the villainy of such thugs.

A few days ago a new Russian mine in the shape of a first-aid kit displaying a red cross was used by partisans to booby trap a supply road. It detonated when the kit was picked up, which killed the truck driver. Besides the already familiar drop of mechanical pencils and fountain pens loaded with sensitive explosives, the Russian air force now also drops small first-aid kits resembling German kits. When the bandages are unwrapped, a highly sensitive detonator cap explodes, causing extensive abdominal and facial wounds.

According to the statement of a deserter—an officer—the Russian air force has the following at its disposal:

—Cigarette cases: when opened will detonate.
—Pocket watches: when one attempts to wind them they explode.
—Grey colored frogs: detonation occurs when pressure is applied to the natural looking body.

At Maloarchangelsk, along the supply road, 100-gram field post packages with German addresses and senders were picked up. When touched, they exploded and caused serious burns. In the same area, small, oval tin cans were found with the German label "oil treatment for mosquitoes and lice," along with a very dangerous explosive effect. And so forth, and so forth.... Yet another wonderful thing which has caused great confusion during the difficult nights near Droskowo....

Listen up! The following has been confirmed by official sources: "Russian sound grenades." The grenade explodes a few meters above ground; after the detonation, a sound is audible for ten seconds, which is very similar to sound of the impact. What causes this sound cannot be explained. Despite a thorough investigation of the impact sites, nothing can be found that would explain what causes such noises.

I could list a good dozen similar examples. They are always the same! Bolsheviks are far superior to us when it comes to waging war in this manner. It is a pitiful superiority, and a dangerous one!

July: Deserters and POWs state that on the other side, comprehensive preparations for underground combat are taking place. The Reds want to capture our advantageous cave position this way; corresponding orders from Stalin have been submitted.

Subterranean combat! The Vosges [a small mountain range in southeastern France] and Argonne [the site of heavy battles between German and France during World War I] combatants of the Great War know all too well that this form of combat takes its toll on the nerves of every man. Day and night, we now lie listening in the deepest parts of our bunkers.

Four weeks ago, we were lying exactly like this in our holes and sap trenches, our ears pressed to the wet ground, listening for the muffled pounding of the pick axes and shovels with which they were digging. To calm our pounding hearts and frazzled nerves, we tell ourselves again and again: as long as there is pounding, there is no danger. What pitiful comfort during these hours! But then we heard shuffling and buzzing when the cases of explosives were installed at the head of the completed tunnel. We knew that danger was growing and growing; if it becomes quiet down there, then it is time—the chamber is fully loaded and any second now an enormous, destructive blast could erupt.

For hours and days, we were literally lying on 1,000 kilograms of dynamite, until the evening of July 14, when its detonation blasted our positional structures to bits, and combat around the still smoking craters began.

Even today, we don't know where or if the Reds are digging their tunnels. It is exactly this uncertainty that is worse than everything else. Again and again, we place our heads on the ground to listen! We are driving each other crazy, each person claims to have heard a suspicious noise on the ground. It is like the loony bin here, as it is very difficult to bring our men to their senses.

I know, however, that even the smallest preparation on the other side will be quickly detected by our leadership, and it is this trust that relaxes me and therefore my men, for nothing is more contagious in the trenches than perseverance and cold blood.

And then something else stirs our spirits and turns even the staunchest of pessimists into happily smiling optimists—the new leave regulations! I am hoping to see my wife and kid in the beginning of August. With all the joy of knowing this though, suddenly a great fear comes down over me. We, who God knows have battled with death and the devil, are dreading that before then we will be hit by a piece of metal, which would rip this whole saintly picture to shreds. All of a sudden, we are now cautious in combat; gone is the stubbornness during heavy bombardments. We are no longer the callous *Frontschweine*, we are civilians in uniform. God knows, I'm just like all the others!

Leave—how long will it be? Will we be able to cope internally and externally at home? Thousands of thoughts and considerations are running through my poor head. Damn it! If the vacation would just get here!

Prisoners are taken during my nightly reconnaissance mission. It is of utmost interest for us to find out about the enemy's mine preparations. According to statements made by captured Bolsheviks, the gophers over there are working night and day. Where the tunnels are being driven forward, they can't—or won't—say, despite our drastic measures.

There is one statement that all four of them have made: this is supposed to be their first substantial undertaking, and the explosion isn't expected to occur for two months. (These guys were right; on October 5, a section 200 meters north of us is blown up.)

For days, trouble has been in the air. Nobody is thinking about going on leave or nice things like this anymore—we just don't have the time for it. Early today at dawn, this week's 14th Soviet tank assault rolled in. Now in the late afternoon, it has finally been pushed back. We closed in on them with tanks and FlaKs, and broke through their lines all the way to a small section of forest. It was very difficult this time. We did it though, and a deep drag on a pipe is our reward.

On the front line, the infantry is waging a stubbornly hard fight. On a hill across the way, where the rubble of a large tank is, where the ground has been turned over a dozen times by shells, where burned tree stumps stand strangely sad against the sunny sky, all hell seems to have broken loose. Our mortars send blasts that ignite fireworks of red lightning bolts onto the ridge, which creates a thick wall of smoke. And since their tanks were snubbed, the Reds are now sending bombers and low-flying anti-tank bombers which mess with the ground combat. Our machine guns are barking, and our grenades hiss as they fly across to the enemy. The droning of airplane engines and the rattling of on-board weapons mix together into an infernal noise, which fills heaven and earth.

There is suddenly a strange tone to the uproar, a tone that sharpens our ears and heightens our senses: enemy artillery! The rounds are crashing about while tired fragments, the late comers, which fall out of the sky with a final mean snarl, splash onto the wooden planks of the trench covers.

They are shooting poorly today, the Reds. They must know it as well, for after the fourth round, there is silence. The front line is growing quiet as well. I am familiar with this; for one hour there will be peace and quiet, only to start up again with full force when night falls, and early tomorrow morning, when the *schweine* come out again with their tanks. Just as a side note—I want to go on leave. It brings tears to my eyes that I can't tear myself away from here tonight. To go on vacation, especially now, seems so incredibly remote!

10 August: I am on the train home, which moves along bumpily, as slow as a snail. It is almost unbelievable, but nonetheless, I am sitting on board a solidly built German passenger train. Each passing telegraph pole brings me closer to seeing my dear Rosel and my little girl again. Luckily the trip is long, because it is difficult for me to leave behind the experiences of the last hours on the front line. It was hard to leave; two of my men fell. The gun-carriage burned out; all my stuff has gone to the dogs.

It's best to sleep; in sleep lies oblivion. Perhaps it will also bring nice dreams, an advance on the happy days ahead of me. What a lucky dog! I am getting teary eyed—now that's unbelievable! Who could understand what is going on inside of me?! A lucky dog isn't supposed to be sad!

6 September: I am back with my unit! The seventeen days of sun and happiness lie behind me like a distant dream. It was an entirely great experience, this leave. Full of gratitude, I think of my love, whom I have to thank for the countless hours of untroubled happiness. Unforgettable will also be my hours with little Erika. Everything, really everything, was full of harmony and sunshine. I have many beautiful, comforting thoughts and memories stored up for the approaching difficult winter days. I received so much new energy and optimism from my time at home. Everything makes sense again. To cherish something like this, and to fight for it, is worth it. Yes indeed, it is worth it!

"*Sakra*! [Damn!]," one of our Bavarians spouts out behind me. That's all he says. There is a deadly silence now. Oh how it's blowing outside. Chalk and mortar dust rain down on us like droplets of flour from the ongoing fire from above. Good old stone ceiling, please hold up and don't let us down!

Orders are supposed to be picked up at regiment HQ this afternoon. I volunteer for this because I can't stand anymore the stifling air that has been depleted of oxygen, nor the torture of stiff bones and numb limbs. How wonderful the fresh air is! It has stopped raining and a humid haze fills the streets, through which the ghostly grey and sad ruins stick out. The fire has died down. Only occasionally does a volley pass over the high buildings. The whining 122s explode with a dull sound. The street is nothing but a mud hole, and thick mud splatters with every step since the gutters are buried under mountains of rubble. The sun

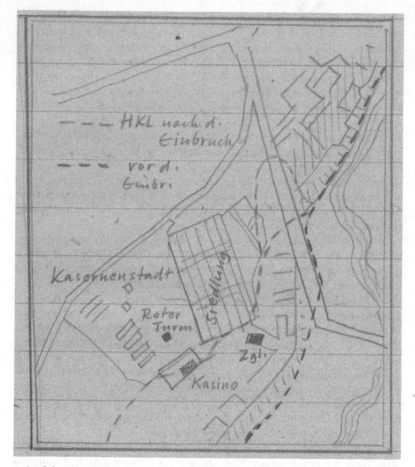

A sketch by Hans Roth showing the center of Woronesh (Voronezh), including the Germans' main line of defense (HKL) and forward positions.

is coming out, but I have no time to enjoy it, because at this very moment the bombing is starting up again with full force. Artillery fire rages over the ruins like rain showers. This damn muck won't allow me to run. I have to cross some backyard where it is worse. I'm hoping I don't trip—dear God, don't let me fall in this manure. The stench from dead bodies is penetrating my nose, and I can't breathe enough fresh air. This sloshing and sliding through the sticky muck seems endless. Over head, there are sounds of planes, and all around the crashing of bombs. There are many blind shells that sink into the mud. Off to the side is the glistening body of a Rata with grey-green wings, which show off the carefully painted Red Soviet star.

Verdammt [damn], I should already be there! There is the main street, which isn't a street anymore, devastated by constant bombing. My map still shows the rows of houses, which have long since been ground to a pulp by shells. Further ahead, where "*Molotov-Platz*" ["Molotov Square"] must be, there is apparently mortar fire; one can hear its barking like a pack of mad dogs. Single shots whiz by at close range with a dull swash.

It's no use. I'm sweating like a monkey [*ich schwitze wie ein affe*], my knees are weak, and I need a cigarette break. Volleys of heavy shells are sweeping over my head in the direction of "*Rote Fabrik*" ["Red Factory"]. Their impacts are not too far away, though not far enough to be protected from their noise and close enough to observe them. A torn up patch of oak trees is cloaked in smoke. Right now, a giant tree trunk is being blown to pieces, with splinters flying all over the place. There is a blind shell from which I crouch down close to a wall. And across the way, more craters are being formed; smoke plumes trail into the air and clods of dirt are being tossed everywhere. Right now a piece of shrapnel explodes with a loud bang; white-grey clouds of smoke and glaring lightning flashes fill the entire street. I stare at this horrific scene, spellbound.

Then, all of a sudden those *hunde* [dogs] start to aim more closely. A burned up projectile hisses as it drowns in the mud. I didn't notice that I had placed my hand over my mouth. There is a loud howling. My God they are huge! Just barely do I reach a partly collapsed basement before the storm begins. A rumbling vibration penetrates the ground all the way to where I am located. What started as a cigarette break has now turned into a long hour of fear and terror.

It's Sunday, and also a sunny day. After the cold and rainy days, it has finally started to feel like May since yesterday. The sky above the ruins of the big city of Woronesh is blue and peaceful. I climbed all the way to the top of the vast ruins of the gun-powder factory, and am now crouching among the molten and bent iron beams of the ceiling. It is a great view from up here; you can see about a third of the entire city. Over there flows the Woronesh, that good old river, with its wide, muddy streambed, which has been a good front for us for weeks, and also a good barrier to the advancing Reds.

One has been able to let his guards down during these August days, even the command. Our trust in the muddy flow of the good old Woronesh has turned into an inexcusable recklessness. Night after night, we notice that the Russians have started piling up huge amounts of stones. Message after message was sent to the division. Air reconnaissance reported that tanks have been assembled in Monastyrtschenko. Except for a few shells, nothing, absolutely nothing, has been done to guard against this encroaching disaster. One fine day the stone dam across the Woronesh was actually finished. Multiple messages were sent to command. Their answer was as follows: "Let the tanks come close, that way they will be easier to shoot down." Excuse me for not recounting the details of how well we did in shooting down their tanks.

16 September: The Russians have gained control of the eastern slope of the southern part of Woronesh. Along with it, we lose the important defense bastions of "casino" and "brick yard," which provide the enemy with a view of the entire hinterland. They are even able to see as far as the Don, with its hills and supply roads. I have already been told how unsuccessful and bloody the counterattack has been, and how the week-long bombing from hundreds of weapons had no effect.

Ever since then, the Reds have been sitting in the "casino"—an enormous pile of rubble where the basements are deep and safe. They have also been sitting in the oven of the "brick yard," which could not be easily destroyed by our Stukas. All this looks like a yellow-brown burned out patch lying there harmlessly in the sunlight.

To the north and the west, as far as you can see, is an ocean of bombed out houses—nothing but a gigantic field of ruins. Smoke is rising from it in all shades of grey. There are also the white and yellow clouds from the new fires, which mix with the violet and grey fog of the smoldering and dying fires. Towering, threatening over them are the monumental stone and concrete fortresses of the Party, the Soviet castles. They had been fortified, and every single one of these buildings has seen bitter fighting; each one has its own bloody history. Whoever fought in Woronesh will forever remember one particular bloody battle for a block of houses, the "Operation Hospital."

There is "Red Square," with the ostentatious Soviet government building; on its façade you could still see a row of small torn-up red flags. Then there is the prison, a huge building with walls more than a meter thick, which even our heaviest guns could only slightly scratch. One side of the building was blown up at the last minute by the Bolsheviks prior to their retreat. Judging by the smell, there must be buried under the ruins a whole mountain of corpses. To the north and northwest is the industrial sector of the town. All the way to the horizon one sees factory after factory, blast furnaces, and steel mills. The engineering works "*Komintern*," which used to have 10,000 workers, is now nothing but a pile of iron and bricks. Then there is the "*Elektrosignal*" factory, which employed 15,000 workers, and the "*Dershinsky*" factory, where each month 100 to 120 locomotives were built. Further to the west stand the sad, black skeletons of the huge burned out airplane hangars. Next to them are the airplane factories, which as you can imagine were gigantic, particularly when you read that 40,000 people used to work there. I could go on and on....

To the south are the straight, square blocks of barracks, which can't be seen at the moment because the smoke from the drumfire is hanging over these cement quarters. Again there is the "Red Tower," partially covered by the dirty yellow plumes of smoke from the gun powder. Everywhere, for as far as the eye can see are ruins and more ruins! The once booming city, with its 450,000 inhabitants, is now a dead city, reigned by terror and death. And yet, it was still worth taking this city, despite the great sacrifices, and to defend it despite the even higher number of casualties. This was the cardinal point and pillar of the front, which had to cover the deployment and attack of the southern armies. Here in particular lies the prerequisite for the success of the operations against Stalingrad and the Caucasus. Stalin, who is well aware of this, is deploying rifle division after rifle division and tank brigade after tank brigade. His goal is to break down this diversionary front. Up until now, we have been able to withstand his enormous pressure, and will continue to do so no matter what happens!

Mangled cables are hanging from the telegraph posts. Swarms of flies buzz over the cadavers of dead horses, which are lying everywhere. One could write volumes about this plague of flies, these shimmering blue-green pests. The penetrating stench of the cadavers attacks one's senses relentlessly, but our nose and eyes are already used to this symphony coming from the ghostly city. The one thing that we are unable to get used to though, is the nasty flies. They are drawn to all the dying corpses under the rubble, and have multiplied to form large swarms too countless to grasp. Birds are also circling over the battlefield; thousands of crows screech above the ruins and fields of death. Again and again, they dive into the depths of the rubble when they see the horrific harvest of death.

Our tired and sweating unit stumbles along the pockmarked asphalt of *Revolution Prospkt Boulevard*, one of the most splendid in Woronesh. Here stand the palatial buildings from the time of the czars alongside the concrete buildings of the Judeo-Bolshevik period—or perhaps better said, used to stand. Through the burned out windows escapes the terror of senseless destruction.

On the inside, we are burned out; on the outside, beaten. There used to be a time when hours of fighting were followed by hours of quiet. That time is over. Sun, moon, and blazing fire all share in illuminating this work of destruction and the slaughtering of people. At times you eat whatever you have, carry your ammunition, or rest for a moment on the ground in the cover of a crater. Our faces have become black and haggard. These days, they are never plump and round, allowing the drudgery of the 24-hour days to be seen in them. Our eyes are red from the smoke and the nightly watches, but our teeth are white from the hard bread. I can't imagine that you could earn your daily bread in a way any more difficult than this.

We are again in position at the "Southern Settlement," the solid part of the bridgehead. The sky is grey and heavy with rain clouds. The earth has been so churned-up that she is bleeding from thousands of circular wounds. Chaotic positional systems trail up the hill. Rifleman holes, bomb craters, and barbed wire tear the landscape into an ugly grimace.

Our bloody "settlement" is bolted up against the breakthrough point! For a month it has been lying beneath the gigantic hammer of destruction. Suffering countless numbers of casualties, the Soviets have worked their way into shouting distance of us. Many elite battalions were allowed to bleed to death just to gain a few meters. Whole Bolshevik tank squadrons are burned out. In the short time from July 10 to August 24 alone, 978 enemy tanks were destroyed. The Soviets' goal to take the last 50 meters to reach the cover of the ruins of the settlement's higher elevation has been left unattainable.

I met up with the troops in Sossua. Since winter, I have been continually traveling between Charkow and Rshew—always right where it's the worst. Meanwhile, our "gypsy unit" has been deployed near Woronesh, intrepidly holding its own, and is now awaiting new orders. A few are missing but overall everything is still holding together. What an incredible miracle!

Orders came today stating that we should settle here in Sossua. The pitiful quarters are supposed to be made suitable for spending winter here. It is unbelievable—shouldn't us poor, relentlessly chased dogs at least get some peace and quiet once in a while?! But who has mentioned anything about an "umbrella-theory" [*Regenschirm-Theorie*—i.e. conspiracy]? With a lot of diligence and patience we went to work on our quarters. Here and there, there are few things that could still be improved, but overall we are finished with our winter burrows.

Now is of course when we will get our marching orders. And indeed, as usual, they arrive timely as ever. One beautiful afternoon, an excited messenger comes running: "Everybody get ready, in two hours the division will be marching!" Adieu "Jaizis" and "Moloka"! It would have been so nice, but it wasn't meant to be. On time, and as ordered, the engines hum their goodbye song and off we go in the direction of Woronesh.

We are rolling! Sweltering heat is upon us like molten lead. Our forced march has been ordered right when it seems to be foul again in Woronesh; though when has it ever been different there. We are prepared to ignore all the problems along the way, all the heat and dust. A few hundred kilometers lie before us and we are needed near Woronesh, urgently needed. We are surrounded by a sad barren landscape; a flat, singularly desolate and unchanging plain from horizon to horizon. There is also dust, hot dust; the hottest dust! And as we march alongside the road, we become covered in the never-ending white-yellow clouds, which at times make it impossible to see for hundreds of meters; so much so that one just stumbles, the infantry marches blindly forward, tenaciously and courageously as usual, with the sun glowing over a shadowless landscape, while temperatures climb to 110° every day.

German barricade during the battle for Woronesh (Voronezh). *(Photo courtesy of www.wwii-photos-maps.com)*

Soviet tank in flames. *(Photo courtesy of www.wwii-photos-maps.com)*

Typical scene of trench warfare
in the vicinity of Woronesh
with German soldier using a
scissor telescope to survey enemy
movement. *(Photo courtesy of
www.wwii- photosmaps.com)*

On the Woronesh front.
*(Photo courtesy of www.
wwiiphotos-maps.com*

The closer we get to Woronesh, the more desolate the land becomes. It hasn't been long since a bitter, bloody battle was fought here. The barren fields and plains extend for as far as the eye can reach. The roads are nothing more than wide paths of dust on a treeless wasteland. They have an eastern feel to them. The caravan roads of Mongolia must be similar. They meander any which way just like rivers, these are duststreams, which flow wide, split into many tributaries, and run wide apart, split again into more tributaries, while others rejoin the main flow, just like a stream.

Then all of a sudden, the road narrows; a bridge, some swampy water covered in grass which we had to drive through, which compresses all the tributaries to a narrow one lane road. As soon as we pass through this obstacle the road flows wide again and with ease into its many tributaries. Its surface has been compacted by countless trucks, its bumps and holes and its greyish-white with a bit of dark grey color resembles the skin of an elephant.

Another 30 kilometers to Woronesh; it must be from over there where the enormous, black smoke plumes are rising. During a short rest, we hear the rumble of gunfire which the wind has carried toward us; an accompaniment to the bitterest combat the Eastern Front has seen so far. Endless munitions columns pass by us; from the front comes ambulance after ambulance, on the

What remains of Woronesh after Germany's struggle to seize the city from Russian hands. *(Photo courtesy of www.wwii-photos-maps.com)*

hood, a big, white flag with a red cross whips in the air—they are packed to the limit! Our faces are serious; we know that the following days will be the fulfillment of our destiny for some of us.

Twenty kilometers left to Woronesh! We are now met by long trains of destitution; the last evacuees of the city—women, children, elderly, the sick and disabled—drag along on both sides of the sandy road to the south. All of them are loaded down with their remaining possessions which have been saved from the rubble. We drive past these sorrowful images for kilometers.

Suddenly there is a singing in the air; small clouds from anti-aircraft fire are floating in the sky. Quick as lightning, we are take cover under the pine trees. With stoic serenity, columns of wretched refugees continue to pass by. Tired and exhausted, they plod through the hot sand. And then, all of a sudden, a sharp whistle, a terrible howling; six or seven low-flying Russian bombers pass over their heads, release their bombs, and fire their weapons into the helpless crowds.

There are no words to describe the horrific bloodbath these dogs have inflicted on their own people. We can only administer first-aid to a few, because we have to move on, have to move on to the front, where the black-as-ink smoke plumes are, and we can already see the flickering flames.

Woronesh

We are sitting in the rubble of an enormous, four-story barracks. Through the shattered windows, across bent and molten iron beams, across the moon-crater landscape of the yard, we have a view of the front all the way up to the "Red Tower."

Only weeks ago, before the big "Casino offensive," this was our favorite observation post. Today its ruins are unoccupied; nobody dares the dangerous climb. Of the last eight people who did, each one of them brought down their fallen or wounded comrades who had previously attempted it, until the moment when nobody returned, all of them finding their grave up high.

To the right of the tower at the end of the barracks lies the "casino," an expression that anyone who has fought at Woronesh knows. Here and a couple hundred meters to the northeast in the "brickyard" sit the Russians. These two points govern the whole sector. They are defending them tenaciously. Thousands must have already bled to death here. For six long days one bombing followed the next on a scale never before seen. For hours there was smoke and fire. Nothing! They don't waver.

After another week of artillery and bombing preparations, we commence the counterattack with our panzers and *Sturmgeschütze* [assault guns]. We tell ourselves that after this incredible, never-before-seen preparation of all the heavy weapons, not even a mouse will survive in the ruins.

There is not much to say. By the evening of the attack, with the exception of a few who remain, our division is destroyed. The loss of life, weapons, and tanks is heavy. The entire undertaking was unsuccessful. By the following day, it is a wonder that we are able to hold up against the enormous pressure from the Reds. Nevertheless, they are able to push us back to our October 20 position and diminish our numbers by many. Their units are fully supported by Stalin's Organs. This night is the beginning of the most critical battle for the bloody city.

The expected all-out attack by the Russians lasted for five long days and nights, until last night. We held on to every meter of the smoking rubble field with desperate tenacity. The losses were great, but again we were able to withstand the mad assault, if only by using our last inner and outer reserves.

Now it is quiet, friends and enemies are lying low in the stony ruins. Through a gaping hole in the torn-up wall I have a view of the depot area that had been battered by hand grenades. This has been the focal point of the assault; just yesterday the last forty Soviet tanks were attacking here. And just yesterday, in the early morning glow, five heavy tanks, which had assembled in and emerged from a ravine, were suddenly standing on our own lines, rolling over our holes and trenches. With their gun muzzles on the ground, like burrowing trunks, they would stick their guns into our covers, until we got them right in front of our anti-tank guns and were able to shoot them down.

German 105mm howitzer on the Woronesh (Voronezh) front. *(Photo courtesy of www.wwii-photos-maps.com)*

My heart is full of grief when I talk about these morning hours, because one of our best men, along with his entire gun-crew, had to give their lives. Karl Wissendorf, you will live on in all our hearts; giving your life and those of your men saved all of us from being destroyed; we will never forget this!

The wide field of the terrible combat lies eerily quiet and sad, with its herd of destroyed and broken up tanks. Their burned out hulls lie in the scorching sun like tossed dice in a lost game. Their gun muzzles are turned up in the air, arrested in the moment of their destruction and their torn chains and wheels lying there like the limbs of the dead. One of them has been thrown on its side by the blast of a bomb, like a helpless lump.

Above this scene which is filled with the scent of smoke and dead bodies, the air glistens in silver waves, until it becomes as thick as a yellow veil by dust blown in by the wind. I am tired, very tired even in my heart!

What a bad day! It is pouring, and a strong, cold wind is blowing through the dead streets, and in through the gaping windows. We have taken shelter in a half-buried basement. There is at least a stove that has been left behind here, which will give some warmth once it's burning. But it is not burning yet, instead it's smoking and stinking in a way that just about tears your lungs apart. The space is way too small for us all, but you couldn't ask anybody to go out in the pouring rain and the heavy fire, which is rumbling across the ruins! And that's why we are squatting between the dirty legs of the man behind us, pressed together like a tin of sardines. But it doesn't matter now; at least we are somewhat safe in this dank hole of a basement for a few long hours until we are relieved in the evening. On top of everything, water is starting to drip into the basement from above! It's damn filthy weather today. The right weather for the Reds to attack; judging by the heavy fire, the *schweine* are up to something.

Every other second a tremble goes through the thick walls from the heavy impacts close by. Now a shell must have torn into the ruins right above. How the rubble resonates! The wooden beams are cracking, dirt and stones are falling from the ceiling, but it's holding up, that good old Russian ceiling!

Ever since that unlucky incursion in the "casino" sector, we are now in a dogged fight for every single ruined city block or street section. An ongoing back and forth of close combat from basement to basement and rubble pile to rubble pile....

There is no use to name the streets, which will forever remain a symbol of unforgettable courage and deep suffering. You may not have maps, but if you ask those who might come home, they will have a lot to talk about; about the minutes of horror among burned out factory complexes, among torn up railroad tracks, and the shredded metal ladders of burned out gas tanks.

During these dark nights, the Reds pounce on our posts to silently bring them down—I say *pounce*, but this word is not strong enough to describe the reality. They know they can't take us over, therefore their actions are desperate.

Everybody knows what human beings are capable of in such a situation, especially if they have weapons. They shout their battle cries like animals, but that does not scare us; they did the same last year, it just sounds more atrocious in the ruins of the city.

These days we are shooting with mortars, anti-tank shells, and multiple-barrel guns. The trajectory of the mortar sometimes becomes near nothing from one house into the yard of another. We take the ruins of five houses and then we give back two just to fight, only to then retake five again. Often enough the numbers are different, I guess you could say there is some variety.

Nighttime is the only time that has remained the same, with its fireworks, burning houses, sparks flying, and the beautiful starry sky. But it is already very cold, and one tries to be close to a burning building, though one is always aware of the possibility that the walls could come crashing down over his night quarters.

Then there are the voices of the night: the chirping of the ricochets, the grumbling of heavy mines, the shattering hits of the fire assaults, and the minute-long hellish music of Stalin's Organs. Over all of this stands the shimmering twinkle of a starry sky, the most beautiful I have ever seen. But its gentle calm is abruptly torn apart by all the flares from the Soviet bombers. From now on, the sky is not for a single second without these artificial stars. These stars are glaring and glistening like cold silver, flickering and unsettled. Their magnesium light is unlike the warm red from the smoldering ruins in which we look for warmth.

Bombs strike with a dull, shattering noise, and glowing fragments rain down upon us. Pressed close to the ground, we lie behind rocky rubble or in bomb craters. Some never stand up again; the stiffness in their bodies can't be undone by the glowing wood embers.

These are the disturbing images which will forever be part of the memories from the ruins of Woronesh: the faces of the men have become old and grey, like heavy shadows from extreme exertion, sleepless nights and never-ending terror, along with tense anticipation and always re-igniting combat, are drawn on their features.

We have been spared nothing by this land: the summer fighting commenced in pouring rain, which filled all our holes with muddy water, making the muck greedily hold on to every step and covering our uniforms with a crusty armor of dirt. Then came July with its scorching heat and the fine, flour-like dust; now the dampness of the rainy, fall days is sweeping over the trenches and the crater landscapes, only to be soon again replaced soon by the ice and snow of the merciless Russian winter.

We are not facing this second year of the Russian campaign as fresh and naïve as we once were. These formerly idealistic daredevils have turned into morose, relentlessly tired soldiers of trench warfare, tough people without a sense of humor. Easily embittered, we view our surroundings with the sharpest criticism. The length of the war has brought with it many changes, to which my comrades react with caustic sarcasm and I with a slight sadness. I am no Renn [Ludwig Renn, German novelist and Nazi opponent] or Remarque [Erich Maria Remarque, German anti-war novelist], therefore no more of it!!

But there is always one thing that keeps us going: the knowledge of the love that people at home have for us frontline bums. The eyes of the entire country are on us, all of Germany is proud of us. Really, all of Germany? Well, with exception of the duds, who don't deserve to be called Germans!

All soldiers at the front have very different fates. There is the lucky one, his unit is deployed in the big offensive operations and as hard as the fighting might be, his engagement is rewarded with changing events and new experiences. He is also rewarded by the knowledge that the whole world at home is excitedly following the course of the action on their maps and through the radio reports of the OKW.

Much more difficult and draining is our kind of war, the kind that the *Frontschweine* experience, whose fate is currently leading them into heavy defensive battles. Naturally defensive combat is mentioned only briefly in the army reports. The accomplishments on our front don't provide a great variety of stories for the war correspondents. The going is tough, and days and nights of heavy fighting follow each other. Here you don't have the great moments, which compensate for even the worst hardships of the offensive. Embittered, we fight for every meter of space: lieutenant, non-commissioned officer, and soldier are lying in dirty foxholes, or if they are lucky, in bunkers; and for days, sometimes for weeks, we have to endure the enemy's artillery fire. Each attack is followed by yet another attack; time and again we have to fall in for counterattack.

When the word heroism is used, it should be for the achievement of the thousands of anonymous trench fighters, who have successfully fought the defensive battles of the last few months.

A senior chief told me the other day: "You should know that the accomplishments of your soldiers will be written in capital letters on the first page of the immortal book of great deeds of the German soldiers in the year 1942, even when the newspapers report less about them than about the obvious successes of the other fronts." We are thankful for the kind words.

It's snowing slightly, and a sharp wind slaps ice cold water onto our faces. All eyes are staring ahead where all hell could break loose any moment. Since first light we have been expecting the Russians to attack. Thousands are waiting and waiting…. Restless, nervous hands check the hooks on the canister of the gasmask, put the hand grenades from the right side of the foxhole to the left and back again to prepare for the defense, they are doing a thousand things that carry no meaning or purpose.

Our comrades of the artillery are standing at their guns, waiting and waiting…. Impatient hands turn the greased screws of the *Libelle* [*Lom-57 Libelle*, reconnaissance glider]. Damn far ahead stand the heavy howitzers, and here again the shells lie ready everywhere. The rocket artillery is checking their fuses again and again, because their destroyer salvo is supposed to break the Russian attack. Everything has to work right in order not to let the superior force of the Bolsheviks overrun us and take possession of more parts of the death city.

We crouch in our foxholes, shivering and freezing.... Though it's not just the cold which makes our teeth shatter! A thousand grey men have their faces turned forward. The success of the defense depends on the good eyes of a handful of men, these advanced position observers, who have to stare through the snow curtain and recognize the danger in time....

The snow drifts are getting thicker. Through meter-wide mud puddles a messenger approaches. Orders from the division! "The moment the enemy attacks, our own infantry will strike back with an immediate counterattack. Anti-tank gunners will support the attack and will take over the assault of enemy tank forces." That's how the message was written on the dirty paper, which means we will have to dodge the enemy fire in order to move into the blind spot of the heavy artillery as quickly as possible.

We are freezing as we stare into the drifting snow with tearing eyes, waiting....

Then, all of a sudden an enormous impact makes the earth explode, and the Soviet annihilating fire begins. Their artillery sends their hail of shells our way, PaKs shoot from inside the houses across the street; tanks are shooting from the sides; flight squadrons are showering us with bombs, and intermittently explode the hard impacts of the mortar.

Storm! Storm through hell! It is hell, the noise and the uproar, the constant detonation of shells of all calibers, the hissing whistle of the bullets in the air, the spray of splinters, the flying dirt from the bursting earth, the constantly quaking ground, the biting and stinking smoke of gunpowder, and amongst all this the hard and fast thuds from the discharges of our own mortar.

We have to get through this inferno; the infantry is storming in front of us. They always have to be diligent; they have to stay courageous and hard, stubborn and cold blooded, and they are not allowed to think for a second that they could die or lie wounded the next minute.

The noise of infantry fighting: the clacking of machine gun fire, the discharges of the carbines, the dry popping of the light infantry guns—all of this sounds like the twitter of small piccolo flutes in this thundering war concert. But nevertheless these light weapons and the men who guide them will decide the battle.

After an hour of bloody close combat the attack is beaten back. The Red storm troopers are finished, at the limits of their strength. Prisoners are stumbling towards us with terrified faces. But with undiminished force, the heavy weapons thunder on, enemy artillery is trying to tear holes for a second or third attack.

For days it has been bitter cold. Today the mercury shows 25° below zero; a thick white snow cover wipes out the sharp contours of the vast ruins. But there are always new impacts from all size of caliber tearing through the beautiful whiteness of the cover, leaving terrible black and red stains. A difficult period is now starting up again; God only knows what lies ahead in the next weeks. This gentle calm is abruptly torn apart by all the flares from the Soviet bombers. From this moment forward, the sky is not for a single second without these artificial stars.

It is strangely quiet along the entire Woronesh sector. People are saying that the Soviets have withdrawn large troop contingents in order to deploy them further south for larger offensives. Let's just wait and see! Our *Landser* are great at spreading rumors. It is highly unlikely that we would have indeed had a few quiet days! Up to now we have always been in the thick of it. I believe that it will continue just like this after fresh reinforcements arrive.

Marching orders are here! How many have we already received during this God-forsaken campaign? We're back on our feet and then loaded onto cargo trains, headed up north again for a change. For 48 hours we haven't looked over the edge of the trench or even across the lightly snow-covered marsh of the front, where underneath its dirty skin hundreds of mines lie. Neither have we looked through the binoculars to watch the Bolsheviks, in their bunkers and deep sap trenches with their machine guns.

For 48 hours we didn't need to duck and huddle in the dirt whenever the enemy would extend his long arm of heavy weaponry over the German positions, as if trying to erase everything that sticks out of the plowed earth. We didn't have to listen to the sound of Stalin's Organs at night, when the darkness is illuminated by the ghostly light of bright flares and the silence is abruptly pierced by the hissing of grenades and the barking of machine guns, which can bring death a hundredfold just seconds later.

The following order: "Company to transfer north," has taken us away from deprivation and the desire to just survive, as well as the constant stress on our nerves, senses and muscles, to the comforting safety of this heated cargo train. We are moving along nice and slowly, kilometer by kilometer to the north. Where to? Nobody knows. It doesn't matter anyway! Warmly packed into straw, we start to doze off until we finally fall into a calm, restful sleep.

The following five days and nights are worry-free, sleep-filled travel across the wide and deadly white Russian plain. Then we are unloaded. Forgotten is the gigantic field of rubble of Woronesh, the city of death. We are again in the flatlands and as protection against the cold and the enemy we have to rely on the dirty, stinking Panje huts. Soldiers, soldiers…! During the icy day we endure snowstorms; during the night short, restless sleep in filthy *Ruski* sacks. Not that we haven't rested our occasionally clean bodies in hundreds of European beds. We have dreamed nice dreams in the fancy baroque beds of French Châteaux that had nothing to do with war; we have lain on straw sacks in English bunkers, and with our hearts thumping we have listened to the impacts of fire salvos and caught bedbugs on Moroccan reed mats. We have had inappropriate dreams on the clean, cool sheets of Belgian boarding school beds of innocent girls whose more or less virgin bodies used to lie there. We have wiped off the dust and sweat of the battlefield on down comforters. We have experienced the most stubborn bedbug attacks from the leather sofas of Polish Jews. In the clean pillow mountains, fresh smelling embroidered covers of the western Ukraine we have dreamed of home. And lately we have gotten to know the terrible Russian sacks in the Soviet paradise.

We have become experts in the hospitality business, and in the future, even the dirtiest and slimiest host will not phase us. We have experienced all degrees of physical humiliation with our own bug-infested bodies. You should see our solemn faces when we find a Panje hut at night before the frighteningly fast approach of darkness which doesn't yet have a pencil note on its door that reads, "Occupied by unit number, whatever."

Even when a full dozen stinking locals already populate the small wooden room, the few of us still fit comfortably inside. A Panje hut eats up people endlessly. We spread out on the floor along with the Russians; whole generations move on top of the wide, expansive stove which takes up almost half of the entire room. Wife and child, man and bugs; eight or ten, or twelve or fifteen are lying up there, but not because we took their space. Even when we are not there they are huddled on top of or behind the stove. For us the archetype of living and comfort is the amount of space. With Russians it's different: first comes the oven. There are those who have simply thrown a few boards together and a roof on top and have their finished Panje hut. That's how we live nicely separated, some on top of the oven, and the others in the rest of the hut, while a small lamp on a little shelf below an icon burns all night.

In spite of the filth and the bugs, we are experiencing a few happy carefree days in these pitiful huts. One or the other even dares to think it possible to celebrate Christmas here in relative safety and respite. But only the absolute idealist would be able to think like that. For me, I act like I always have during this damn campaign. You just put dirty laundry in a water bucket and you look forward to putting on a clean shirt for once—never mind that we just received marching orders. This time we have to deploy especially fast. The wet laundry is stuffed into our backpacks, and 30 minutes later we are marching south toward an unknown destination. Judging by the pace of the march something is on fire somewhere.

After a record march we reach Kastoruoje. New combat-ready troops are sent our way, and in a few hours the new battalion of army *Panzerjägers* is ready for action. Despite the great honor—not many units become "Wehrmacht" troops—we are not sure how to feel about this. Things look fishy in the south; the many ambulances we encounter are not exactly elevating the mood.

After a short visit with our Hungarian brothers-in-arms we reach Rossosch, where the Italian A.O.K [*Italienischen Armee-Oberkommando*] is located. There

I am met by serious faces. In bad French one asks this or that person where things stand; the short conversations are unclear and nervous.

In the evening, in a biting snow storm, we reach the position of the *Alpini-Corps*. That same night a tank-supported attack by the Soviets is halted and the enemy is beaten back across the river Don. The young division suffered its first losses.

In the following clear, freezing cold and moonlit night the enemy pushes across the ice of the Don once again with their giant steel guns. The battle lasts until the morning hours. One can tell, however, that we haven't known the Russians since just yesterday, that a lot is feigned over there, for the Red *schweine* are trying to fake large attacks in order to divert us from other positions. This is confirmed by prisoner testimony.

These observations and predictions are forwarded to the Italian commando stations. Everything is done through the German communications staff. For ours the situation is discussed in bad school French. There is no agreement; the German communications officers are judging the situation differently (probably more accurately) than the Italian gentlemen. More things are translated, the German officers would like to pound their fists on the table, but they have to be courteous toward their brothers in arms and smile politely! Valuable time passes! Nothing happens—poor *schweine* in the trenches, they have recognized for a while that a catastrophe is approaching. Dark premonitions are blackening the heart. Once again the well-worn photos of sweethearts, wives, and mothers are wandering through the hands of the infantrymen. Not a good sign!

In the night we are withdrawn from the Alpini position. This happens head over heels this time. At first light we scoot across the frozen swamps of the Kalitwa toward the south while staying close to the front. Here things are volatile! What a bad beginning! In Orobinsky we are meeting up with the first German infantrymen. Run down and bloody, they look at us with grey faces and without saying anything. A real frontline pig knows what's going on. Even without words we know that a big disaster is looming ahead, as the smell of dead bodies is hanging in the air. Things are looking foul.

The front rolls and swells, creating a wall of mud behind which I seek shelter from the icy wind drizzling down into the shallow dirty yellow creeks. A wild confusion reigns on the bumpy, frozen village streets. Dangerous nerves have taken over.

The artilleryman, who is usually an easygoing, animal loving country bumpkin, beats on his poor, skinny horse in a way that is heartbreaking. The tormented animal bucks and the reins get tangled with an oncoming PaK carriage. The usually calm and patient truck driver breaks sharply, and the back of the heavy truck slides sideways and hits an infantry vehicle loaded with small packages. A chaos of vehicles and men, the responsible parties are screaming and swearing and the Italians are barking and yelling in their pitched voices.

Speaking of Italians! All of a sudden I come to a realization and it becomes frighteningly clear what is going on here. I had already been wondering on the way down why we were encountering so many small and large groups of Italian soldiers in loose packs without any leaders. After exchanging a few words with a comrade who has more information about the situation, it becomes clear to me: those guys are taking off; they are running away just like their officers, who have already saved their own valuable lives. A handful of Germans are left behind to bleed to death faced with a force twenty times superior. These oncoming packs are also blocking the roads for those what want to come to the aid of our condemned comrades. Full of hate and disgust, we look into the faces of those running away. Cowards, you have taken way the faith in comradeship-in-arms forever. You have been and will remain traitors!!

The German high command is putting pressure on the Italian A.O.K., trying to get them to stop the oncoming flood. And once again, there is translating and negotiating without results, because the panic-inducing rumors of the fleeing—today I know it must have been an entire army—causes even the "courageous" Italians in the hinterland to pack their bags. The great comrades of the neighboring *Alpini-Corps* want to save the honor of their countrymen; feverishly they are trying to establish positions where they can regroup those who are fleeing.

The ground is frozen too deeply. Too late, everything is too late! It is bitter cold and biting icy wind chills you to the bone. We are therefore glad to get orders at noon to move into our positions. The second company with wonderfully equipped vehicles and guns is withdrawn, to go back into position a few kilometers further south. We never saw them again.

Our unit has been deployed to Zapkowo, where we try to settle down and get somewhat comfortable in the primitive bunkers. My special attention is on the Italians. If the situation were not so deadly serious, one would have to laugh wholeheartedly. With downcast eyes, like thieves, one after the other is taking off. Their faces are yellow and it probably doesn't look much better in their pants.

Trucks that do not start right away in this deadly cold are simply left behind. Nobody takes on the transportation of the enormous food supplies that are stored here in large warehouses. Too bad that guards are still posted in front of them; otherwise we would know what to do.

With the evening comes food and good news. Now that our stomachs are filled we are looking confidently toward the next hours. Everything will be fine. In the morning there will be an attack, and a police regiment is moving in for reinforcement. A large battery close to the big mountain of Zapkowo will go into position during the night in order to play the accompanying music to the attack.

It's an icy, clear and moonlit night. It is barbarically cold, about 35° below; without gloves our skin would stick to the metal of the weapons. In the direction of Orobinsky, the sky becomes a trembling firewall for a few minutes from the impacts of Stalin's Organs; her thunderous drumming reminds me of the best times. Through the thunder and crashing we were unable hear the soft singing and familiar chugging of the Ivans. All of a sudden a gurgling rustle ... we have just enough time to kick ourselves in the butt before there is an enormous explosion on the ground. A hundred meters away a second bomb hits, bits fly in the air like fireworks. My neighbor, who is a metal worker in his civilian life, is reminded of the shower of sparks from a welding torch. This guy is not altogether wrong!

From this point on the thunder of the explosions is constant. The bombers aren't paying any attention to us anymore; instead they are dropping bombs in clusters at the entrance of the town where the road becomes very steep. Damn, that must be just the spot where one of us saw the heavy battery a little while ago. We are in deep shit!

A little before midnight, a high ranking officer comes to me in my bunker. He is the commander of the heavy battery; desperately he tells me that for the last two hours he has tried to move up the mountain unsuccessfully. The road is completely iced over and the guns are sliding sideways. For two hours the *Ivans* have been dropping bombs there; half of the battery is blown to pieces, a mush of blood and metal is lying in the street. It must be terrible. The man is so angry he has tears in his eyes. We are supposed to help and move in with our traction engines. It is very difficult to explain to him that we have just enough gasoline for an emergency, in case we have to evacuate the most valuable parts. No Italian position gave us any gas. The German soldiers can bleed; the Italian gentlemen need the gas to flee.

Bitter and disappointed, he goes back to the rest of his battery, which is still being bombarded by the Russians. We are feeling terrible. We couldn't help our good comrades from the artillery, and tomorrow we can't expect any help from them. It will be a pitiful attack without their heavy fire. And all of that because of a few liters of gasoline, because of the stinking Italians!

Things are looking bad. We attacked this morning; the police regiment is bleeding to death under the overwhelming pressure of the Russians. Even us Germans can't hold on any longer. Large sections are already surrounded; others have been blown to smithereens by Stalin's Organs and by tanks.

Before midday Russian tanks unexpectedly break through into the town. Systematically they shoot at all vehicles, setting them on fire; we ourselves are then hunted down like rabbits. We can't advance through the deep snow; someone falls, is grabbed by the tracks of the T-60, and crushed to a pulp. One can only talk about this with a few weak words—what remains hidden is the terror and the horror of it all.

At noon we have to evacuate the town, we can't hold it any longer! Shrapnel is flying all over the streets from the constant impacts, and the biting smoke obscures our vision. Reception camp Zwanowka! Everyone who is able to escape destruction gathers here.

Good god—what must we all look like! I wouldn't bet a dime on my life. In an hour at the latest the enemy tanks will be here. We have nothing to put up against them. Nothing!!

Ahead at the road junction a mounted messenger is approaching—they still have these in this war?! There is no time to admire him—vroom!! Bull's-eye! Man and horse burst into atoms. My stomach turns sour. Damn it! Even we don't see things like that every day!

In the evening I receive orders to bring all secret documents to safety and to try to break through to Krinitschnaja. I take the regiment assistant along; an enemy tank had rolled over both of his legs. The poor guy screams at every hole in the bumpy road. Everything is so wonderful that you just want to puke! On the road I run into an Italian transport with ten heavy trucks. These Italians are busy throwing the shells that are desperately needed on the front into the ditch so that they can get away faster. All I can see now is red; senseless rage takes hold of me and like the devil himself I drive right into the trembling pack. Supposedly I was even shooting, according to what the driver told me later. It's possible I'm not aware of what I did. It doesn't matter, for things were exploding left and right.

Hundreds of Italian trucks are standing around everywhere, left behind by the cowardly pack. Other than a few exceptions, all of them are scooped up by the Russians an hour later. One can't even think about it. Just like that they left the food supplies for an entire corps behind—that was supposed to last until May '43. The Reds are all over it now, stuffing themselves with all that wonderful food. About 80,000 cans of meat, tons and tons of lard, hard sausage, 500 sacks of coffee, 20,000 liters cognac, etc. Not to mention all the other stuff. Just two days ago we had a glance into the large warehouses and smiled at a few hundred hams with our mouths watering. What a pity, what a pity!

Zwanowka had to be evacuated also. We retreat under heavy fire and O.B. is seriously wounded. Reception camp moves to the east along Golubaja-Kriniza. In Golubaja, close to the sheep farm, is the division post. Since this morning the Reds have been attacking with strong air power. Four fighter planes fly over the sheep farm around noon, apparently not paying any attention to us. Ten minutes later they return. Before we can take cover bombs are raining down on us. But there are no explosions. Duds! The men are just getting up from the dirt in order to discuss the bad Russian ammunition, when the earth explodes around us. It suddenly occurs to me—timed fuses. Black, stinking smoke is all around me. "The gas is burning," somebody shouts. Out of the smoke a small

German soldiers defending
the line around Rossosch.
*(Photo courtesy of www.wwii-
photosmaps.com)*

Camouflaged Soviet tank under attack
in Rossosch. *(Photo courtesy of www.
wwii-photosmaps.com)*

Russian comes running, the driver of the gasoline truck, like a human torch he stumbles a few steps, then the burning roof of a house slides down and buries him.

Covered in blood, Heinz Stichel breaks down; Eichler is lying next to his vehicle with his legs shattered. Yellow clouds of gas are rising out of the bomb craters; right there lie the completely torn apart bodies of Mueller and Fritz Knoll, poor, good boy! Little Nolte, our excellent head physician, is sitting against the torn up wall of a Panje hut! He looks into the distance, as if he were dreaming; everything around him no longer involves him—he must be thinking of his baby boy who was born eight days ago. A faint, narrow line of blood is running across his boyish face; on top of his head I see something white—his brain. In a very low voice he is saying just one word: "Pity!"

For the past few days we have been in Rossosch, eighteen or twenty kilometers behind the new front; only one company, already diminished by 50%, remains to face the enemy. In a short period of time the young, strong division has been beaten up, and over a hundred men are missing. How many of them might still be alive behind enemy lines?

December 24: Christmas Eve! Across the snow and ice and through the black, stormy night, our thoughts are with our families at home, where at this hour the candles of the Christmas tree are casting a gentle light on the children's beaming faces—Erika! Where a pretty, young wife with moist eyes is holding the Christmas letter from her beloved in her hands and her thoughts are reaching out far away—across the ice of ancient old rivers, across the tattered Russian forests where the wolves are hauling, across the rubble of large cities, which have lost their horror under a sad, drab snow cover; past the pitiful Panje huts, all the way to her loved one. Silent night, holy night....

Silent?! The thumping and roaring of the front is making the windows shake. Holy?! Ahead, the Red murderers brandish their tenfold superior force against the wretched German reception post. The drunken, yelling thugs stick their bayonets into the twitching bodies of our wounded comrades. "Peace on earth!" God in heaven when will that be again?

The candles on our little *Tannenbaum* have burned down, we have read the many, lovely words from home, it's warm in our little room and it is warm in our hearts. I am happy and content. Don't I have all the reason to be? We are not facing the enemy and we have received a hundred good things to eat and drink. A little bit of good wine has chased the bad ghosts of this bloody battle away; what remains are the appreciation and gratefulness to be alive. Who doesn't dream of the comfort of being with wife and child—at home, Germany!!

The Red flood has come to a standstill, as a small dam, a thin front of brave, German men does not budge; they are holding their position! It's another story in the south, where the enemy has advanced to the west and the southwest, having taken over Millerowo and now standing threateningly close to Rostow.

Despite our pride about the recent successes we can't get any enjoyment due to the thunderstorm that is breaking loose in the south. Our recurrent question is whether the Hungarians will hold their positions in the north?

Our days in Rossosch are carefree; the daily attacks by the Russian bombers can't disturb our peace of mind. We enjoyed a quiet and contemplative New Year's Eve with a bottle of champagne, reminiscing about the turmoil of the year 1942. What is going to happen in the coming new year? It is fortunate that we don't know. After all that we hear and see, I believe it will come to a decision in 1943. We have used up a lot of our energy in the east and the west, and it is only the Russians who are mobilizing their best resources.

15 January, 1943: The sky is clear this morning; the temperature is around -30° C. White layers of fog are covering the Kalitwa swamps. Our comrade Herbert has a weak bladder and leaves the room at 0500 hours, slamming the door. He reenters the room, white as chalk, screaming: Russian tanks! I am immediately wide awake and go out onto the street. I can clearly hear the rumbling of tanks, and shortly afterwards an explosion. Damned, these bastards must be very close. Now they appear on the other side pushing one after the other through the gardens; they stop, fire, and lumber toward the center of the city. Ten, fifteen, eighteen, twenty heavy blocks of steel—T-34 and KWI—reach the bridge. The infantry dismounts and fans out. Six heavy tanks drive by in close distance without noticing us, continuing on to the railroad station. These bastards want to cut our troops off. It is time for us to get ready.

We don't have heavy weapons or explosives; we have almost no troops left in the city. We throw some of our belongings onto the carts and slowly move to the main street along the buildings for protection. Black clouds of fire hover above the city. Stukas are dive bombing on the Russian tanks like hawks, thus distracting the Red bastards from us. We broke through the ring after one hour. Burning Rossosch now lies behind us, the last tanks fire shells into our convoy. Escape!

Every soldier on the Eastern Front is familiar with the harshness of the Russian winter: chaos and terror is everywhere; tanks have been abandoned, disabled or burning vehicles lie along the roads; there is constant bombing by the Russians; food supplies are burning; there are long waits in snow banks, and we are frostbitten. The slightest injury can cause major problems, for medical service is non-existent. Nobody helps you anymore; everyone is on his own. The weak ones die in the gutter or in the blizzard.

Ten or twenty fear-stricken men are hanging on the sides of a truck and are being crushed to death in the convoy. Some have lost their gloves, their fingers are frozen stiff; they are weak and fall down, only to be killed by the trucks that follow along in the convoy. Begging, whimpering, cursing and shooting.... Whoever has been subjugated to this wretched experience will never forget it for the rest of his life.

The terrible has now happened: the Hungarians in the north are retreating, or you could say that the entire army is fleeing in panic.

Nikolajewka! The night is illuminated by hundreds of fires. Bombs are falling constantly. The air is filled from the noise of the explosions, the rumbling from collapsing buildings, the fiery explosions of vehicles filled with gasoline, and the screaming of injured people. Panic-stricken horses are galloping across the burning streets trampling everything in their path.

Where should we go? Should we follow the stream of refugees to Walniki or should we turn to Budjennij which is closer to the front? I am using all my influence to convince my comrades to go to Budjennij as the next destination.

Russian tanks have broken through everywhere. After Budjennij, I am totally familiar with the terrain, which is of utmost importance for all unforeseen events. On the next morning I receive a message that close to Walniki Russian tanks have attacked and destroyed our entire convoy. God help us!

Budjennij has been abandoned! Walniki has been abandoned! Retreat to Wolokonowo. Wolonokowo too has been conquered after a bitter fight with Russian tanks! Escape—retreat—desperation.

We reached Bjelgorod in almost total exhaustion. If somebody had told me a quarter of a year ago that I would see Bjelgorod again I would have declared him insane. In case somebody had predicted in my presence that the front line would be here again, I would have broken every bone in his body.

And yet everything is now the same again as it was a year ago. The bloody sacrifices of the entire summer have been in vain. God give us the strength to endure and keep us from being weak.

Kursk

Arrival in Kursk. The military command of the army ordered us to get the last heavy artillery and transport vehicles ready as quickly as possible. Two companies were established with the remaining troops and the soldiers on vacation who were waiting at the railroad station. Woronesh has been abandoned, Kastornoje has fallen, Sektikry is being threatened. The flood of the Reds is rolling toward the west like an avalanche, crushing everything in its path. Kursk will be overrun very soon.

Occasionally I meet old comrades who have struggled through to our position. Their pale faces are contorted with terror and deep despair. They tell us about their horrible experiences. Heinz Scheele from Latuaja arrives and talks about the attack of Russian tanks on a hospital train: partisans blew up a railroad bridge near Kastornoje. Two trains filled with helpless, injured soldiers were stuck on the tracks. In that moment Russian tanks arrived and launched shells at the train cars. This was an easy target for them. After half an hour only smoldering remains are left on the railroad tracks. The last scream and the last whimpering have since died off. One of the thousand of catastrophes in these days has come to an end.

The Reds have reached Ponyri, the important railroad line to Orel; Schtygri has to be abandoned. Kursk is now also in jeopardy. The military command orders the defense of the city, but the rank and file soldiers feel that this is useless, that it is too late. The motivation of the armies, divisions, and the hundred thousand soldiers is at its lowest point. This is the consequence suffered by most soldiers who fought on the murderous front for 41 days and nights without any break, while their comrades were having a good time in France. You can only endure this up to a point. And, God help us in case an unforeseen emergency arrives.

Damn we are tired, our hearts are broken! God knows, we are totally committed soldiers on the front line! We trust our leaders and accept heavy burdens without complaint and with an open heart—but let the spoiled soldiers in the west act as soldiers. Don't talk to me about the English invasion. Let the Tommies come. They will never return when we fighters on the Eastern Front pull off their "roast beef legs."

The enemy is now at Kursk's gate. Food supply, equipment, and spare parts depots have been cleared out, and the last medical corps has evacuated the city. Bombs are raining down on the buildings day and night. The railroad station is burned out and totally destroyed. No train is under steam anymore for its many expectant happy vacationers.

Railroad Station Kursk—this was the dream of a hundred thousand German soldiers! This is where the bliss of four weeks of indescribable vacation began; it is here where I climbed onto the train with a pounding heart yearning for my home, Germany! The terrain is now covered with deep bomb craters; the barracks where we received our food supply is burned out; the sign advertising "vacation trains to Germany" has been torn to shreds by the bombs. Isn't this like a symbol, or maybe an admonishment to wipe away all sweet thoughts about vacation, homeland, wife and children, to open the heart for the horrible fight for our very existence? There will be no victors or losers in this fight, only survivors and permanently marred human beings!

The situation is now serious. Once more I receive orders to secure any remaining sensitive documents and records. The rest of the important communication equipment is transported in a second truck. During the night we arrive in Sudsah via Lijgoff.

7 February: The next morning we continue marching in the direction of Sumy. The streets are covered everywhere with snow and crowded by the retreating Hungarians. There is an endless convoy of sleds and tanks. What a miserable bunch! They lumber through the snow apathetic and somber, their feet covered with rags, heavy hiking poles in their fists, and some are carrying only their rifle case—they discarded or sold their rifle a long time ago. Yes, they sold their own rifle! The sleds are loaded with loot or goods for which they have traded. These are no longer soldiers but riffraff. Their own downfall was caused by themselves.

By the afternoon it is only 14 kilometers to Sumy. We are hungry and freezing. The icy storm rattles our bones. Fourteen kilometers more and we will enjoy a warm shelter.

The village Schewtschenko is on the right, a forest is on the left and ahead of us. The deep red sun sets over the treetops. It is a peaceful picture that reminds us of our homeland, since forests are rare in this area, yet we are so accustomed to them. Nobody can hold it against me for being nostalgic about my home. I am cherishing my beautiful memories.

Suddenly, we are faced again with the harsh reality; a single loud bang knocks us over. Constant flashes of light appear at the edge of forest and now also at the villages located further above. Three shots hit our windshields, several pieces of shrapnel fall to the left and right. Let's get out of the car immediately! We are wedged in by the Hungarians' last vehicles. Ahead of us are a German car and a truck. Everywhere Hungarians run in all directions, panicked. None of them shoots—they don't have any weapons left anyway! All we hear is screaming, whimpering, the singing and chirping of machine gun fire, the dull thump of the mortars, and the howling of the anti-tank guns.

Our two trucks swerve on the snow-covered road. The Hungarian sleds are blocking the road. We beat on the guideless horses, and with superhuman strength succeed in tilting the sleds off the road. We now remain the only target and are now attracting fire from carbines and guns. We are in a stupor. We have to get the trucks ready! We succeeded. The first truck starts moving. The cover of the truck is hit by machine gun fire. The carbine was shredded into two pieces in the hands of my comrade, Deuschle. But our track is rolling. Fire bombs hit the snow in front of us; 2cm anti-tank projectiles drop on the side of the road! Damned bastards! I stand on the running board of my truck and look around! Black smoke billows from the truck cover, the gas is burning! We are close to our destination and it is over! The second truck is lost as well; a burning Ford blocks the road.

Now we have to run for our lives! We run through snow that is up to our knees; we are surrounded by rifle fire. Totally exhausted we arrive in the evening in Junakowka. It is incredible: none of us six comrades have sustained any injuries. God help us in our future!

The village had been cleared and leveled. In the forest are traces of approximately 200 partisans or remaining Red Army troops. It is not our task to verify this. The area of the attack is horrific even after the snow has blown over the mangled corpses. Smashed sleds, trucks, cars, dead horses, and about

80 fallen Hungarians lie on the ground. A German car was riddled with bullets like a sieve. It is covered with soft snow, as if to pity the distorted bodies of our comrades. At a short distance, in the middle of the ruins, is the German truck which provided a path for us though the snow. The sergeant and the soldiers are dead, killed by shrapnel! And now I recognize my truck. I am tremendously relieved. A quick check reveals that the truck has been pillaged but the documents are still there. Some of the boxes have been opened. The motor is still okay, but the loading structure and the cover have been heavily damaged.

The second truck has burned down to the tires, blackened iron rods lay in the snow—a sad picture. But we are happy since we still have the second truck including its valuable load. In the evening we arrive in Sumy and are temporarily on safe ground. Sumy is now being threatened from the south. Far on the west side the enemy has broken through and is now near Romny, half the distance between Kursk and Kiev.

The air is totally calm on this icy cold February morning. The sun rose on a cloudless sky. Its yellow-red sphere provides a stark contrast to the pale, grey sky. Above the horizon are stripes of green interspersed with shades of pink. The icy air generates a crackling sound. Day and night are reflected in the hollows of the snow, which when uncovered by the sun light, shimmer with a blue light, mysterious as the light in a grotto. Where the sun beams hit the snow, the colors change to the paleness of a corpse, touched by a vibrant, reddish breath.

With our tired legs we shuffle through the snow; ragged horses pull the six sleds. Attached to the first sled is an *Akja*, a toboggan which is weaving left and right in its attempt to follow the tracks. It is a silent convoy, a death knell. The *Akja* carries a precious load, the body of our leader, First Lieutenant Simon! His corpse has been with us for eighteen days and nights as a token of our comradeship. During this, shots from the enemy were being fired above his body, intending to destroy us. We finally broke through the Red ring; our first lieutenant is with us, and this is good!

We can't stop now. Charkow has been abandoned due to pressure from the enemy. The large depots and buildings have been blown up; the beautiful mansions dating back to the times of the czar have been burned down.

Stalingard-Rostow-Charkow: the big triangle is now in the hands of the Reds and lost for us. We desperately cling to every village and city. But the enemy is too strong. We have to retreat after a few hours of bitter fighting. Our faces are grey; bitter desperation settles in our hearts as our toughest enemy. It is -40° C; the snow level is as high as our bodies. The steaming, agitated and exhausted horses can't even pull the empty sleds anymore. Our small group becomes smaller and smaller, only half of them are still able to fight. Injured soldiers, many with frostbite, load their carbines and shoot. They lumber through the snow; their faces are contorted with pain. In the midst of the blizzard, some fall behind and lose their group, which was supposed to support them.

The tanks of the Reds arrive everywhere. All of a sudden silhouettes can be seen on both sides of the road. Our Stukas always arrive on time to get us out of this mess. We continue to rush through the snow. Everything is so totally useless! The icy cold numbs us so much that we are losing the will to survive. Who cares about the shrapnel of the tank shells and ricocheting bullets from the enemy carbines? We are tired, incredibly tired.

After the relatively mild weather of yesterday and the day before— temperatures ranged between -15° and -29° degrees C—a sudden change in the weather. A whistling, piercing wind sweeps through, pushing ahead the dry snow in wide sheets. A dirty, grey sky, in which the sun is glued on it like a lemon yellow, starts to fade.

We have met up with other retreating troops that have suffered equal losses and are now forcing our way together as a considerable fighting power toward the northeast. During the day we take turns fighting or sleeping in snowdrifts. At night we sneak past villages that are occupied by the enemy. Provisions and ammunition are scarce but the mood is better, because here and there we keep hearing about new divisions that are supposed to be attacking from the south.

A thin sickle of a moon is hanging in the ink dark night. With the fall of darkness we have moved away from the enemy. At first the road is blocked by a snowdrift. Then there is hissing rifle fire and loud thuds in the snow from exploding shells. Assault troops are filing along the waves of the snowy desert. Corpses are lying around everywhere, there were many fatalities. And we continue to march, a forever lasting and painful rush though the deep snow.

We are now sitting in a dank basement around a fuel drum which substitutes for an oven, and are enjoying the comfortable heat. This morning we broke through the last line of the Soviets. The dark blood from our dead horses still sticks to our uniform from when we had to lie along the highway behind their still warm corpses. These short and shaggy horses from the steppe saved the lives of some of our comrades.

But let's not spend any more thoughts on this anymore. As a matter of fact we don't even want to reflect about the past! We just want to sit around silently and hold our icy cold hands to the fire and feel the warmth streaming through our bodies, slowly, very slowly. And as we look at each other we are trying to smile. Where is the winter? At the front door? Where is the horror? We have probably passed the last barrier. Outside, death is still haunting the streets. Heavy Soviet artillery is shelling the northern part of the city. But we're just sitting around a glowing fuel drum and trying to smile. We are quite safe and are now getting homesick. We yearn to join our brave and courageous army division. We heard that they fought gallantly.

But right now we have only one question, how can we get to Orel? With a few tricks and some cigarettes we secure several flat railcars [*Rungenwagen*] to head up north on this beautiful evening. (Beautiful is certainly not an apt word in this context considering the icy blizzard whipping across the railroad tracks.) The trip turns into an endless misery, and the rumor spreads once again that these are the foot soldiers' final weeks in the East.

The hissing curse "*scheisse*" [shit] is an expletive used by generals and privates alike and is now used also by the Russian civilian population. This crude expression is symptomatic for the entire state of the war. It characterizes the disappointment and rage, reluctance and impatience. But a bit of humor alleviates everything, even if it is just morbid humor. But not to despair; in case we don't get a meal, if our vehicles get stuck in the mud or snow, if our machine gun is covered with layers of ice when we change positions, when we miss the mail from our home country, we use only one word: *scheisse*!

We stop in Gomel for two hours. This is the area where the "glorious" 8th Italian Army has settled down. It is not a friendly reunion. A rumor is going around that some of these guys haven't been allowed to take any vacation for two years, and that several regiments have been decimated. I don't know whether this correct, but this certainly should teach them a lesson.

We are now in Orel. We left the vast partisan-infested forests and the air attacks behind us. On the same day we rejoin our comrades who were deployed in Orel. We are now at home; ready to face our next adventures.

This is the time when an invisible force sucks all color and light from the surrounding landscape and immerses it with a grey layer which is the desolate national color of this country. Very often this country is depressing—but never as poignant as in this hour. It is now five o'clock, yet it is dark in our bunker. The narrow slit offers only a pale grey view to the outside. Our little stove is glowing, the fire cracks and spits. In these grey hours we can enjoy the warmth of the fire. This is not possible during the daytime, since it would betray our position to the enemy.

It is beyond comprehension that, despite the proximity of the front, we are still able to enjoy a quiet moment, a moment where we can dream and reflect. Surrounding our little stove is not only a cloud of warmth but also our silent emotions. We sit around and smoke, interrupting the silence with only a few sentences.

The sun sets, blurring the outlines of the landscape mellowing our hardship at the front.

And now it is time for toasted bread. Our stove has reached the right temperature and now the pleasant ceremony of the soldier starts. We cut large slices of the dark bread and place it on a plate in the stove. The slices turn brown and crispy; the unforgettable smell of the bread fills the cramped space of the bunker. It is a smell which reminds us of long lost days, of the coziness and the pleasantness of the world. There are many ways to toast the bread, which permits you to distinguish the characteristics of the people in the bunker: the greedy person, the easy person, the unconcerned person, and apathetic person. The experienced toaster is patient, but will start dreaming when he stands at the stove and becomes distracted from the bitter reality, if only for a short time.

A pitch black night has now fallen outside. The first shots are fired, shells howl in the icy snow storm. The fleeting pictures of our homeland pass quickly; the fine blue smoke from our toasted bread has vanished; the trenches demand once again the full attention of every soldier. In come the impacts from shells; more and more impacts—thousands, tens of thousands—countless shells without any break. One cannot distinguish anymore between each explosion. It is now a continuous noise of bursting and cracking, a never ending infernal noise. The time does not pass, every minute feels like an hour.

We crawl into our bunkers and snow dugouts. In the beginning we are still talkative, but then we become more and more silent. We are hoping that the explosions will stop and the enemy will attack. Right now we have to endure this endless drumbeat.

Outside the landscape slowly changes its snowy appearance. Shrapnel destroys the camouflage and shakes the snow from the branches. The howling storm whirls the snow in all directions. But the noise of the explosions is drowning out the howling of the wind. The explosions singe the earth and eat up the snow which has turned into a green and black mass covering the ground. Hot pieces of metal—tiny splinters and jagged pieces as big as your palm—howl through the air. This has been going on for three days and nights, interrupted only by short breaks. The fire stops only when the Bolsheviks attack. But since we beat them back every time, despite their tanks and superior numbers, their horrible shell fire starts again every time and engulfs our positions with a widespread and incomparable vengeance. And then, slowly the whiteness of the snow turns black.

The Reds deploy their people and weaponry brutally and recklessly. Here and there they succeed in breaking through our front. Their losses are just as heavy as ours. A few comrades are lying quietly at the bottom of the trench; snowflakes have settled on their stony faces.

It is Sunday. An eerie quietness covers the desolate landscape after the embittered fights during the last three days. The naked winter soil is exposed by the torched Bolshevik tanks. And there are many such dark blotches in the terrain, motionless and silent.

We get used to the fact that enemy attacks continue to be followed by more attacks, even after we mowed them down more than ten times. We get used to the earthen-colored masses of enemy troops which seem to grow out of the soil and advance like a steamroller, yesterday, today, and certainly tomorrow.

Many times we ask ourselves during the few, quite hours between the attacks: did the dead awaken again?

All thoughts stay focused on the present moment when barrages surround us day after day, when volleys of explosive charges are hurled at us, grenades

Map of the Orel sector of the Eastern Front.

howl without interruption, when bombs explode and tanks shriek. All our actions and thoughts are concentrated on survival. And we learned to hate. We have seen our comrades lying on the ground, barely recognizable; even so, he was dear and precious to us. Late in life we learned to hate, this wasn't in our nature; and to think that everything used to be so smooth before. But it is not too late.

We receive our mail. The content is more serious than it has been during the past weeks. It reveals to us the mood in our homeland and their worries about us. Our fights are tough and relentless as never before. We know that they are aware of this back home. It is now a fight for survival, a fight for everything.

Orel

About twenty white beams are scanning the sky. This is the night of the bombers. Yesterday Russian planes dropped propaganda leaflets; they announced terror attacks and advised the civilian population to leave the city. Bombs of all sizes fall through the night. Countless fireworks and magnesium cluster bombs—also known as *Christbaume* [Christmas trees] illuminate the night sky with a dark red glow, the exploding anti-tank shells fall down like sinking stars and the yellow flashing of shrapnel bombs—a true *Hexensabbath* [witches' Sabbath]. This night brings heavy losses for our men and our weapons. On account of these hellish nights, our meals for the next weeks consist only of margarine and minimal rations.

It has now become quieter on the front. On one early morning we are told to move from our present position to support our comrades further back. We are six kilometers behind the main front line, which is very close to the rear limit. After ten hours of refreshing sleep which was interrupted only twice by Ivan's bombs, we are in a good mood and enjoy our breakfast. It is a picture of almost tranquil peace under such circumstances, and we are very astonished when our *babushka* gets busy moving all her pitiful belongings to safety. She takes the few pictures and the completely blind mirror from the wall and removes the icon out of the corner. I ask her what the purpose of this is, but she hesitates to give me an answer. My comrades pack their belongings in the meantime. Our experience with previous retreats has taught us that when the civilians start to pack their belongings, it is time for us to get ready as well.

In January we were in Budjennij and Walniki; in February, Woltschausk and Bjelgorod. It is always the same—we establish our billets in the village huts, or in the stone buildings which at least have windows.

The local people greet us with joy and servility, reading every wish from our lips. We lay down to recover from our previous sleep deprivation. When we wake up we call Matka [one of the women in the hut], as the fire went out during the night and we are freezing horribly. But nobody shows up. We look around; the entire family has vanished.

We wait hours for an explanation, hours of almost unnatural Sunday quietness. Suddenly fire and explosions surround us again. We are already familiar with this grinding sound, interrupted only by short moments of silence, and then the heavy shower of the barrage impacts. The infernal concert started at sunset and lasted without break almost until midnight. And then, suddenly and abruptly, it stops just like it had begun. Then we hear the alarm. The Soviets have broken into the city; the nightly fight for the buildings has started.

The civilian population had already escaped from Bjelgorod a week before its capture by the Soviets. But we scoffed at such an ambush by the Reds, for we had considered it impossible. The front was far, very far. Then one morning there were no more civilians in our billet, but the Russian tanks were in front of the buildings.

We learned our lesson. With mixed feelings we remember now the hasty preparations of our *babushka*. Our good mood is gone. All the civilians in the other quarters have also vanished without a trace. The famous rats have left the sinking ship.

We should dismantle our telescopes; we are going to be facing a lot of problems! We have known these guys long enough. The civilians usually stay in their huts like cockroaches; they don't flee when they are threatened by bombs or grenades. But the civilians have now escaped, since they were expecting the Red attacks to go building by building. Their communication system is creepier than all the tribal drums in Africa. By nightfall almost every civilian has disappeared, silently like a bad stench.

There is an unusually loud rumbling and cracking around 1900 hours toward the front. A little bit later a messenger from our regiment arrives and alerts us that the Reds have broken through the front line and are now at a distance of 1000 meters from the village.

The fight for the village endures two days and nights. We have a tough time of it until we succeed in pushing the Soviets back. On the third day the HKL [*Hauptkampflinie*—main front line] has been reestablished. And at the same time, the civilians return, friendly and innocently smiling like children as if nothing had happened.

The bullet-riddled windows have been repaired, the damaged walls have been covered and the shredded roofs have been resealed. Babushka, Matka, and the children work from dawn to dusk. In the evening the large family sits around the stove or lies on the floor. At the edge of the village is our ammunition depot. While this is not the best, it isn't a problem since Ivan has not paid us a visit for long time and it is very well camouflaged. The snow is already very soft, but the wind is still icy. At night we sink into our straw beds totally exhausted.

Again, like the other nights, we yearn for our Russian hosts to retire so that we can get a good night's sleep on our straw mats. But nobody moves. We try to hide our heads in the pillows. During the afternoon our hosts stayed in the sticky but warm huts. Later on they disappeared with their wives and kids into the potato storage. When we found them, they were grinning sheepishly, but did not talk to us.

We finally get our rest and swear that we will shoot anybody who disturbs our sleep. Suddenly we wake up. Fragments from the window are lying on my body; glass shards and debris is everywhere, and near the stove a palm-sized splinter is sticking out of the clay wall. And now it is rumbling and cracking everywhere. Ivan's airplanes fly until two in the morning. I count 53 bomb explosions. One-third of the village is destroyed by the time they left. But at least they did not succeed in hitting our ammunition depot, which would have flattened the entire village.

In the morning the entire clan appears again and repairs their houses yet again as good as possible. For three more nights they continue to sleep on the oven, only to disappear later again in the potato storage. Meanwhile, we catch on to what they are doing. We pack our belongings and also seek cover in the sticky potato holes.

Tonight the Russian bombers return once again and destroy half the remaining village. The rest is smashed to smithereens from the exploding ammunition depot. Once again the Russian civilians were better informed. They have their own underground communication network with the Russian front. Our GFP [secret field police] tried very hard to crack their communications system. But it was futile!

I have been standing on the road to the front for hours, waiting to guide the trucks into their positions. Platoons are pushing forward, the artillery rumbles by; the ground vibrating from the grinding wheels. To my rear I can see the flickering glow of cigarettes. My spade bangs against my gas mask at every step. A horseback rider gallops forward. Somebody asks what time it is: it's two in the morning. A canteen nearby is brewing fresh tea. The smell of tea with rum wafts over the road. Cooking utensils are rattling. Ahead of us is a thundering noise, sheet lightning illuminates the sky—the muzzle flash of the heavy artillery. In between is the tak-tak-tak hammering of machine guns, just like the second hand of a pocket watch. Finally at three in the morning our platoon trucks arrive, which had been delayed due to attacks by *Ivan*.

After a peaceful cigarette we advance. The road gets worse and worse, strewn with potholes.

In Mattuoje we come upon the firing zone. The impacts are now close to our road. Vehicles are rushing back. Somebody shouts from the last vehicle: "The ammunition truck has been hit!" At the edge of the village is a bright, darting flame which illuminates the trajectory of the enemy artillery. Now it is getting

The German front in the East on May 10, 1943.

serious. Somebody shouts: "Stop! More fire! Take cover!" The ground trembles from the multiple dull thuds. We cling to the ground as if it could provide us with protection. Splinters are buzzing and whirring by, only to be interrupted by the dull thuds in the distance, the shots from the next round. But we have to advance. Our platoon has to be in position by morning.

We reach the corduroy road, the worst stretch of all. There are countless bomb craters on both sides, and we are attacked again and again on the ground; Russian fighter planes are strafing us.

What remains of the village of Blashkatowo consists of no more than smoldering beams, broken household goods, and lonely chimneys in the center of destroyed houses, blazing huts, and the disgusting smell of burning flesh. We are close to our target. At 0520 hours our platoon is in position, but two good comrades are missing.

The muddy season! Bright sunshine follows snow and hailstorms which have swept across the steppe. The thaw starts to settle in after three sunny days. On the fourth day it is so warm that the water mixes with the soil and dissolves everything into layers of mud and dirt. Last weekend the melt water reached up to our knees and filled up the creeks and gardens. The surrounding landscape is a giant lake. Our vehicles are stuck. It takes us three to four days to move a single vehicle which before took only an hour.

We are lucky that our boots arrived on time, which has at least provided us with minimum protection against the icy water. Everybody is preparing to live like an amphibian. Proven medicines against common illnesses are dispensed, just like the previous year. The weather is horrible; in addition we are under severe attacks day and night.

Something wonderful happens during these days. A battalion of young soldiers with fresh faces and new equipment arrives. Their boots are shining and their pots and pans have never been used on a Russian stove, though we noticed this much later. The wonderful thing is that they were marching in rows of three and were singing! We step out of the heavily shelled huts and bunkers which have been our home and are unable to comprehend such a miracle. We stand there silently in our camouflage, caked with dirt, and we touch our stubbly faces in disbelief. They march along a series of small grave mounds with crosses on top and I get the impression that their voices tremble for a moment. We lower our heads in silence and look down on our wet, clay encrusted boots. Somebody cracks a joke, a cruel joke under these circumstances: "They will stop singing pretty soon." But nobody laughs, nobody agrees with the joker. We all know that these young comrades from the homeland will march the final two or three kilometers to their positions in rows or single file. Each will hold his rifle in his hands to avoid banging it against their cooking utensils. For a moment they will be astonished when they get instructions to

Mother's Day 1943: "You will know what I am saying by this little drawing. To my darling, hugs and kisses, from Hansel, 4 May, 1943." *(Photo courtesy Christine Alexander and Mason Kunze)*

empty their pants and coat pockets and place everything in their breast pockets. And they will shiver to the bone when they understand the purpose of this order. The same happened to us when we jumped into the trenches. The icy water reached up to our waist and flooded our boots; our pants clung to our thighs. But they will endure it, just like we did. They will enjoy the blessing of the bunker stove; its heat expels the water in our pants and socks into milky rivulets. And when their uniform has the proper clay crust, nobody will be able to distinguish them from us anymore.

They think a lot about us and we almost feel tenderness toward our young comrades. We envy their singing which refreshes our old memories.

This winter has been very harsh to us. It could have frozen our hearts, banned the laughter from us and caused us to forget our songs. The bitter cold, the howling snowstorms, the days without food, and the nights without sleep have imprinted deep wrinkles on our stubbly faces.

Occasionally we receive these overly clever letters from home asking us about the mood on the front. We shake our heads in disbelief over such stupid questions. Silly civilians! We are soldiers fighting on the front!

A storm is brewing over the steppe to the east, the second storm from Mongolia. We have to lean our bodies against the storm. Step by step we dig into the ground and thus succeed in holding our position. Don't ask us how we are able to survive this winter. Never ask us at home to talk about this. When one grinds his teeth during the long winter months, he has difficulties opening his mouth later on. Don't ask us in the future. We stand our ground silently and fight—and we will continue to fight. We never want to think about it, we want to forget everything. And now our comrades are passing us with a song on their lips. We hold the belief that our heart is armored with ice and steel. And now that we feel it beating again we are aware how the long winter has been ravishing us. Our young comrades should continue singing. We should stand side by side: we, out of the purgatory of the long winter, and our comrades with their young hearts and innocent confidence.

Overnight a fresh wind started blowing off the clouds which had been covering the sun. Within a week the water and mud, against which we had been fighting a losing battle, has disappeared. But nobody is quite yet ready to believe in the miracle of springtime. The first dust clouds which are blown along the dry roads still generate suspicious looks. Maybe nature is playing a cruel joke with us. But we are happy that spring has arrived in such a pleasant way.

It is now quiet in our sector. Occasional assaults by enemy artillery; a few attacks by Red aircraft. Our bunkers are secure and are withstanding the bombs. They have been fortified with planks and railroad ties. Until a short while ago we didn't trust such peace on the front, just like the unusually mild weather. But now it looks like Ivan has finally surrendered. From time to time we are even able to relax for one or two hours. We reminisce often about the tough weeks of the "winter battle at Orel."

The main focus of the battle during the second half of February has been on the west side of Orel, to be followed a few days later on with an unprecedented ferocity on the southeast side of the city. The enemy concentrated strong battalions, tanks, and heavy artillery at both locations. It was therefore not surprising when the thunder of the artillery started on an icy February morning.

What has occurred so far at this undefeated section has been pure hell. Even experienced fighters in the trenches have never encountered such a ferocious attack. The Russians launched a massive attack with infantry consisting of 120,000 to 200,000 troops, 400 tanks and 120 to 150 batteries, which was an extraordinary number on the Eastern Front. It is almost unbelievable that the German divisions could withstand such an overwhelming onslaught, but it is the enemy who was fully aware of this. Last but not least, the high loss of troops and materiel, caused by futile attempts to break through in the same sector, has taught the Bolsheviks a lesson that the defenders will hold their ground despite their own vastly superior forces. The Bolsheviks' goal to cut off Orel in a pincer operation from the north to the south at the same location has motivated them to deploy these gigantic resources. We realized from the first hours of the massacre that it was essential to defend the prominent bastion of Orel, the most eastern point of the entire front. We were also aware of the fact that we could meet the same fate as our brave comrades in Stalingrad.

Besides the north-south pincer with attack points at Bolchow and Ponyri, the Soviets have deployed two more spearheads west of Shisdra, in the direction of Brjzusk, and at Ligoff. Furthermore, the forest area of Karatschew at Gomel is a giant area of marshes 500km wide, which is completely impenetrable during the winter time. It is also occupied by thousands of partisans and regular airborne troops. Every other deployment of replenishments has been robbed by bandits. All that we can do is hold our position to the bitter end. There cannot be any deliberation about our methods. Our position was very clear. Our only chance at survival is to defend ourselves. It is a tough battle for men who have nothing to lose. It was this horrible realization that made everything so easy at the time. Many soldiers marched to their death with a smile on their pale faces.

23 February: The barrage of shells and heavy artillery has commenced, covering the German positions and fortifications. Bombers drop their loads in rows along the trenches and, in addition, armored fighter airplanes nosedive over the battleground and target us with their machine guns.

And then the first wave of the Bolshevik infantry and tanks starts rolling in. It is both horrifying and unique. But we are not supposed to talk about this. We defend ourselves with a courage reinforced with desperation, and handle our weapons like skilled craftsmen.

It looks like everything is to no avail. Too fierce are the recurring attacks on our positions and everything that moves or sticks out of the icy cold winter landscape. Too vicious are the ever-present fighters which fly in groups like white lumbering birds of death with their rattling machine guns close above the main HKL. There are too many tanks and much too much infantry: seven infantry divisions and four tank brigades just in the first days of the attack! The enemy succeeds in breaking through, deploying infantry and later on new tank brigades. In the first five days, 121 tanks are destroyed, only to have 80 new ones deployed the very next day! The poor weather conditions render the deployment of our Luftwaffe difficult. The losses are very high. Every day brings with it a new crisis which we can only overcome with efforts that are beyond our human strength and our own blood.

1–6 March: During these first days of March we move to the southern sector where a new focal point is forming. The enemy has deployed four armies and an air force command into the area between Kursk and Orel. Again and again they attempt to break through the gaps in the decimated divisions of our right wing and to move around our entire southern wing. The battle has now reached its climax. Since the beginning of the offensive at the end of February, the enemy has suffered 35,000 troops dead, 280 destroyed tanks, and 140 downed aircraft.

In spite of such huge losses, the fighting spirit of our enemy remains undiminished. Their push is directed to the west. We continue to fend off their forces to the southwest and north of Orel. In between, the enemy attacks our flanks with their motorized divisions and tanks. At the same time they deploy strong forces on three more positions: to the southeast of Orel, at a location closest to the city, to the north of the Schisdra section, and to our west. All attacks are supported by heavy artillery, not to mention the countless tanks.

7 March: We destroy 77 out of 90 heavy tanks. The fights continue with an incredible ferociousness until March 10, with heavy losses on both sides. The situation continues to teeter on the edge of a knife. Our ammunition and food supply are being exhausted—the most important supply lines are threatened or are under heavy attack by the enemy. We come to the bitter conclusion that this might be the end. Two days more and everything will be over.

12 March: The miracle happens. The usual massive attack in the morning doesn't occur. There is still a lot of metal flying around, a mere pittance though compared with the previous days. Yet we stopped believing in miracles a long time ago, and have the suspicion that some kind of deviltry is behind this absence of heavy attacks. Our senses are sharpened for the next assault. But there is no change, not during the night nor during the next day. We receive a message that our troops launched a counterattack in Charkow, which is most likely the reason behind the mystery of the sudden diminishing number of combat operations. There are still a lot enemy units in the area which are now facing new realities. Their operational purpose is now in jeopardy and they are apprehensive. The battle at Orel is over.

An early springtime with bright sunshine follows the second terrible eastern winter. With gratitude we look up from our trenches which are filled with the runoff from the melting snow, to a bright and blue sky. The shining sun in the center is like a symbol for the confidence in our victory. We are going to make it!

Springtime has arrived faster than we expected. The last snow melted weeks ago. Due to the summer heat and drought, the mud which covered the entire landscape vanishes within days. On the front we are again masters of our destiny. Platoon after platoon rolls over the roads covered with thick dust clouds from the panzers, *Sturmgeschütze*, mortars and long-barreled guns. This smells again like a major offensive. In a few weeks we are going to attack. *We?* I don't believe it. I guess we will be rounded up later on and then deployed to fight on the front. But let's wait and see.

The first comrades have left already on leave, and it will be my turn in a few weeks. And now I am overpowered again by an eerie feeling that, so close to reaching my goal of a thousand happy dreams, something could happen to me. A persistent toothache, headaches or diarrhea—suddenly everything assumes major significance. The recurring question is: I hope I am not going to get sick. I am in a bad mood these days!

Our Luftwaffe and the enemy air force have been very active during these past few days. Day and night dozens of bombers or fighter aircraft fly through the sky. And this is always a telltale sign: when the "*Totenvögel*" [birds of death] dart about, either we or the enemy are planning major events. It is like a movie theater for the frontline soldiers. But this show is not without dangers.

6 May: There is a lot of activity today. At the light of dawn a squadron of Soviet bombers flies over our front line. Suddenly they make a sharp turn; they dive down and approach our position at high speed. Gauging from experience, they should now open their bomb bays and death should start to rain upon us. But nothing happens. Instead we are now hearing the familiar howling sound of our fighters. We brace ourselves against the walls of the trench and watch the events unfold in the clear morning sky where they are fighting for life and death. The tight, evasive maneuvering and shooting have started. Our fighter aircraft dive down on the slower bombers, whose gunners are attempting to shoot them down. The muzzle fires from the machine guns and the onboard cannons sparkle in the sky. Our fighters make their attack and then steeply pull up again with their engines howling to get on top of the enemy bombers. A

Soviet bomber in the sky starts to tumble, dips his right wing, and then spins to the ground to explode in bright flames. Within the next three minutes four more Soviet bombers meet the same fate. On this day 74 Soviet aircraft were shot down in our sector.

Yesterday our first *Tigers* arrived and positioned themselves in a broad line behind our sector. This gives us a reassuring feeling, since the Reds are also assembling their tank units on the other side. The front is brimming with FlaKs of all calibers and sizes.

We are quiet and confident since winter is over, and the sun belongs only to us.

Editors' note:

As Hans Roth's third and last journal ends he's within weeks of going on leave, and so he may have missed the climactic Battle of Kursk, which commenced on July 5, 1943. At Kursk, the largest tank battle in history, involving up to two million men, the Soviets finally proved that they could withstand a good-weather German offensive. From that point onward the Soviets held the strategic initiative in the East, and the Germans could only attempt to delay their counter-invasion of Europe while simultaneously trying to hold off the Western Allies, who were invading German-occupied territory from the sea.

Hans Roth's military experiences after his third journal ends in May 1943 are unknown, though it is likely he was working on a fourth journal when he died, which by some very slim chance of fate may yet emerge.

It is only documented that he lived for one more year, as the documents on the following pages attest. In an official notice to his wife, Rosel, from the German Army High Command (OKH) he was reported missing as of June 25, 1944.

At that time the 299th Infantry Division was on the front line of Army Group Center, southeast of the city of Vitebsk. The previous year's combat had taken place primarily in the southern sector, and the Germans expected a renewal of Soviet offensives in that direction. However, taking advantage of their superior mobility, thanks to motor vehicles and other supplies from the West, the Soviets had secretly shifted the axis of their advance to the center of the front.

On June 22, 1944, the third anniversary of the German invasion, the Soviets launched Operation Bagration, a gigantic surprise offensive that caved in the opposing front. In German annals, the disaster is referred to simply as "the Destruction of Army Group Center." Of half a million Germans on the central front, 350,000 were lost as they faced 2.5 million Soviet attackers.

The 299th Infantry Division was among the first German formations to be hit by the juggernaught, and was immediately overwhelmed. After all his narrow escapes during the war, Hans Roth was finally, evidently, forced to succumb. The official notice from OKH to Rosel states that as of June 25, 1944, he was *vermisst.*

Final Documents

The official notice from the German Army to Rosel, describing how her husband had gone missing southwest of Vitebsk as of June 25, 1944. The message ends with wishes of good health and good luck for his eventual homecoming, though to anyone reading his journals it should be doubtful that Hans Roth would ever allow himself to be taken prisoner.

DEUTSCHES ROTES KREUZ
IN DER BUNDESREPUBLIK DEUTSCHLAND
S U C H D I E N S T   M Ü N C H E N

DRK-SUCHDIENST 8 MÜNCHEN 40 INFANTERIESTRASSE 7a

Frau
Rosa Roth
Frankfurt/M.
Johanna Kirchnerstr. 20

UNSER ZEICHEN:
N 4 a - 12   TAG:
(IM ANTWORTSCHREIBEN NICHT VERGESSEN)

Betr.: Ihr Suchantrag nach Johann Wolfgang R o t h , geb.28.8.12, in Hanau/M.

Sehr verehrte Frau Roth,

im Rahmen unserer Nachforschungen wurden alle uns zugegangenen Angaben und Informationen über das Schicksal Ihres Angehörigen überprüft. Über die individuellen Ermittlungen hinaus haben wir besonders die Möglichkeit untersucht, ob der Verschollene in Gefangenschaft geraten sein könnte. Dabei ist den Kampfhandlungen, bei denen Ihr Angehöriger und weitere Soldaten der gleichen militärischen Einheit vermißt wurden, genau nachgegangen worden. Das Ergebnis ist in einem Gutachten festgehalten, das Ihnen Aufschluß über unsere Nachforschungen und Einblick in die für den Verschollenen entscheidend gewordene Phase des Kriegsgeschehens gibt.

Wird am Ende der Darstellung auch der Schluß gezogen, daß Ihr Angehöriger zu den Opfern des 2. Weltkrieges gezählt werden muß, hoffen wir dennoch, Sie durch die Bekanntgabe des Nachforschungsergebnisses von jahrelang ertragener Ungewißheit zu befreien.

Der Verschollene wird nach unseren Unterlagen noch gesucht von

./.

Wir dürfen an Sie die Bitte richten, dem/der/den Suchenden von dem Gutachten Kenntnis zu geben.

Für Ihre freundliche Mithilfe bedanken wir uns herzlich.

Mit vorzüglicher Hochachtung

M. Heinrich
Direktor

Anlage:
1 Gutachten
1 Empfangsbestätigung
1 Merkblatt

FERNRUF: SAMMEL-NR. (089) 18 80 31 · FERNSCHREIBER: 05 23 977 · POSTSCHECK: MÜNCHEN 851 00
BANKEN: LANDESZENTRALBANK MÜNCHEN KTO. 700 019 14 · BAYER. VEREINSBANK MÜNCHEN, ZWEIGST. AM NORDBAD, KTO. 900 101

XII.69

A post-war notice from the German Red Cross, informing Rosel that they had no further information on her husband.

5 2UR IIII.345/50

B e s c h l u s s .

Der Graphiker Johann R o t h

geboren am 28.8.1912   zu   Hanau am Main

zuletzt wohnhaft in Frankfurt am Main. Johanna Kirchnerstrasse 2o

wird für tot erklärt und der Zeitpunkt des Todes auf den   25.Juni 1944

festgestellt.

Die Entscheidung ergeht kostenfrei und wird nach Ablauf der einmonatigen Beschwerdefrist nach Veröffentlichung in der Verschollenheitsliste rechtskräftig.

G r ü n d e .

Frau Rosa R o t h geb. Wolff, Frankfurt am Main. Johanna Kirchnerstrasse 2c

hat als   Ehefrau

die Todeserklärung des oben Genannten beantragt.

Der Antrag ist gem.§§ 1 Abs.1,3-7, 14-16,18 des Verschollenheitsgesetzes vom 7.1o.39 und dem hess.Gesetz v.6.7.48 zulässig und begründet.

Durch eidesstattliche Versicherung der Antragstellerin vom   3.8.1950

sowie durch Nachricht der Abwicklungsstelle vom 11.7.1950

ist glaubhaft gemacht, dass der oben Genannte als Angehöriger der deutschen Wehrmacht am Kriege teilgenommen hat, im Gefahrengebiet vermisst worden und seitdem verschollen ist.

Die Auskunft der Abwicklungsstelle der deutschen Dienststelle zur Benachrichtigung der nächsten Angehörigen von Gefallenen der ehemaligen deutschen Wehrmacht in Berlin-Wald innslust hat vorgelegen.

Das Aufgebot ist durch Bekanntmachung in der Verschollenheitsliste A

Nr. 1o18   am it 1.9.1950   veröffentlicht worden.

Vom Leben des Verschollenen ist bis zu dem auf den 23.1o.5o

festgesetzten Zeitpunkt keine Nachricht bei Gericht eingegangen.

Als Zeitpunkt des Todes war gemäss § 9 Abs.3b des Versch.Ges. der

vermisstentag   festzustellen.

Die Kostenentscheidung beruht auf der Verordnung v.4.1o.49 (R.G.Bl. I S.194 und der VO. des hess.Justizministers v.17.9.49 Just.Min.Bl. Nr.19).

Frankfurt am Main, den   23.Oktober 1950
Amtsgericht Abteilung 52
gez:Dr.v.Wüllerstorff.Amtsgerichtsrat
Ausgefertigt:

Justizangestellte als Urkundsbeamtin
der Geschäftsstelle des Amtsgerichts
Abteilung 52

Frau Rosa R o t h
Frankfurt Main
Johanna Kirchnerstr.2o

Der Beschluß ist rechtskräftig.

Frankfurt (Main), den ...

Geschäftsstelle des Amtsgerichts
Abteilung 5.
Justizinspektor

Another official notice to Rosel, this time from the Bundesrepublik, dated October 1950, confirming that her husband, Hans Roth, had been lost in the war.

Suggested Reading

The editors have relied on a number of published works to explain the context of Hans Roth's original journals. Among these are:

Careell, Paul. *Hitler Moves East, 1941–1943*. Winnipeg, CA: J.J. Fedorowicz Publishing, 1991.

Einseidel, Heinrich, Graf von. *The Onslaught: The German Drive to Stalingrad*. (Foreword by Max Hastings.) New York: W.W. Norton & Co., 1984.

Glantz, David M. *Kharkov 1942: Anatomy of a Military Disaster*. Rockville Centre, NY: Sarpedon Publishers, 1998.

Guderian, Heinz. *Panzer Leader*. New York: E.P. Dutton & Co., 1952.

Hoyt, Edwin P. *Hitler's War*. New York: McGraw Hill, 1979.

Lemay, Benoit. *Erich von Manstein: Hitler's Master Strategist*. Philadelphia: Casemate Publishers, 2010.

Manstein, Erich von. *Lost Victories*. Novato, CA: Presidio Press, 1982.

Meyer, Kurt. *Grenadiers*. Winnipeg, CA: J.J. Fedorowiz, 1994.

Mitcham, Samuel W., Jr. *The Men of Barbarossa: Commanders of the German Invasion of Russia, 1941*. Philadelphia: Casemate Publishers, 2009.

Niepold, Gerd. *Battle for White Russia: The Destruction of Army Group Centre, June 1944*. London: Brassey's, 1987.

Seaton, Albert. *The Battle for Moscow*. New York: Sarpedon Publishers, 1993.

Warlimont, Walter. *Inside Hitler's Headquarters, 1939–45*. Novato, CA: Presidio Press, 1990.

Zhukov, Georgi K. *Marshal Zhukov's Greatest Battles*. (Ed. and with commentary by Harrison Salisbury.) New York: Harper & Row, 1969.